Supervision in the Me
Health Professions

A practitioner's guide

Supervis al health
professic andatory
registrati has been
written t of those
involved

In *Su* ong with
her guest illustrate
ways of t ples, she
explores

- How
- Wha
- Wha

Supervisi ractical
and indis mental
healthcar herapy,
counsellii

Joyce Sc byshire
Commun for the
Doctor o effield.
She has o tice.

Supervision in the Mental Health Professions

A practitioner's guide

Joyce Scaife

With contributions from
Francesca Inskipp, Brigid Proctor,
Jon Scaife and Sue Walsh

Brunner-Routledge
Taylor & Francis Group

HOVE AND NEW YORK

First published 2001 by Brunner-Routledge
27 Church Road, Hove, East Sussex BN3 2FA

Simultaneously published in the USA and Canada
by Taylor & Francis Inc
325 Chestnut Street, 8th Floor, Philadelphia PA 19106

Reprinted 2002 by Brunner-Routledge
27 Church Road, Hove, East Sussex BN3 2FA
29 West 35th Street, New York, NY 10001

Reprinted 2004 by Brunner-Routledge
27 Church Road, Hove, East Sussex BN3 2FA
270 Madison Avenue, New York, NY 10016

Brunner-Routledge is an imprint of the Taylor & Francis Group

© 2001 Joyce Scaife; individual chapters, the contributors

Typeset in Times by RefineCatch Limited, Bungay, Suffolk
Printed and bound in Great Britain by
Biddles Ltd, King's Lynn, Norfolk

This publication has been produced with paper manufactured to strict
environmental standards and with pulp derived from sustainable forests.

Cover design by Jim Wilkie

British Library Cataloguing in Publication Data
A catalogue record for this book is available
from the British Library

Library of Congress Cataloging in Publication Data
Scaife, Joyce, 1950–.
    Supervision in the mental health professions: a practitioner's
 guide / Joyce Scaife; [with contributions by Francesca Inskipp . . .
 [et al.].
        p. cm.
    Simultaneously published in the USA and Canada.
    Includes bibliographical references and index.
    ISBN 0-415-20713-4 (hbk)—ISBN 0-415-20714-2 (pbk.)
    1. Mental health services—Administration. 2. Health services
administrators. 3. Mental health personnel. 4. Supervisors.
5. Personal management. I. Inskipp, Francesca. II. Title.

RA790.5.S285 2001
362.2'068—dc21   00-059261
        §
ISBN 0-415-20714-2 (pbk)
    0-415-20713-4 (hbk)

For George and Edith

Contents

List of illustrations   ix
List of contributors   x
Preface   xi
Acknowledgements   xii

1 **Introduction**   **1**

2 **Supervision and learning**   **15**
JOYCE SCAIFE AND JON SCAIFE

3 **The emotional climate of work and the development of self**   **30**
JOYCE SCAIFE AND SUE WALSH

4 **The contracting process and the supervisory relationship: avoiding pitfalls and problems**   **52**

5 **Frameworks for supervision**   **70**

6 **Group supervision**   **99**
BRIGID PROCTOR AND FRANCESCA INSKIPP

7 **Ethical dilemmas and issues in supervision**   **122**

8 **Use of audio and videotapes in supervision**   **145**

9 **Live supervision and observation**   **160**

10 **Creative approaches**   **173**

11 **The influence of different models of therapy and counselling on the supervisory process**   **189**

12 **Learning logs in supervision**   **206**

13 **Challenge and evaluation**   **215**

14   The supervisor's role in coursework   **231**

Conclusion   239
Appendix 1   Self-assessment schedule for supervisees   240
Appendix 2   Examples of rating scales of supervision   243
Appendix 3   Sample consent form   245
Appendix 4   Core skills in the helping professions   247
Appendix 5   Sample notice for clients   250
References   251
Author index   268
Subject index   274

Illustrations

Figures

2.1	The experiential learning model	28
3.1	Levels of the helping system	31
5.1	General supervision framework	75
5.2	A process model of supervision	85
5.3	A cyclical model of supervision	90
6.1	Overall map for running group supervision	103
6.2	Russian dolls	106
10.1	A drawing of the client as a fish	176
10.2	A man drowning in a glass of beer	178

Tables

6.1	Typology of groups	104

Contributors

Brigid Proctor and **Francesca Inskipp** met at the first BAC (then SCAC) Trainers' Conference in 1973 when they were both employed as full-time counselling trainers – Francesca at NE London Polytechnic and Brigid at SW London College. Since then they have been engaged in the development of counselling and supervision training as trainers, supervisors, external assessors, consultants and writers. Joint publications include a set of three audiotapes and two booklets entitled *The Skills of Supervising and Being Supervised*, produced in 1989. In 1993 and 1995 they produced *The Art, Craft and Tasks of Counselling Supervision*, two workbooks – *Making the Most of Supervision* and *Becoming a Supervisor*, both illustrated with audiotapes. They have both published books on counselling and counselling skills and Brigid has a new publication *Group Supervision: A Guide to Creative Practice*.

Dr Jon Scaife is a lecturer in Education at the University of Sheffield. His background is in physics and mathematics, and he became interested in learning as a result of teaching these subjects. He is now interested in learning and knowing *per se*.

Dr Sue Walsh is a senior lecturer in Clinical Psychology at the University of Sheffield. She completed her Ph.D. at the Social and Applied Psychology Unit, University of Sheffield and her clinical training at the University of Exeter. Her primary interests lie in the interface between clinical and organisational psychology.

Preface

Supervision, particularly as a component of initial training, and increasingly as a contributory element in continuing professional development, is deeply embedded in the cultures of the helping professions. This is despite the claim (Holloway and Neufeldt, 1995) that there is no research on standardised and empirically validated training programmes for supervisors. Client outcome is the ultimate test of the effectiveness of supervision. But the relationship between supervisor interventions and client change is subtle and complex. Not surprisingly, attempts to account for and understand this relationship have produced little of substance, and serious methodological deficiencies prevail (Ellis, Ladany, Krengel and Schult, 1996; Holloway and Neufeldt, 1995; Russell, Crimmings and Lent, 1984).

Nevertheless, when Holloway and Neufeldt (1995) ask, 'Would you choose to see a therapist who had never received direct supervision of her or his work?', the likely answer would be 'No'. The message from this to practitioners is to use the available literature on supervision to inform our own practice and experiences in supervision. This book is an attempt to broaden the supervision literature, both by taking a panoramic view of the work of other authors and by drawing on my own experiences.

Jon Scaife and Sue Walsh jointly authored with me Chapters 2 and 3 respectively. This reflects the fact that my ideas about learning and about emotions at work have developed enormously through the many lively and enjoyable conversations we have had over a number of years.

I first encountered Brigid Proctor and Francesca Inskipp through the very helpful sets of books and tapes on supervision that they had produced. Having listened to their work on tape I invited them to lead a supervisor training workshop in which these two 'retired' counsellors delighted and entertained us whilst ensuring that we went away with a wealth of new ideas and evolving skills. Their experience of group supervision is much wider than my own and I wanted this breadth to be reflected in this book. My grateful thanks are due to Jon, Sue, Brigid and Francesca, both for their contributions and also for their inspiration in my work.

Acknowledgements

In my career I have been very fortunate to work with many colleagues who have stimulated and contributed to my ideas about supervision. These include, in particular, many supervisors and supervisees to whom I am especially grateful for allowing me to try out my ideas and for sharing their ideas about supervision. Many thanks also to those who commented on earlier drafts – Jon Scaife, Gerry Kent, Margaret Roberts, Sue Walsh, Penny Allen, Mike Pomerantz, Jan Hughes, Zoe Bradshaw, Linda Buchan and Liza Monaghan.

Special thanks to Hannah, Jonny and Jon for putting up with me when I was plugged into the keyboard rather than to their needs, and to Pat and Ray for a peaceful and loving place in which to write.

Acknowledgements are also due for permission to reproduce illustrations as follows: Routledge and Cassell for Figure 3.2, which was published on page 46 of *Counselling Supervision* by M. Carroll in 1996 and adapted from illustrations in *Supervising the Counsellor: A Cyclical Model* by S. Page and V. Wosket in 1994; the American Counseling Association for Figure 10.2, which was published on page 157 of volume 28 of *Counselor Education and Supervision* © ACA in an article by Ishiyama in 1988: reprinted with permission; Figure 6.1 which was originally published on page 57 of *Supervision in the Helping Professions* by P. Hawkins and R. Shohet in 1989.

Chapter 1

Introduction

I believe that the word 'supervision' conjures up a variety of ideas and emotions in people. The prior experiences of practitioners in the helping professions can lead them both to seek and to avoid further involvement in the process. I have met people who have felt wounded by the words of a supervisor twenty years earlier and are still smarting. There are others who feel unsupported if the work context does not offer ongoing supervision throughout their professional career.

I became interested in supervision when first faced with the prospect of becoming a supervisor, and after my initial experience of the role. I was worried about being 'found out' as an inadequate practitioner and I had the idea that supervisors required much expertise and *gravitas*. Despite my pre-qualification training, it was the first time that my clinical work had been observed in progress by anyone and I found the experience nerve-racking. After this I set out to 'arm' myself with information and ideas that would protect me from such experiences in the future.

This book is an attempt to draw together ideas from sources I have discovered over the last twenty years, to describe some of my own experiences in supervision and to attempt to make them useful to people who are interested in developing their own ideas and skills in supervision. It is principally intended as a book for practitioners and I hope that it reflects both the scientist-practitioner and reflective-practitioner groundings of the helping professions.

Different chapters address the purposes for which supervision might be undertaken, ways of understanding supervisory processes and ideas about how to carry out supervisory tasks. Some of the dilemmas that accompany the role are explored, including ethical and other philosophical issues. The quality of the supervisory relationship is taken as central to the achievement of the aims of supervision, especially in regard to the construction of a climate of safety which allows the vulnerabilities of the participants to be shown and managed.

Professional helping is carried out within a number of different disciplines that include counselling; psychotherapy; educational, clinical, counselling and health psychology; psychiatry; social work; nursing; art, speech and language, and occupational therapies. The book is addressed to these and related professions. It is also intended to be of relevance to work across different client groups, and whilst reference is made to 'the client' this is not to imply that the client is an adult or an individual – the client could just as well be a child, family, group, carer or organisation.

Some terms are used interchangeably. The supervisee is variously described as the therapist, professional helper, clinician, and practitioner. The work carried out is referred to as therapy, counselling and case-work. This approach is meant to indicate an inclusiveness that represents the diversity of terms used in different helping professions, in all of which supervision is a feature of training relationships and/or continuing professional development.

This chapter discusses some of the different ways of viewing supervision in order to clarify for the reader the underlying assumptions upon which the remainder of the book is based.

What is supervision?

Aims and purposes of supervision

A distinction between the purposes and functions of supervision is helpfully made by Carroll (1996). Following Carroll, the primary purposes of supervision are defined here as ensuring the welfare of clients and enhancing the development of the supervisee in work. In order to effect these purposes the supervision should perform the functions of education, support, and evaluation against the norms and standards of the profession and of society. This is the case irrespective of employment arrangements and applies both in private practice and public service.

Many attempts have been made to define supervision, but, as with all such attempts, none entirely does it justice:

> Supervision provides an opportunity for the student to capture the essence of the psychotherapeutic process as it is articulated and modelled by the supervisor, and to recreate it in the counselling relationship.
>
> (Holloway, 1992: 177)

> Supervision is a working alliance between a supervisor and a worker or workers in which the worker can reflect on herself in her working situation by giving an account of her work and receiving feedback and where appropriate guidance and appraisal. The object of this alliance is to maximise the competence of the worker in providing a helping service.
>
> (Inskipp and Proctor, 1988: 4)

Supervision is that part of the overall training of mental health professionals that deals with modifying their actual in-therapy behaviours.
(Lambert, 1980: 425)

[Supervision is] an intensive, interpersonally focused one-to-one relationship in which one person is designated to facilitate the development of therapeutic competence in the other person.
(Loganbill, Hardy and Delworth, 1982: 4)

An intervention provided by a more senior member of a profession to a more junior member or members of that same profession. This relationship is evaluative, extends over time, and has the simultaneous purposes of enhancing the professional functioning of the more junior person(s), monitoring the quality of professional services offered to the client(s) she, he, or they see(s), and serving as a gatekeeper of those who are to enter the particular profession.
(Bernard and Goodyear, 1998: 6)

These definitions serve to orient the reader towards the meaning of the term 'supervision', whilst acknowledging that the meaning given to the word will differ between individuals. There will be no attempt here to offer a definitive meaning of the term 'supervision', since words mediate between the meanings located within the speaker and the listener so that, 'strictly speaking nothing we know can be said precisely' (Polanyi, 1958: 87–88). However, because the term has been used differently in different countries and in different traditions of counselling and psychotherapy, its usage is further explored below.

Pre-registration and post-registration supervision

Sometimes 'supervision' is used only to describe relationships in which one person is a student or trainee and the other a qualified professional, or relationships in which the supervisor has managerial responsibility for the work of the supervisees. When used in this way (for example, Morrison, 1993), a distinction is drawn between 'supervision' and 'consultation', the former involving a position of authority for the supervisor which includes a mandate to direct the supervisee if necessary.

The definitions of supervision listed above include the notion of the supervisor being a more senior member of the profession, even if the supervisee is fully qualified to practise. In contrast, attempts have been made to include peer relationships under the definition of supervision and distinctions have been made by the use of terms such as 'training supervision' 'practitioner supervision', 'peer supervision', 'peer consultation' and 'consultation'.

In this book the view is taken that whilst there are significant differences in the process of supervision when the partners in the relationships are at different stages of their careers, there are sufficient commonalities to discuss all of them under the term 'supervision'. Were it obligatory for the supervisor to be the more senior partner, it would prove extremely difficult for some counsellors and therapists to arrange their mandatory ongoing supervision as their careers progressed. Supervision here is used to describe what happens when people who work in the helping professions make a formal arrangement to think with another or others about their work with a view to providing the best possible service to clients and enhancing their own personal and professional development. It thus includes what some authors have defined as 'consultation'.

Individual and group supervision

Some definitions emphasise a one-to-one supervisory relationship. Whilst this is the most common mode of supervision in many of the helping professions, group supervision can offer a rich tapestry for learning and development with a range of possible formats and leadership roles, examples of which are described in Chapter 6 by Brigid Proctor and Francesca Inskipp.

Commonality and difference of therapeutic model

Another notion is that the supervisor's tasks are to provide and model exemplars from which the supervisee learns. Whilst that can be a helpful process, the approach of this text is that it is also possible to learn from a supervisor who draws on a different model or models from that being adopted in the therapy by the supervisee. It would be important explicitly to negotiate whether the supervisor and the supervisee are working from similar or different models of therapy. Examples of supervision which draw on different models are presented later in transcripts from Scaife (1995), and Bernard and Goodyear (1992).

Features that characterise supervision

The term 'supervision' is used here broadly to cover a range of arrangements, but a number of common features are regarded as characterising supervision:

- The purposes are to secure the welfare of clients, and to enhance the services offered to clients by their therapists. In so doing, the supervisory focus may be almost exclusively on the needs and experiences of the supervisee.
- Supervisory relationships should either preclude the simultaneous existence of other role-relationships between participants (friendships,

managerial relationships), or where dual relationships pertain this should be acknowledged and the implications addressed.

- Supervision is characterised by an agreement or contract (with varying degrees of formality) which specifies the purposes, aims, methods, term, frequency, location, etc. of the supervision.
- It should not be an aim of supervision for the personal development needs of the supervisor to be met by the supervisee, but supervision is appropriately addressed to the personal and professional development of the supervisee.
- Supervision can serve formative, restorative and normative functions (see Chapter 5).

In pre-registration training, supervision is also characterised as follows:

- The effects of supervision are to socialise the new recruit into the profession, to replicate institutional canons and to propagate the norms of the profession.
- The supervisor performs a gate-keeping function which allows for the exclusion of those deemed to be unsuitable for membership of the profession.
- Supervision occurs in the context of a power imbalance in which the evaluation of the work of those in training can have a profound impact on their subsequent lives at work.

This is not to argue that supervision is the panacea for dealing with work related issues; its aims and purposes can also be achieved through less formal relationships, and the existence of the features above does not necessarily guarantee that the aims of supervision will be achieved.

People at work have their needs met in conversations, ranging from those that take place in the kitchen over a cup of coffee to those that occur in review sessions with managers, in team meetings and the like. Informal conversations and formal ones undertaken for purposes other than supervision may lead to similar outcomes, but would not have the features designated to constitute supervision for the purposes of this text. Nevertheless, supervision does not have to be something that is overly special in order to achieve the aims and meet the defined purposes. One of the most important factors in whether the supervision is useful for these purposes is the interest that the supervisor has in supervision and in the supervisee. When this is the case, all else is likely to follow (Nelson, 1978; Engel, House, Pearson and Sluman, 1998).

Responsibilities in supervision

A number of different parties constitute the stakeholders in the supervisory process. At the least these include the client, therapist and supervisor. In addition, the work most often takes place in a host agency which will have norms and mores of its own. In pre-registration supervision there is also likely to be the involvement of a host training body such as a university or other institution of higher education.

All of the participants and agencies that constitute the supervisory system have roles and responsibilities, and will influence the process of supervision to a greater or lesser extent. In this section, the responsibilities of the different stakeholders are explored and the author's views presented.

The client

Before considering the responsibilities of clients, a decision regarding the identity of the client needs to be reached. In different contexts the client may be an institution, the referrer, the carer, the identified client or their family. The client is the person or system that seeks change for the purpose of relieving distress or solving problems. The client may be seeking change in another rather than in self, as is often the case, for example, when a child is referred. In such instances the person presented as the problem may become the client, but not necessarily at the point of referral. Problems can be solved through many different approaches and through various processes of change. For instance, a child may be referred with sleep problems, the resolution of which might include a change in the child's pattern of sleep, the parents coming to accept that they can tolerate and adapt to the child's pattern of sleep, redefinition of the problem as a marital–sexual one in which the sleep pattern focuses attention elsewhere, or a move of house as a result of which the neighbours no longer complain about disturbance in the night. The problem might also be defined as arising from a socio-cultural context in which infants are expected to sleep alone rather than in physical proximity to their parents and could be resolved by resisting contextual pressures and allowing the child into the parental bed.

Once the client has been identified, the definition of the problem and the decision to work towards change usually lie with the client, albeit with the help of the therapist. Whilst the therapy may not begin with this degree of clarity, an appraisal of motivation or capacity for change at a more or less formal level is part of the ongoing assessment. Where the client is indefinitely committed to no change, continuing efforts are likely to be experienced as frustrating for the therapist, and costly for the purchaser. If the work is to be successful, commitment to change cannot rest solely with the therapist or supervisor. Ongoing assessment of motivation to change is the responsibility of the therapist and supervisor.

The responsibility of the therapist/supervisee

Responsibilities to clients

In the therapy, the responsibility of the practitioner is to participate in and to strive towards creating the conditions that will facilitate change for the client. Whether or not clients respond is up to them. In addition, supervisee therapists have responsibilities to act ethically and within the professional guidelines established both by their employer and by their professional body. Actively participating in supervision and remaining open to learning as part of continuing professional development helps therapists to ensure that they are fulfilling these responsibilities to clients.

Responsibilities for supervision

Supervisors sometimes assume that the burden of responsibility for what happens in supervision, and the outcomes of it, lies principally if not exclusively with them. Supervisees also fall into the same trap and as a result may approach supervision passively, as if it is something done *to* them, not something in which they have responsibility for making sure that their needs are met. When the responsibilities of the supervisee are abdicated, a set of unreasonable expectations of the supervisor may be created. Understanding of the different responsibilities of supervisors and supervisees can be drawn from considering a parallel between the supervisee–supervisor system and the client–therapist system. Essentially, the supervisor is responsible for participating in and creating the conditions in which learning and development can take place, and in which the client's needs can best be served; but whether the learning opportunities are grasped is the responsibility of the supervisee.

Inskipp and Proctor (1988) have developed an excellent set of materials to aid supervisees in identifying and developing their skills in taking this responsibility, from which the following list is derived:

- Considering how to share your current understanding of your strengths and points for development with the supervisor.
- Taking a position of openness to learning which includes communicating your thoughts and feelings in supervision.
- Noticing what you find threatening in supervision.
- Noticing how you typically show defensiveness.
- Identifying your own ideas about boundaries in supervision and working out how to let your supervisor know should they begin to stray beyond them.
- Being prepared for and having the skills to negotiate disagreement.
- Identifying your expectations about the focus of supervision.
- Being clear about the roles that you expect of your supervisor.

- Working out how to stay in control of feedback that might be given by the supervisor.
- Examining your views about having your work observed either directly or indirectly.
- Working out how to show your supervisor your fears and anxieties without undue apprehension in anticipation of negative evaluation.
- Letting the supervisor know what is proving helpful and unhelpful to your learning and development.
- Acknowledging errors with a view to learning from them.

The responsibilities of the supervisor

Depending on the context of the supervision, the supervisor has various wide-ranging responsibilities for the client, the supervisee, and for ensuring that the mores and standards of their own and the supervisee's employing body and any involved professional and training institutions are maintained.

For the welfare of the client

Supervisors will need to identify with whom the responsibility for case-work lies. In pre-registration training this will often be with themselves, whereas in post-registration arrangements it is more likely to be with the supervisee. For example, in a survey of counsellor supervisors working in private practice, none of the respondents regarded themselves as legally responsible for their supervisees' work (King and Wheeler, 1999). The location of this responsibility should influence the manner in which supervision is conducted. In the former, supervisors will need to have a more 'hands-on' awareness of the work being undertaken in order to effect their responsibilities to clients and in order to protect themselves and their supervisees from potential litigation. Even in post-registration arrangements, supervisors have responsibilities towards clients and cannot 'unknow' things that they have been told or have observed in supervision.

The dual responsibility for the client and for the supervisee can give rise to some of the most difficult dilemmas for supervisors. The needs of the two parties may conflict, and in such circumstances supervisors need to steer a course that is fair to both and which they themselves can tolerate, albeit with a sense of discomfort. Such a conflict of interest can arise, for example, as a result of the supervisee experiencing debilitating levels of anxiety in the presence of clients so as seriously to impede the formation of a relationship in which the client is able to change. The supervisor is faced with the dilemma of ensuring that needy clients are provided with adequate help, whilst simultaneously aiding the supervisee in dealing with her or his anxiety. Paradoxically, the supervisor may find that raising the issue with the supervisee further escalates anxiety levels. However, for some supervisees, clear statement of a problem confirms what they already implicitly knew and allows them to undertake the task of remediation with the help of the supervisor.

Generally speaking, where the client is at risk or where someone else is at risk from the client, supervisees will value the input of the supervisor in helping them to steer a safe course. A dilemma arises if the supervisor believes that the supervisee is not taking the danger sufficiently seriously. The supervisor is responsible for pursuing the matter further with the supervisee until satisfied with the course of action agreed and taken. Dilemmas can also arise should supervisors find themselves questioning whether the supervisee should be practising at a particular time. Whilst there is clearly a gate-keeping function in pre-registration supervision, a course of action is not so obvious in practitioner or peer arrangements. Where the difficulties are acknowledged by the supervisee, the supervisor's role may be to help the supervisee to determine how to act. In the face of a failure to acknowledge and act appropriately, the supervisor may be faced with taking the matter outside supervision, discussing *how* not *whether* to do this with the supervisee. In private practice supervisors are particularly sensitive to the tension between practitioners needing to stop working for personal reasons but needing to continue practising for financial reasons (King and Wheeler, 1999).

Whilst the supervisor's responsibility may be clear, there is evidence that supervisors find it very difficult to take matters beyond the supervision itself. King and Wheeler (1999) found that counselling supervisors in the UK were very reluctant to invoke the British Association of Counsellors (BAC) complaints procedure even if obliged to do so. When undertaken, the process had been experienced as distressing for both supervisor and supervisee. King and Wheeler advocate a cautious approach by supervisors in private practice to agreeing to take on a supervisee, but point out that, paradoxically, counsellors with less experience or skills, in whom the supervisors had least confidence, might find it most difficult to obtain supervision from well-regarded colleagues.

Supervisors need to be clear that they share responsibility for the welfare of their supervisees' clients, and that this may present conflicts with their responsibilities to their supervisees. This is discussed further in Chapter 7.

To the supervisee

The supervisor cannot make the supervisee learn and develop but is responsible for participating in, and working to create and manage the supervisory process so as best to facilitate the supervisee's learning in the service of the work. Many of the skills required are versions of the skills of supervisees. In addition supervisors have responsibility for the process of establishing a contract for supervision and for being open to development of their own knowledge and skills in the process of supervision.

Supervisors are responsible for effecting any designated tasks that arise from the regulations of other involved parties. Where a number of different parties are involved, this can generate dilemmas regarding the priority of different needs where these conflict. For example, if an employer pays for the supervision of one of its employees, and it emerges in the supervision that the supervisee is acting ethically but against the stated aims and objectives of the employer, to whom do supervisors owe their principal allegiance – the supervisee or the purchaser of the supervision? It is best to establish this before entering into the supervisory arrangement. When the arrangement is clear and in the open, the supervisee can make an informed decision about what he or she can safely reveal in supervision and what would compromise the supervisor. In this instance, the supervisor can in any case help the supervisee to explore the options for acting both ethically and within the aims and objectives of the employing body. Where no change results, the supervisor will be able to act according to the initial agreement regarding primary allegiance.

To the employer/s

Different employers may be involved in a supervisory arrangement. Supervisees may be employed by their own agency but undertake work in the supervisor's agency. In this case, it will be necessary to establish the specific responsibilities of the different parties and how disciplinary and grievance procedures will be effected in the rare event of their being necessary. An additional complication arises when the supervisee works in the supervisor's agency but on a voluntary or self-funded basis. Supervisors will need to clarify their responsibilities to their own agency, including the liability of the agency for the work of the supervisee. Whilst the majority of supervisory relationships work to the satisfaction of all parties most of the time, the rarity with which serious difficulties arise makes it essential that the supervisor take responsibility at the outset for clarifying the procedures to be followed in such unfortunate circumstances.

To the training institution

Where the supervisee is in training it is the responsibility of the training institution to inform the supervisor of its expectations, but subsequently it becomes the responsibility of the supervisor to act in ways congruent with the agreements that have been made in relation to the expectations and standards of the training institution. Should the supervisee be required to produce case material based on the work done under supervision, the supervisor has responsibility for ensuring that appropriate clients are available that enable the completion of such work. Training institutions usually require that the supervisor make a formal assessment of the supervisee's work. Supervisors will need to familiarise themselves with assessment procedures and have responsibility for working out how they can best carry out their role in such a way as to include both formative and summative evaluation.

To the profession

In supervision of pre-registration training, the supervisor may also have a significant role in and responsibility to transmit the values and standards of the profession. This can be more or less conscious and explicit, but the underlying values of the profession are likely to be manifest in the way that the supervisor thinks and acts. In a research context, this tendency to act consistently with the 'school' in which one's development has taken place is described by Kuhn (1962). Ekstein and Wallerstein (1972) describe this socialisation into the profession as the development of professional identity arising by association with senior members of the trainee's own professional discipline.

In this section the responsibilities of stakeholders beyond the more immediate triad of client/therapist/supervisor have been explored only peripherally, but the supervision takes place in a wider context which confers responsibilities beyond the immediate triad. In agreeing to provide supervision, by implication the supervisor accepts the responsibilities associated with each of the agencies concerned and as a result must deal with the implications that arise.

Boundary issues

Personal and professional

The extent to which the supervision focuses on personal issues is determined partly by the model of therapy in which the parties are engaged. Historically, for example, whilst there has been disagreement in the psychoanalytic school about the extent to which the same analyst might both analyse and supervise a student (Doehrman, 1976), the feelings experienced by the supervisee have nevertheless been regarded as a legitimate and desirable focus of supervision.

The emphasis on the personal is a matter for negotiation in the supervisory relationship. It is important that the supervisor does not stray beyond the territory agreed and also that the supervisor is aware of the supervisee's other sources of support in the event of life events or other personal issues compromising the work. The issue of personal and professional development is explored in greater depth in Chapter 3.

Supervision and therapy

Whilst there is a clear distinction between therapy and supervision in terms of a focus on learning for life as distinct from learning for work, there are also commonalities of purpose regarding development and change. Supervisors are likely to draw on a set of skills common to both tasks that include active listening, collective meaning-making, information giving, supporting and challenging. Additional dimensions relevant to the supervisory task include evaluation and probably a greater degree of supervisor self-disclosure.

Because of the commonalities in the supervisory and therapeutic roles, supervisors need to beware of straying from the task of supervision, particularly where they are invited into the role of therapist by the supervisee. It is useful always for the supervisor to have in mind the question 'How is this relevant to the work?' as an aid to maintaining the boundary between the two different roles.

Supervision and teaching

In supervision, it is appropriate at times for the supervisor to act as a teacher either by giving information or by more generally focusing on the learning of the supervisee using enquiry and exploration. The common aims of increasing knowledge and skills are relevant to both roles. But supervision covers a wider territory through its restorative function in which the supervisor helps supervisees to understand and manage their emotions at work. Supervision is also less likely to be constrained by an externally determined curriculum. Supervisees working with clients will generate a personal curriculum for their learning based around the specific encounters of their day-to-day work.

Dual relationships: friendships/managerial relationships

Where participants in a supervisory relationship have no prior or ongoing relationship that was established for other purposes, there is a greater freedom in which to work out the new relationship. Many people participate in managerial supervision at work and it is a moot point to what extent this concurrent role-relationship restricts and limits the potential achievements of the supervision. When one person has power to influence the progression and promotion of the other, there is bound to be some influence over what takes place in supervision. This dual role-relationship is likely to pertain in pre-registration training as well as in other managerial relationships. The influence of the disparity in status may be contained by discussion during and following the contracting process, but its influence may readily be underestimated.

One approach to this dual relationship is for the supervisee to have supervision with both a line manager and an independent supervisor. The profession of counselling, in particular, has recognised the benefit of such an arrangement which provides a context for the exploration of issues which the supervisee might feel uncomfortable about exploring in a managerial relationship. The contracting process then has an important function in reaching agreement about which matters should be discussed with which supervisor.

Where a choice of supervisor is possible, people may be tempted to select someone whom they know and like. Supporting evidence for this was reported by Lawton (2000) in a study of qualified counsellors working in further education colleges. She found that convenience of location and familiarity with the supervisor took precedence over all other considerations. In many cases this will present no problems and may facilitate the development of a very effective supervisory relationship. However, where the relationship extends beyond the context of work, potential problems arise. If the supervisor makes a negative evaluation of the supervisee's work, there is a risk that this could lead to a redefinition of the relationship from friend to enemy. Where supervisors prioritise the friendship, are not prepared to compromise it, and thus withhold the negative evaluation, they are failing to fulfil all aspects of the role that they have contracted to provide.

In my experience, people tend to be reluctant to acknowledge the potential difficulties that can arise when friendships and formal work relationships coincide. Attempts to manage this have led people to agree not to meet each other outside work for the duration of their relationship in supervision, and this may prove satisfactory. Such an arrangement clearly acknowledges the potential for blurring of roles and allows role conflict to be addressed as an agenda item in supervision.

Choice or allocation of supervisor

The degree to which people may select their own supervisors as opposed to having them allocated will often be influenced by their stage of career development. The greater the opportunity to choose, the more likely will be the supervisee positively to anticipate engaging in the supervisory process. Where choice is possible, there is a view that experienced practitioners benefit more from the challenge and stimulation of a new approach rather than gravitation towards the familiar (Page and Wosket, 1994). Particularly during training, supervisors are more likely to be allocated by the training institution. Supervisors will have reputations in the training community deriving from their previous input, and this can have extensive repercussions for what subsequently takes place.

Generally speaking, supervisors perform this role through choice and are interested to carry it out well. Supervisees who are allocated a supervisor whose reputation generates concern have a responsibility to consider how this might affect the establishment of the relationship, and would benefit from discussing this with the person responsible for the allocation. Supervisors have a responsibility to be interested in their reputations in the professional community and to seek feedback with regard to their supervisory role. In the knowledge of their reputation they can bring it into the contracting process by suggesting 'You may have heard that . . .', which signals that reputations are appropriate material for discussion and exploration.

In a similar fashion, supervisees themselves acquire reputations which may also be handled though disclosure and discussion. Secret knowledge is likely to generate adverse effects that will interfere with the process of supervision.

It may be considered that 'bad' reputations are more problematic than 'good' ones. However, supervisees allocated to a 'good' supervisor who fails to conform to expectations may struggle to make meaning of this failure, and may conclude that the fault lies with themselves.

Wherever feasible it is desirable for there to be an element of choice of partner in supervisory relationships, including a built-in review process which enables partners to reassess the suitability as both develop and change.

Summary

This chapter has explored the definitions and parameters of supervision. The term is used widely to encompass both pre-registration and post-registration arrangements. The features that define supervision as opposed to other work relationships have been identified, and the commonalities and differences with other roles and tasks have been reviewed. The different responsibilities of the parties involved in supervision have been explored. The next chapter moves on to focus on a particular task of supervision – that of aiding the supervisee's learning and development.

Chapter 2

Supervision and learning

Joyce Scaife and Jon Scaife

Whatever else is accepted as a purpose and aim of supervision, the development of the supervisee's knowledge, understanding and skills is almost invariably a central component. This chapter explores some general ideas about learning, how it is accomplished, and how supervision might contribute. It also addresses how the supervisor might help supervisees to understand more about their own learning styles and highlights the responsibility of supervisees for their own learning. The task of the professional helper requires the application of knowledge to practice. The linking of theory and practice may be one of the preoccupations of the supervisee and a significant focus of supervision. This chapter is addressed both to the construction of knowledge and to its application in the skills of helping.

Views about knowledge

Knowledge-in-action

In professional training there is some emphasis on the learning of theory that is usually taught within a curriculum defined by the training institution or professional body. There is also a practice component and it is typically this that is supervised. The knowledge acquired in coursework, or through the reading undertaken at any stage in a professional career, could be described as 'declarative knowledge'. It consists of theories, concepts, principles and facts that can be stated by the supervisee (Bransford and Vye, 1988). This might also include the capacity to describe techniques and approaches to intervention. When this knowledge is applied in practice, the process of application may be referred to as 'procedural knowledge'. This form of knowledge is regarded as tacit and automatic and is referred to by Schön (1987) as 'knowledge-in-action'. Knowledge-in-action takes place during skilled performance and its features may not be amenable to verbal explication. Even when key features can be described, learners cannot acquire the skilled performance without their own active involvement.

Skilful performance necessarily involves procedural knowledge. This can be seen by considering performances such as riding a bicycle, playing a sport, making music or learning to speak a second language. There is not time consciously to think of all the knowledge that is applied whilst effecting these skills, even if it had a conscious form. Bringing some features to awareness can even undermine performance; for example, thinking too hard about particular aspects of a golf swing. Since professional helping involves the skills of interacting with others, procedural knowledge is a necessary feature. Binder and Strupp (1997) argue that what is specifically needed is a particular sort of procedural knowledge that allows for on-the-spot appraisals and reappraisals of the problem situation whilst simultaneously acting within it. Following Schön they refer to this as 'reflection-in-action'. They suggest that true therapeutic competence and effectiveness involve becoming proficient in the capacities for reflection-in-action and improvisation. These capacities are central to ideas expressed in the literature on adult learning and they will be returned to later.

Philosophical underpinnings

Views about learning particular skills are predicated upon a set of underlying assumptions and beliefs about how knowledge of the world is obtained. In Britain there is a long-standing tradition of empiricism, which stresses the essential role of the senses in the creation of knowledge. A legacy of the seventeenth-century philosopher John Locke is the widespread assumption that the mind is a container into which knowledge flows through experience. Many teaching and training approaches are consistent with this doctrine, i.e. lecturing, and imitative methods such as the apprenticeship approach. Positivism is a strong form of empiricism in which knowledge is seen as advancing through systematic observation using the methods of natural science. Metaphysical knowledge concerning concepts such as goodness, beauty and justice is rejected from a positivist viewpoint as it does not appear to derive directly from the experiences of the senses. Metaphysical knowing might be regarded as the knowledge of the heart as opposed to the knowledge of the head. The distinction is elegantly illustrated in the following quote:

> When you understand all about the sun and all about the atmosphere and all about the radiation of the earth you may still miss the radiance of the sunset.
>
> (Whitehead, 1926: 279)

In contrast with empiricism is innatism, or nativism, in which the mind is regarded as having an embedded, innate knowledge-bearing structure. In this view, the possibilities for learning are determined within the individual during development, and learning becomes a realisation of innate potential, at most selected, but not otherwise determined by the environment. The widely held views that people are characterised by fixed abilities (she's naturally musical) or general intelligence (he's not very bright) illustrate an implicit commitment to innatism.

The 'nature–nurture' argument has persisted in one form or another from the time of Socrates and Plato, and the question of the explanation for the origin of knowledge is still not settled. Nevertheless, if you ask people to think about what and who have influenced their learning they can generally identify some factors to explain how they have come to learn what they know. The responses usually include explanations that owe much to their experiences, but are also likely to include responses that identify feelings not directly attributable to the observable. This chapter explores theories about how people learn, both from experience and through development.

Relevance of theories of learning focused at the level of behaviour

Within the empiricist tradition there have been various views about the status of mental content. Behaviourism is at the end of the continuum in focusing on what can be observed rather than on mental content. Behavioural theories seek to account for learning through the interaction of the individual with the environment. Conducting supervision from this standpoint, one would expect that learning might be facilitated by the supervisee observing the work of the supervisor or other therapists either live or taped. The supervisor acts as a model for supervisees who may reproduce elements of what they have observed in their own work. This can be of particular relevance where the procedures are relatively common across work with different clients – for example, in introducing oneself and the way of working, or in following a standard assessment procedure. Other behaviour that could be modelled includes responding to certain events in the work where safety is at a premium, such as assessment of risk where a client is threatening suicide, or explaining to the client the issue of confidentiality and its limits.

In addition to being observed directly, the supervisor may provide a model by illustrating what to say, making suggestions with: 'You might have said . . .' or 'I might have said . . .' Supervisees who are at an early stage of training often have not learned the different style of communication undertaken in therapy in which typical social conventions might be breached. The sorts of questions or statements used in therapy might in other contexts be construed as 'rude' or might require the use of language normally reserved for intimate relationships. Examples include asking clients diagnosed as anorexic how much they weigh, asking suicidal clients about the plans that they have made to kill themselves, in sexual therapy asking questions about erectile functioning, or in a childhood soiler asking about the consistency of the stool. Supervisees may avoid such issues in their attempts to be therapeutic. Seeing how it might be done is likely to enhance the confidence of supervisees since they might emulate the supervisor.

Whilst some learning can derive from observation, further development can hinge upon behaviour rehearsal or practice, perhaps with opportunities for feedback from the supervisor. This can be accomplished through role-play in supervision or by supervisees practising alone or making recordings of their attempts to bring to supervision for further discussion.

Practice can be regarded as enhancing the development of technique and is of relevance in the learning of any number of practical skills. When technique has become fluent, its execution can be said to be 'overlearned' and hence relegated to a less conscious level (Frostig, 1972; Gilbert, 1957). It may not be possible to identify how this change to less-conscious awareness of the components of the task took place. Mastery of technique, as in other skills such as playing a musical instrument, enables fluent performance in which the performer can concentrate on other issues such as self-expression or full attention to the client. In the domain of therapy, 'self-expression' might equate with the style of the therapist.

This concept of overlearning connects with the ideas of Bateson (1972). He proposed the idea of habits as being mental economies that free the mind to focus elsewhere. Attention needs effort whereas habit occurs at a level of automation. In supervision, the development of such mind-freeing habits may be facilitated by the supervisor. The supervisor may provide an exemplar to be carefully observed by the supervisee. Through emulation these behaviours may become 'normal' for the supervisee in the context of the work. The supervisor might identify salient actions that are central automatised phenomena.

The behavioural concept of reinforcement is also applicable to the supervisory situation. At times supervisees value positive feedback in the form of a 'well done', or a specific compliment. Some supervisees regard *any* sort of evaluative feedback as preferable to the uncertainty of none at all. In addition, and ultimately perhaps of greater importance, is the reinforcing experience of success which occurs when therapists observe the positive outcomes achieved by their clients as a result of therapy. In this regard, it is helpful if the supervisor is able to arrange for the supervisee to work with at least some clients for whom good progress might be predicted.

Thus, the behavioural tradition offers a number of ideas that can be applied in supervision to aid the supervisee's learning and development. The chapter goes on to explore other ideas relevant to this supervisory task.

The concept of mind and the plastic brain

In Western thinking – dominated from Descartes until this century by Cartesian dualism, but now strongly challenged – brain and mind were classified, respectively, as material and non-material things. Since it was held that only material things could be studied, the consideration and exploration of aspects of mind such as understanding were neglected. Recent work in diverse disciplines (neuroscience, psychology, artificial intelligence and philosophy) has led to widespread rejection of the dualist separation of mind and brain and has consequently allowed the concept of mind to become a studied phenomenon. One post-dualist view is that consciousness is an 'emergent property' of brain, along with a concept of self. Brain science is thus able to shed light on mental processes and content. This work has defined 'plasticity' as a key property of the brain:

> Talk of the brain as hard-wired is misleading . . . The key to our magnificent abilities as anticipation machines involves fixing gross architecture while leaving the development of connections at the micro-structural level undedicated and adaptable.
>
> (Flanagan, 1992: 46)

Flanagan's point is that whilst the large-scale structures of the brain are common to human beings and are the result of evolution at the genetic level over multiple generations, each of us has our own flexible fine structure of neuronal connections:

> the plastic brain is capable of reorganising itself adaptively in response to the particular novelties encountered in the organism's environment.
>
> (Dennett, 1991: 184)

Work by Edelman (1992) has led to an understanding of the development of neuronal structures in the plastic brain in terms of a process of selection that parallels Darwinian natural selection, though operating on time-scales of seconds, and perhaps minutes and hours, rather than on multiple lifetimes.

Edelman proposes that a genetically inherited human 'value system' is at the root of learning – for Edelman, value means the capacity to discriminate in ways that have conferred relative survival advantage. For example, organisms that can make value distinctions between environmental factors such as hot and cold are likely to be at an advantage over those that cannot. When an individual's value system 'fires' in response to something, this firing process strengthens the currently active neuronal pathways. Alternative pathways are weakened in comparison. This process of neuronal group selection is an example of plasticity in the nervous system. Change in behaviour, including mental behaviour, that results from a process such as this is learning. Learning occurs as a result of physiological change in the brain in which stable neuronal pathways are constructed.

Ideas such as those of Edelman, Flanagan and others paint a picture of unique brain structures and unique learning having arisen in each individual. Each person's neuronal 'street map' will have evolved during her or his life to fire to different stimuli. People comprising the supervision system will bring these different learning histories to the relationship. It follows that it would be helpful to create a supervisory relationship in which tolerance, exploration of difference and curiosity about the individual and sub-cultural learned beliefs underpinning the approach to the work may be expressed.

The interpersonal dimension

A selection process that is quite distinct from Edelman's theory of neuronal group selection is proposed as operating within the 'environment' of the human social system, or a sub-set such as the helping professions. This is cultural selection through the selection of ideas; the selection of what to learn. To a degree each profession that works to alleviate human suffering will have devised its own sub-cultural ideas of what is considered appropriate to learn and what is excluded. In learning the profession, individuals become encultured within that school of thought, the tenets of which do not always become obvious except when coming up against people schooled in alternative professional cultures.

An exercise designed to show how individual beliefs and convictions are implicitly brought to supervision and influence the process was designed for a supervision workshop as follows. Participants were divided into three groups, each given the same task of wrapping an egg. Each group was given a different card on which were written the directions for what should be achieved in wrapping the egg. One group was invited to wrap the egg for aesthetic effect, the second for durability, and the third for economy. Upon completion, the products of each group were passed to another group whose task was to give feedback and critique the product. Initially some of the comments made about other groups' efforts were negative to the point of being scathing. Emotions ran high. After a few minutes of loud debate and laughter, one person asked another group's members why they had wrapped the egg in that particular way, and there was a gradual realisation that the different groups had been assigned different values from which to approach the task.

Since supervisors comprise only one element of the supervisee's environment, to what extent can they contribute usefully to what is learned? Carl Rogers (1974) has questioned this (italics are his):

> I have come to feel that the only learning which significantly influences behaviour is self-discovered, self-appropriated learning. *Such self-discovered learning, truth that has been personally appropriated and assimilated in experience, cannot be directly communicated to another.* As soon as an individual tries to communicate such experience directly, often with quite natural enthusiasm, it becomes teaching, and its results are inconsequential.
>
> (Rogers, 1974: 276)

Rogers takes the view that for meaningful learning to take place, the learner must be at the centre of the process. In questioning whether another can assist the learning he rejects the idea of direct communication of knowledge as useful. The question then becomes whether the supervisor can do something else that acknowledges the central position and the values of the learner and from which learning can result. An alternative and more optimistic position than that of Rogers was taken by Gagné (1967). According to Gagné, actions such as supervision or teaching involve:

> The institution and arrangement of the external conditions of learning in ways which will optimally interact with internal capabilities of the learner, so as to bring about changes in these capabilities.
>
> (Gagné, 1967: 295)

In this view, the task of the supervisor is to work out, together with the supervisee, what supervisory environment and interventions will best connect with the current knowledge and beliefs of the supervisee.

The implications of these ideas about knowledge and learning for supervision are:

1 That the supervisor's actions and resources are in competition with other aspects of the learner's environment for the learner's attention.
2 That in order for learning to take place, what is to be learned must connect with the underpinning pre-existing values and current knowledge of the learner.
3 That in addition to observation, description and experience, there are internal implicit processes that are less amenable to analysis and study that also contribute to learning.

Personal learning styles

Pask (1976) argues for two distinguishable processes involved in the learning of complex material – building a description of what may be known (a conceptual model of how topics interrelate) and building procedures that represent a more detailed sequential study. Individuals may show a dominance of one of these processes over the other. Those who show a preference for the development of an overview are described as holists, who tend to adopt a global study approach. Those preferring procedure-building are described as serialists, who adopt a local approach to study whereby they focus on local facts and details. The holist typically focuses on several aspects of the subject at the same time.

Ford (1985) explored to what extent postgraduate students could adopt either holist or serialist strategies. Two groups of students were identified, each showing a preference for one strategy. They were then taught with two different teaching strategies designed to suit either holist or serialist learners. The majority of students showed evidence of greater learning taking place as a result of the teaching designed to suit their learning style.

Pask's is not the only attempt to identify distinctive individual learning styles. Riding (1992, 1994), for example, identifies nine categories of learning style based on the dimensions of analytic–holist and verbaliser–imager. He accounts for these differences in terms of the individuality of human brains, not at the neuronal level but through differences of brain activity.

The implications of these ideas for supervision are that supervisees might find it helpful to identify their preferred learning styles and the way these styles vary with the task. In the light of this knowledge the supervisor might strive to create the conditions for learning that would best suit the preferred learning style.

Methods for the exploration of personal learning styles

A number of questionnaire methods are available for exploring personal learning styles, for example the Study Preference Questionnaire (Ford, 1985), the Short Inventory of Approaches to Study (Entwistle, 1981) the Cognitive Styles Analysis (Riding, 1994) and the Manual of Learning Styles (Honey and Mumford, 1992). In addition, a number of paper and pencil based assessment methods have been devised by Pask (1973).

A technique for exploring which environments and interventions have previously enhanced the supervisee's learning has been described by Judy Hildebrand (1998a). She invites supervisees to draw a professional 'genogram' of their previous learning. This can be pictorial, in words or images according to the preferences of the individual. The task is to map the historical influences on learning that have been of relevance to the way the person conducts her or his work. This might include people and relationships, books (including novels), films, 'gurus', personal crises, and so on. The exercise is private with a view to the supervisor asking, 'What would it be helpful for me to learn from your having done this exercise?' 'What does it tell me about the conditions I should try to create that will be most helpful to your learning in supervision?'

A further method for exploring personal learning style is to offer a problem that acts as a metaphor for an issue in professional helping, and to ask the supervisee to attempt to solve it. The supervisee then thinks about how he or she approached the task – through a logical and steady progression, with impatience, through guesswork and the like. Information about supervisees' approaches to this problem might shed light on their approach to problem-solving in general. Examples of such tasks are described in Scaife (1995).

Piaget's ideas applied in supervision

Piaget (1972) proposed a theory of knowledge growth through a process of equilibration, which arises from the interaction between individuals and their environment. Equilibration is a process of resolution of incompatibilities that can occur between what the person currently knows, and the perception and meaning made of an event that does not fit with current knowledge. The person's response to a perceived 'gap' or conflict is typically initially conservative (i.e. resistant) then conservatively adaptive – the knowledge system accommodates the disturbance that gave rise to the perceived gap or conflict with as little change as possible. If this fails to resolve the conflict, the knowledge system changes so that such disturbing events are no longer disturbances because they now fit. The transient resistance has melted away and a new practised response remains. This is regarded as stable until a further incompatibility is perceived.

Some implications for supervision derive from this aspect of Piaget's theory. Firstly, it is necessary for a lack of fit to be perceived before it can be responded to. If the gap between the understandings of the supervisor and supervisee is too great, it may not be possible for supervisees to perceive that something has occurred that is of relevance to their learning. This is encapsulated in the four stages of learning readiness described by Inskipp and Proctor (1993). They describe a cycle in which learners move from a comfortable state of unconscious incompetence in which they are unaware of not knowing or possessing a skill. Recognition of not knowing leads to a less comfortable state of conscious incompetence (or self-conscious incompetence). This may arise as a result of having seen another perform the skill, or when something is tried unsuccessfully. There is then a decision to be made as to whether to attempt to learn the skill in the knowledge that the process of learning will be accompanied by clumsiness and failure.

The next stage is that of conscious competence when the skill can be performed with intellectual effort. Finally, the stage of unconscious competence is reached when the skill is overlearned and can be performed without conscious effort.

A first step may be for the supervisor to draw the attention of the supervisee towards that which it is intended for her or him to learn. If the supervisee does not perceive this as material to the learning, he or she might respond with incomprehension, with resistance or avoidance. As hypothesised by Piaget, a conservative initial response would be expected. When there is a significant gap in knowledge and experience between supervisors and supervisees it may be very difficult for supervisors to 'de-centre' and understand the current status of the learner with respect to the knowledge that they wish to impart, a point made by Donaldson (1978).

For example, in teaching interviewing skills it was the intention of one of us and a colleague to ensure that we addressed issues of difference, and in particular ethnicity, gender, age and disability in the session. To this end, we asked the group members to identify their own features as might be noticed by a client on first meeting. People talked about their age, gender, ethnicity, hearing losses and the like at some length. The feedback from this session was that issues of difference had not been addressed. On further exploration it became apparent that the learners had not identified their own personal features as relevant to learning about difference – they were at the stage of focusing exclusively 'out there' on the client, not yet including themselves as a feature of the therapeutic system. On reflection it would have been helpful for my colleague and I to bridge from our own characteristics to those of clients in order better to connect with the position of the students.

In the application of Piaget's ideas, some authors go so far as to prescribe that the teacher or supervisor instigate a series of problems specifically designed to produce a state of disequilibration in relation to the topic to be learned (Rowell, 1989). Our own experience, both in our learning and in that of supervisees, is that sufficient unsolicited examples present themselves such as to create a frequent state of uncertainty, often accompanied by the unpleasant emotional states of confusion and anxiety. It would not be surprising should a self-preserving defensiveness constitute a normal response.

The application of Schön's ideas about learning

Here we return to the idea introduced earlier in the chapter, that counselling and therapy are skills that depend on the acquisition of procedural knowledge. Binder and Strupp (1997) argue a case for the development of capacities for reflection-in-action and improvisation. They regard treatment manuals as offering a sketchy map of the therapeutic terrain on which moment-to-moment movements must be improvised. The method that they recommend for the development of these skills is through structured sequences of therapeutic problem-detection and problem-solving exercises under conditions that simulate actual clinical experiences. This would fill what they see as the current gap between classroom teaching and work with clients in which the material brought by the client cannot be controlled.

They argue that video-records and segments of real or simulated therapy situations could be used, both to illustrate theory and to provide opportunities for coaching and practice of skills in interpersonal processes. Supervisors may be in an ideal position to offer such simulations and exemplars.

The adult learner

Some of the ideas explored in the sections above are explicated further in the literature on adult learning. Adult learning might be distinguished from learning *per se* in that it acknowledges the capacity of adults to reflect on their own learning in addition to participating in it. Brookfield (1986) suggests that, 'educators should assist adults to speculate creatively on possible alternative ways of organising their personal worlds' (p. 233), 'developing in adults a sense of their personal power and self-worth . . . and fostering a willingness to consider alternative ways of living' (p. 283).

Mezirow (1985) identifies three ways of acquiring knowledge: instrumental learning, dialogic learning and self-reflective learning.

Instrumental learning

This kind of learning is based on a traditional scientific paradigm of knowledge and the pursuit of scientific truths or laws of nature. It involves a prediction about observable things or events that are to be supported or proven incorrect. Learning is directed towards determination of cause–effect relationships, and the knowledge gained is instrumental in nature with a view to increasing individuals' control over their environment. This approach is consistent with an empirical view of knowledge.

This kind of learning might be applicable to those aspects of the work in which the helper might need to exercise control over the environment – for example, managing time boundaries, being able to interrupt respectfully or managing the respective contributions of family members in a family meeting. Instrumental learning might best be facilitated through some of the methods associated with behavioural approaches.

Dialogic learning

In this type of learning new meanings and understandings are viewed as emerging though dialogue. Significant learning is viewed as involved with moral issues, ideals, values and abstract social and political concepts with no simple yardsticks for judging right or wrong. Rather, the validity of knowledge is always provisional and new information is viewed as leading to repeated revision of judgements.

Mezirow suggests that for many areas of knowledge there are no correct answers. The learner needs to develop understanding of the relationship of values to context and be open to acknowledging the validity of different views on a subject. The task of the supervisor is to build self-esteem, helping learners to trust their own assessments of situations even where these go against received wisdom. This involves the creation of a context of safety in which underlying assumptions, values and beliefs may be shared and discussed.

Self-reflective learning

Both this and dialogic learning connect with the ideas of Edelman, Rogers and Piaget in acknowledging the importance of values in influencing learning, the centrality of learning constructed by the self rather than directly transmitted by another and the importance of environmental challenge to an existing meaning or perspective.

In self-reflective learning:

> The learner is presented with an alternative way of interpreting feelings and patterns of action; the old meaning or perspective is reorganised to incorporate new insights. We come to see our reality more inclusively, to understand it more clearly and to integrate our experience better. Only the individual involved can determine the validity of the reorganised meaning scheme or perspective.
>
> (Mezirow, 1985: 21)

Self-reflection may be aided by the supervisor's taking an enquiring approach to work carried out or observed by the supervisee. This can be by asking the supervisee questions such as, 'How did that feel?', or 'What might you have done differently?' Questions could also contain alternatives to the meanings made by the supervisee or to the 'normative' meanings of the culture in which the work is being carried out. For example, an assumption tends to be made that where a family of origin is capable of providing adequate care for a child, this is a better option than the child being looked after by alternative carers. Where this assumption is made, it could be challenged by the supervisor and supervisee discussing the advantages of both staying in the family of origin and of being looked after by other carers.

The relevance of context

Weil (1993) argues that the tasks for the supervisor are to help supervisees to recognise factors that limit their understanding and behaviour, and to help them to develop a critical consciousness with respect to their own assumptions, behaviour and effectiveness in different situations. There is also the need to help supervisees to understand the values of the systems in which people work, and the parts that they play in maintaining the status quo or in unsettling these meaning systems. These issues are explored further in Chapter 3.

The emphasis in an adult learning context on developing critical reflection is explored further by Mezirow (1988), who views the most important aspect of adult learning as problem-posing rather than content-mastery or problem-solving. He emphasises that adult learning and education do not occur in a social vacuum. This acknowledgement of a social and political context is particularly important when looking at historical views held within the helping professions. The body of knowledge changes over time. A vivid illustration of this is provided by instances of the pseudo-science that has underpinned racism in the late nineteenth century and the twentieth. James Hunt (reported in Fryer, 1984), an expert in the treatment of stammering, held a theory of innate differences between black and white people. He founded the Anthropological Society of London in 1863, and a summary of his annual presidential address was as follows:

- That there is as good reason for classifying the Negro as a distinct species from the European as there is for making the ass a distinct species from the zebra: and if, in classification, we take intelligence into consideration, there is a far greater difference between the Negro and the European than between the gorilla and the chimpanzee.
- That the analogies are far more numerous between the Negro and the ape, than between the European and the ape.
- That the Negro is inferior intellectually to the European.
- That the Negro becomes more humanised when in his natural subordination to the European than under any other circumstances.
- That the Negro can only be humanised and civilised by Europeans.
- That European civilisation is not suited to the Negro's requirements or character.

In looking back it is hard to comprehend the development and propagation of such ideas within the professional community without reference to the prevailing social, economic and political climate. History suggests that future generations looking back will find aspects of our current canon of knowledge just as alien, and maybe similarly distasteful.

Experiential learning theory

Learning to be a professional helper involves the construction of new knowledge and the development of skills in its application in practice. Experiential learning theory (Kolb, 1984) attempts to account for the process by which this learning takes place. Kolb describes a cycle of learning in which there are four stages; namely, 'concrete experience', 'reflective observation', abstract conceptualisation' and 'active experimentation' (see Figure 2.1). The cycle repeats and may be entered by the learner at any of the four stages, but the stages are followed in sequence. For example, at the stage of concrete experience, the supervisee might discuss in supervision methods for identifying the client's schemas using a cognitive behavioural approach. He or she then tries to use these methods with a client. The results of this are brought to the following supervision in which the supervisor helps the supervisee to reflect on her or his experience through a process of enquiry. This might lead to new

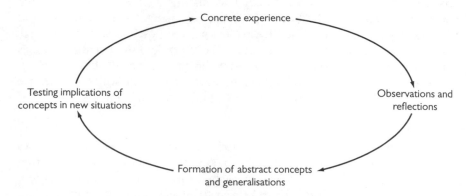

Figure 2.1 The Lewinian experiential learning cycle. From Experiential Learning: Experience as the Source of Learning and Development by Kolb, D. © 1984. Reprinted by permission of Prentice-Hall, Inc., Upper Saddle River, N.J.

understandings at the level of abstract conceptualisation, arising from which the supervisee tries the method differently on the next occasion.

The key features of experiential learning are:

- Learners are involved in an active exploration of experience. Experience is used to test out ideas and assumptions rather than passively to obtain practice. Practice can be very important but it is greatly enhanced by reflection.
- Learners must selectively reflect on their experience in a critical way, rather than take experience for granted and assume that the experience on its own is sufficient.
- The experience must matter to the learner. Learners must be committed to the process of exploring and learning.
- There must be scope for the learner to exercise some independence from the teacher. Teachers have an important role in devising appropriate experiences and facilitating reflection. However, the transmission of information is but a minor element and the teacher cannot experience what the learner experiences or reflect for the learner.
- Experiential learning is not the same as 'discovery' learning. Learning by doing is not simply a matter of letting learners loose and hoping that they discover things for themselves in a haphazard way through sudden bursts of inspiration. The nature of the activity may be carefully designed by the teacher and the experience may need to be carefully reviewed and analysed afterwards for learning to take place. A crucial feature of experiential learning is the structure devised by the teacher within which learning takes place.
- Openness to experience is necessary for learners to have the evidence

upon which to reflect. It is therefore crucial to establish an appropriate emotional tone for learners: one which is safe and supportive,
and which encourages learners to value their own experience and to
trust themselves to draw conclusions from it. This openness may not
exist at the outset but may be fostered through successive experiences
of the experiential learning cycle.

• Experiential learning involves a cyclical sequence of learning activities. Teaching methods can be selected to provide a structure to each
stage of the cycle, and to take learners through the appropriate
sequence.

(Weil, 1995: 14)

This kind of open-minded problem exploration is advocated by Coulshed
(1990), who argues that the more staff are encouraged to rely on so-called
rational decision-making tools, procedural manuals and routinised service
delivery methods, the more they stop thinking for themselves. Such blinkered
responses can lead to narrow and superficial discussions in supervision, trap-
ping supervisor and supervisee into a happy conclusion that all is inspected
and under control.

Experiential learning theory prescribes a particular role for the supervisor
as a facilitator and designer of environments to support learning. It takes into
account many of the ideas noted earlier in the chapter. Supervisors' knowledge of theories of learning is likely to underpin their approach to supervision when attending to the 'formative' purpose of the task. In addition, the
cycle might be referred reflexively to a supervisor's learning of supervisory
skills.

Summary

In this chapter we have explored ideas about the nature of knowledge, skills
and learning. These ideas have included the relevance to supervision of
behavioural theories of learning, the concept of mind, personal learning
styles, Piaget's and other constructivist views regarding the growth of
knowledge, experiential learning and the adult learner. Connections and
distinctions between these ideas have been discussed and their application
in supervision explored.

Chapter 3

The emotional climate of work and the development of self

Joyce Scaife and Sue Walsh

This chapter focuses on the role of the supervisor in relation to the emotions of supervisees because these affect and are affected by their work. It also addresses the role of personal issues, personal histories and personal qualities in the work of supervisees, and the supervisory task of facilitating the development of self-understanding and knowledge. Supervision can perform the functions of support and the development of self. This chapter aims to encourage supervisors to give consideration to these aspects of their role.

There are two themes within the chapter. The first addresses how work contexts, events, and the attitudes and behaviour of clients and colleagues can have significant consequences for the emotional state of people working to help others (i.e. the influence of work on self). The second theme considers the issue of personal and professional development and how the personal qualities, values and beliefs of helping professionals are of central importance in their work (the influence of self on work). The development of self-awareness is often referred to in the helping professions as 'personal and professional development'. The chapter moves from a focus on wider cultural and institutional influences to specific relationships between clients and therapists. In the final section some exercises designed for the exploration of values and beliefs are described.

The emotional climate of organisations – its effects on supervisees

Professional helping often takes place in institutions which are influenced by the wider social, political and economic context. In an ideal world, people might hope to experience their institutional context as compatible and congruent with their own values and aspirations, but this cannot be assumed or guaranteed. Within the institutions in which we work there are social, political and economic forces that can be construed as dangerous, disturbing and destabilising, which may evoke feelings of vulnerability in the employees. Political changes can reverberate throughout organisations and lead to staff

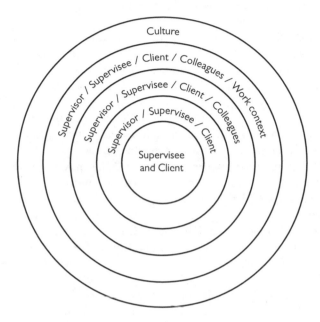

Figure 3.1 Levels of the helping system

experiencing dislocation and alienation from the tenets upon which the employing organisation becomes based.

Morrison (1993) argues that practitioners in the helping professions expect to experience some primary stress arising from the work they undertake, but are far more distressed by the secondary stress arising from the organisation's response to them when this happens. He offers a theoretical framework to explain the damaging effects of this process on staff: The Professional Accommodation Syndrome (Morrison, 1990).

The ethos of the employing organisation and the motivation of individual employees can be at cross-purposes. People's motivations for becoming professional helpers can be explained at a number of levels, which include family scripts and wider cultural values. At the level of the individual, people usually express a desire to be useful in the service of others – they want to help. Employers may have other priorities – to make a profit, to cut costs, to reduce waiting lists, to increase bed occupancy and the like. One view would regard employees as 'economic cogs' whose role is to undertake the tasks of the organisation. An example would be the concept of 'scientific manage-ment' (Taylor, [1911] 1998), in which the worker is reduced to executing management thinking.

Faced with the task of attempting to help another individual, these insti-tutional priorities may be frustrating and restricting in terms of the action to be taken that would best suit the case. The incompatibility of the purposes of the individual and of the organisation can produce a sense of misery, helplessness, outrage and alienation.

In training contexts additional constraints and potential conflicts result from the involvement of the third party; namely, the training institution. The priorities of this institution are likely to include successful completion of the course by as many students as possible. In a university, the status of staff and students may depend on seeming to know more, or, for example, publish more, than colleagues. Bernard and Goodyear (1998: 76) highlight this particularly in relation to postgraduate students when they state, 'the achievement orientation, competitiveness and evaluative nature of the academic climate tend to exacerbate anxiety'. Such a climate may be fostered further by a 'marketplace' political context in which funding of public services such as universities and the health and social services depends on outputs and quantification.

During the 1980s and 1990s in the UK, the change of emphasis in the political climate away from caring to production and output was reflected in the language used in these contexts where 'patients' and 'clients' became 'service users' and 'customers'. University staff gave up 'teaching' in order to 'deliver the curriculum', and when library books were borrowed on loan there were no longer other 'readers' but 'customers' waiting. Treating the health and public services as a marketplace economy is almost certain to be accompanied by distress and a reluctance to make the transition in meaning for staff who entered their professions in order to 'care' or to 'teach' rather than to 'deliver'.

Supervision can serve a restorative function for helpers afflicted by this sense of alienation and dislocation by offering a reflective space in which the influence of these conflicting ideas can be understood and moderated.

In our opinion, the effect of the organisational context and climate on the supervisee is a legitimate focus of supervision. Different contextual dimensions might be analysed in order for supervisees to develop a clearer understanding of their own position and the influences to which they are subject at work. Pearce and Cronen (1980) offer a hierarchical model for this purpose, whilst other authors (Hoffman, 1991; Scaife, 1993c) propose a more heterarchical relationship between the elements.

In our experience such analyses can help people to make sense of their position in the work system and this may help to take the sting out of what may have been construed as personal. For example, a particular service revealed a repeating pattern of schism and recovery following each attempted appointment of a clinical leader. Responsibility for the management and development of the service was vested in the post of service manager. Not surprisingly, the vision of the service manager and the clinical leader sometimes, if not regularly, conflicted. As these conflicts escalated, it became inevitable that one or other of the holders of the lead roles departed in response to the unbearable levels of frustration. In the lead up, other staff were caught up with conflicting loyalties and became wounded in the battle. The difficulties were usually attributed to the problematic personality of one or other individual. For some of the staff, explorations undertaken in supervision facilitated a distancing in which new and more tolerable meanings emerged.

Learning cultures

Hawkins and Shohet (1989) describe a number of working contexts or cultures and the climates that they produce. These include the 'personal pathology culture', the 'bureaucratic culture', 'the watch-your-back culture', 'the reactive/crisis culture', and the 'learning/developmental culture'. They argue that nearly all organisational cultures are a mix of these types but that the learning/developmental culture allows reflection on experience with a view to making sense of this in a way that allows the experience to challenge one's way of seeing and thinking about the world. We would argue that such a culture effectively provides nurture for its staff and clients with contingent personal and professional development mediating the negative experiences that can be induced by elements of the work context.

In order to create opportunities for restoration, reflection and developing meanings, a focus on the *process* of learning rather than the outcomes (information or knowledge) is desirable. For example, a colleague described how he was educated in an institution by people whose vision of education happened to be to develop understanding rather than to acquire factual knowledge. On taking up a place at university he was amazed to find that he had significantly greater understanding of the subject than many of his peers with better grades than his own who had been educated to pass examinations.

If the process of learning is valued, to not know is the impetus to try to find out rather than to pretend to know already. It implies a focus on questioning and curiosity rather than on premature closure. Premature closure may be advantageous in certain contexts – for example, emergency health services where decisions must be made quickly. But most work in mental health and social services is not carried out in conditions of emergency. If supervisees can see that the supervisor's interest is in facilitating learning then the context of safety will allow them to disclose uncertainties and minimise the sense of threat that can lead to a veneer of competence and resistance to learning.

Relationships with colleagues

Professional helpers are likely to spend a significant proportion of their lives at work. Shared interests offer ground for the development of intimacy with colleagues which could threaten pre-existing close personal relationships and partnerships. Supervision can help people both to manage their needs for intimacy at work and to maintain appropriate boundaries. The emotional demands of working with distressed clients may heighten this tension between the need for intimacy and the need to separate.

Close proximity with colleagues who are experienced as annoying, harassing, boring or dim-witted can evoke hostile emotions that make work an undesirable place to be. Work offers as much opportunity as life outside work for the experience of pleasure and displeasure in the company of others. The difference is that at work it may be impossible to avoid colleagues who distract, annoy or irritate. To add further complexity, these people may occupy positions of influence in which they cannot be avoided and as a result of whose actions careers can be made or broken.

Supervision may provide the only context in which it is possible to stand back from relationships in order to analyse and understand the interpersonal processes taking place and to construct action plans in order to alleviate the distress arising from them. Some contexts can be experienced as particularly unsupportive to the development of successful working relationships. For example, multidisciplinary teams may be the source of tensions that can undermine rather than facilitate good working relationships (Roberts, 1985). Professional bodies have attempted to help their members with this issue by providing guidance on responsibilities within such teams (for example, British Psychological Society, 1998b). By definition the professional helpers who constitute the team bring with them different training, have been encultured into different professional schools of thought and as a result see the work through different lenses. Tensions are inevitable, particularly where the structure of the team elevates the views of one discipline above others. Instead of the multiple lenses providing a comprehensive overview, competition can generate factions and splits within the team and differences of opinion can become personalised. Good arrangements for supervision outside managerial arrangements can provide a medium for minimising any adverse effects of conflicting perspectives in multidisciplinary teams.

In our experience, the range of emotions aroused at work in relation to clients is at least equalled if not exceeded by those evoked by colleagues! After all, these feelings can in some ways be given freer rein since one is not setting out to help colleagues in the same way as setting out to help clients, and the expectations about behaviour from within the two roles (colleague, client) are quite different. However, it may be just as necessary to develop an understanding of emotions evoked in relationships with colleagues who can exert a daily influence on mood state, future promotion, sharing of workload and the like, as to explain and contain them in relation to clients. Supervision may be the place in which a more distant perspective can mediate the effects of relationships with colleagues.

Emotions generated within the supervisory relationship

The supervisory relationship itself is a sub-set of relationships with colleagues. It is sometimes argued that supervision implies a complementary relationship in which there is a difference in status between the participants (Wynne, McDaniel and Weber, 1986). This feature is of particular relevance when supervision occurs in the context of a training relationship in which the supervisor has a formal and crucial evaluative function. It has been argued that this structural feature of the supervisory relationship makes it inevitable that intense emotional reactions will develop in the relationship in one or both partners (Doehrman, 1976).

When working well, supervision offers a containing relationship in which many issues, including relationships with colleagues, can be usefully explored. However, at times it may be the supervisory relationship itself that comprises the source of grief for either or both parties. Ladany, Hill, Corbett and Nutt (1996) found that one of the frequent reasons for nondisclosure in supervision was a poor alliance and that negative reactions to the supervisor were the most frequent type of nondisclosure. This is not surprising given the structural feature of differential status of the participants in many supervisory arrangements. In the study of Ladany *et al.*, most nondisclosures to supervisors were discussed with someone else, typically a peer.

Salzberger-Wittenberg (1983: 12) argues that an adult entering a new relationship with a teacher is inevitably anxious and that feelings associated with earlier relationships with authority figures are evoked. 'Any new relationship tends to arouse hope and dread, and these exist side by side in our minds. The less we know about the new person the freer we are to invest him with extremes of good and bad qualities.' She argues that helpers such as teachers, counsellors and doctors are often imbued with immense power for good and evil. More realistic expectations include the hope that the other will help through her or his greater knowledge and experience, that one will be treated with tolerance, and that one's unreasonable demands will be understood yet met with firmness.

The differential status of participants, particularly in training supervision, cannot be denied. However, its influence can be circumscribed by acknowledgement of its potential impact and discussion of how it may be contained. Since beginnings are crucial to what follows, it is important that care is taken in the contracting process, and this is discussed further in Chapter 4. An essential feature of a good working alliance is a feeling of trust between participants.

It is important to acknowledge that creating a good beginning establishes the foundations for the development of trust, which in turn allows for the possibility of openness and risk-taking. However, often this is not enough and it will be important to acknowledge that the development of trust is an ongoing and evolving process. In particular, making sense of any threatened ruptures in the relationship, such as when the supervisor has to give the supervisee difficult feedback, is important. Such experiences are invaluable for the supervisee, and if handled well can create a stable sense of trust and hopefulness in the relationship such that openness and assessment can go hand-in-hand. In general, a respectful attitude towards the supervisee and to other colleagues can go a long way towards the creation and maintenance of a climate of trust in supervision.

Personal and professional development

People deciding on a career in the helping professions bring with them a wide variety of expectations regarding the relevance of self both to the work and as a focus of supervision. Different views are also characteristic of the different helping professions and of different theoretical models regarding the extent to which the exploration of self in the work is seen as relevant. At one end of the continuum is the view that the experience of personal therapy is essential to competence. In the centre is the view that whilst awareness and development of self in work is crucial, this can be achieved through a range of methods. At the other end of the continuum the emphasis is more specifically on skills learning with little attention given to how personal issues might be relevant in the work. We take the view that it is impossible to leave self aside when undertaking the roles and tasks of the therapist or professional helper, and learning about self in work is a central feature of an ethical stance in relation to the work. The understanding and development of self in work is referred to as personal and professional development. This differs from personal therapy, although undertaking personal therapy might be a method by which personal and professional development takes place. The following sections explore how self is relevant in the work of professional helpers, and how supervision can provide avenues for the exploration of these issues.

Developing an understanding of personal qualities and experiences as they affect and are affected by the work is seen as central to professional development. Learning psychological methods, approaches and techniques is viewed as occurring in the context of these personal qualities. Whilst personal growth is not necessarily a primary goal of supervision, it is an instrumental goal that works in the service of making the supervisee a better practitioner (Bernard and Goodyear, 1992). It has been argued that a keen sense of self-awareness, insight, and control of one's feelings and behaviour are necessary if one is to be empathic and understanding with clients (Middleman and Rhodes, 1985).

What is personal and professional development?

The essence of personal and professional development is an ongoing learning process about aspects of the self in relation to others. An aim is to develop the capacity simultaneously to be affected by the client's communications, whilst reflecting on a range of meanings of the communication and choosing how to respond to the benefit of the client. Without a good understanding of self, the therapist is more likely to participate in habitual patterns of responding developed in the client's or his or her own life histories.

Aspects of self that constitute the domain for personal and professional development in the work context may be understood in three categories:

1 Acknowledging the personal impact of client work

The whole spectrum of feelings experienced towards people outside work can occur just as readily towards clients. These can include feeling elated, angry, useless, sexually aroused, confused, depressed, amused, disgusted and the like. Such feelings can be very difficult to handle when experienced in relation to clients. Feeling bored, angry or hostile towards clients can be particularly difficult to admit and acknowledge when one is seemingly supposed to feel warm and empathic. Those clients that get under the skin can be taken home in the head and ruminated upon endlessly unless there is a process for making meaning of these feelings and using them to inform the work. We would contend that keeping distant from clients as a result of failing to acknowledge these feelings would significantly hinder the work, and thus we do not see avoidance as an option.

Mollon (1989) gives examples of how clients' behaviour towards novice therapists can generate feelings of inadequacy that interact with the more general feelings of incompetence associated with early stages of professional development. In one case example, the client had requested the assistance of a psychologist as she reported to have found previous encounters with the medical profession unhelpful to her long-standing anxiety state. Initially the therapist felt hopeful and attributed the client's dissatisfaction with previous attempts to help to inappropriate medical interventions. As sessions developed, the client conveyed a feeling that the psychologist should do something other than listen and talk, and her stance in sessions was passive – the psychologist feeling that she herself was expected to identify topics. The client frequently questioned whether the work was going to be of help to her, thereby dismissing the activity in which the therapist was currently engaged as having the potential to be of help. Whilst the client's behaviour was not overtly hostile, it was experienced by the supervisee as a sustained attack on her state of mind and her professional identity.

Supervision enabled the novice therapist to obtain a more distant perspective on the case and to make a meaning of the interaction with the client which provided information about the client's other and earlier relationships. This allowed the focus of the work to move to the current interaction between client and therapist, and to the nature of the relationship between the client and her parents. Mollon argues that a task of supervision is to bring the supervisee's anxiety and mental pain into the discourse so that feelings of incompetence and disillusionment regarding the capacity of psychotherapy to be of help can be seen as meaningful material that informs the work.

It is not just that working with clients can generate *negative* feelings that can be problematic for someone trying to occupy a professional helping role. Goffman (1968: 79) asserts that, 'A . . . general way in which human materials differ from other kinds, and hence present unique problems, is that however distant the staff tries to stay from these materials, such materials can become objects of fellow feeling and even affection.' Making sense of these feelings and working out how to respond as a human being whilst maintaining professional boundaries is an appropriate focus of supervision.

The second category of issues that constitute the domain of personal and professional development is the influence of life events.

2 The influence of events outside work on relationships at work

In every life there is an ongoing series of transitions which affects self to varying degrees. These can include major life events such as bereavements, ill health, the formation and breaking of relationships, births and the like, but also a broken leg, a car accident, moving house, falling in love and taking a holiday in a different culture. Each of these events can generate change in the meanings that people make in their lives. People may experience anger, profound sadness or elation, and these feelings, mediated by thoughts and ideas, are brought to work and influence the ways in which it is undertaken.

Each person's emotional context for the work and her or his values and beliefs about the world are thus in constant transition. Exploration of this in supervision can help to identify how these experiences might help or hinder the work. For those who have experienced a recent bereavement, the sadness evoked by being in the presence of a bereaved client may lead therapists to be unable adequately to attend to the client's needs as they become overwhelmed by their own. On the other hand, the experience may ultimately help the therapist to understand how the client's grief may be capable of exerting such a debilitating effect on the client's ability to function.

It is not proposed that the supervisor intrude excessively into the supervisee's personal life, but instead that a focus of supervision is appropriately on the effects of life events on the work rather than on the events themselves and that it is permissible for supervisees to bring such matters to supervision. Supervision is also a forum in which the influence of people's values, beliefs and personal characteristics on their work can be explored.

*3 The influence of personal life history, values, beliefs and personal
characteristics on relationships at work*

If we acknowledge the psychological significance of individual differences, it
follows that each person will approach the work differently, even when adopting the same model and techniques. Often, one's beliefs and values are taken
for granted and do not come into focus except when brought up against
difference. This can occur when travelling and visiting a different culture, or
by meeting individuals who hold different beliefs from one's own. Issues of
difference encompassed by ethnicity, gender, disability, age and sexuality
are explored further in Chapter 7. Below, issues of personal appearance,
personality and temperament, and values and beliefs are discussed.

HOW WILL I COME ACROSS?

The first thing that clients are likely to notice about their therapist is her or his
appearance and general manner. The influence of first impressions may
attenuate over time but is likely to affect the initial process of engagement not
only between client and therapist but also between supervisor and supervisee.
Features such as age, gender, disability, height, weight, skin colour, dress and
hairstyle are mutually assessed at some level before a word is spoken. Some
features are enduring and relatively immutable whilst others are more amenable to change. It is worth considering what clients might make of badges,
see-through clothing, jewellery and the like, and this may be an appropriate
focus of supervision.

Sometimes these factors have an influence from the beginning to the end of
the work. A referral was made to one of us after the client had attended a
public meeting led by a middle-aged male who favours formal dress and a
serious manner. Although not identified at the point of referral, it later transpired that the client had specifically wanted to work with this therapist
whose appearance had conformed to what he perceived as the features of
someone who could help. He did not want to be seen by a female whose style
was less formal. The work was 'stuck' from the beginning, although not
identified as such by the therapist until several sessions had taken place. Had
the issue of the client's preferences regarding the personal characteristics of
the therapist been taken to supervision earlier, much of the frustration
experienced by both client and therapist might have been avoided. Supervision offers a forum in which the participants might declare the first impressions that they perceive themselves to make and check this against the actual
first impressions of the other.

Some personal characteristics might benefit from explicitly being introduced to a client at the outset, particularly if there is reason to believe that the
client may have expected someone different. 'I may seem very different from
the kind of person that you expected to work with and, as you get to know

me, if you feel that this is an issue that is getting in the way I would like you to tell me so that we can work out if you should continue with me or with someone else.'

This would not usually constitute part of an introduction to the work of therapy or supervision but can be used to constructive effect if cues suggest that a specific personal feature is adversely affecting the engagement process or is known to 'throw' people on first meeting in a more general social context.

Another strategy might be to ask colleagues, friends and relations how they think others perceive you on first meeting. Ideally choose someone who is prepared to be open and direct and someone whose opinion you respect! These approaches to this issue are congruent with, for example, a systemic model of therapy. The influence of personal features and characteristics on the therapeutic process might be managed differently within other models, and the example of transference and counter-transference is discussed in a later section of this chapter.

USE OF PERSONALITY AND TEMPERAMENT IN THE WORK

Extensive research in temperament and personality (for example, Thomas, Chess and Birch, 1968) has provided evidence for individual differences that have a degree of stability from infancy to adulthood. These qualities will influence the way in which people approach and are experienced by others in their work, irrespective of the model or theory adopted. For example, some people are generally quiet and calm, others more extrovert; some people are adept in the use of humour, others are more serious. These qualities may be a focus of discussion in supervision. A supervisee might be interested to explore how they can use a personal quality that is apparent in their personal life to more effect in their work.

VALUES AND BELIEFS

Personal biases can inadvertently or explicitly result in therapists encouraging clients in particular directions without considering the full range of options and exploring what is most suitable for the client. For example, those who hold the view 'marriage is for life' may not create space for clients to consider leaving their partners as a solution to their difficulties. Those who have a desire to look after and make things right for their clients may not foster the development of problem-solving skills in the client. Therapists who believe that it is never a good idea to suppress emotions may not acknowledge this as an adaptive response for some people some or all of the time. Bringing these values to awareness enables them to be examined, their effects on the work explored, and a conscious decision taken as to how to use them in the service of the work. There are a number of enlivening and honest books which explore the way in which the practitioner can helpfully be aware of the connection between self, values, and client work (see Yalom, 1989; Casement, 1988).

This does not imply that a therapist cannot hold beliefs and values, only that awareness of them encourages the possibility of understanding that they are not universal and that the client's may be different. Where such differences pertain, the most helpful route for the client may not necessarily be that which in similar circumstances would also suit the therapist.

Processes in the exploration of the personal

In some psychotherapies (such as psychoanalysis) exploration of personal issues has been a required undertaking during training, usually through concurrent personal therapy. Other approaches to the work (such as systemic family therapy) have viewed reflection on personal values and beliefs as essential to training and ongoing practice, but see this as being accomplished through alternative mechanisms such as group work specifically focused on personal and professional development (Hildebrand, 1998b). Some approaches include multiple mechanisms within which trainees can find those best suited to their own learning needs (Walsh and Scaife, 1998).

We take the view that the exploration of personal issues and of self when undertaken with a lens that consistently focuses on relevance to and implications for the work is an essential component of an ethical approach. It may happen that such exploration is more generally beneficial to supervisees, having spin-offs in their private lives. This is serendipitous and not the purpose of supervision. The boundary between supervision and therapy needs to be kept in mind.

Personal and professional development can be addressed by a range of different mechanisms, but is likely to arise in supervision and can be explored whilst continuing to adhere to appropriate boundaries. Where supervision leads to the identification of personal issues that would benefit from exploration outside of supervision, the partnership can continue the discussion by working out where and with whom the supervisee can continue the exploration.

In making a distinction between supervision and therapy, Mollon (1989) says:

> Both should provide a space for thinking, but the tasks are different and the points of focus are different. In supervision, it is the therapy that is the 'patient' and the supervisee's feelings and fantasies are examined only insofar as they might throw light on what is happening in the therapy. The crucial task is to create a supervisory setting in which uncertainty, ignorance and feelings of incompetence can be tolerated and discussed – a culture quite different from the one of 'being supposed to know'. . . .
>
> (Mollon, 1989: 121)

Mollon regards the state of 'being supposed to know' as characterised by the profession of clinical psychology. Holt (1969) believes that this expectation develops much earlier and provides evidence that it is already present in the thinking of primary school children.

Some of the literature focusing on personal and professional development and the emotional context of work tends to emphasise the negative, or the ways in which these issues can adversely interfere with the work. Our own orientation is to regard personal qualities, life experiences and emotions generated at work as having the potential for both positive and negative valence. The task of supervision is then to help in the identification of both the usefulness and hindrances that arise from personal factors.

Transference and counter-transference and their relevance as a focus of supervision

There is not the space here to devote to a thorough review of the impact of transference and counter-transference upon the supervisory process. However, some broad definitions and starting points are useful. If the reader is interested in exploring in more detail the enactment of these two fundamental analytic principles as they are used primarily within psychoanalytic therapy there are a number of texts which may be useful (Casement, 1988, 1990; Hinshelwood, 1994; Laplanche and Pontalis, 1973).

Transference is a process by which the patient invests the therapist with meaning which belongs to the patient's internal world (Casement, 1988); for example, when the patient perceives the therapist as their withholding and judgemental father. Counter-transference is the way in which an analyst feels as an indicator of the patient's state of mind (Hinshelwood, 1994); for example, when the therapist experiences the client as boring or seductive. Depending upon the nature of the supervisory model provided and the skill of the supervisor, such processes, which are traditionally located between the therapist and her or his client, can usefully be located between supervisor and supervisee. For example, one of the authors has the experience of discussing in psychodynamic supervision a very angry 'borderline' client. A mirroring process occurred between the therapy relationship and the supervisory relationship. In the former, the client was experienced by the therapist as constantly attacking her for not making anything better and for being useless. In the latter relationship the therapist began to feel that her supervision was poor, her supervisor ineffective, and began to arrive late for sessions as a mark of unexpressed contempt for her supervisor. It was only when this process of re-enactment between therapy and supervision was reflected upon in the supervision that the therapist felt held enough in her own anger and fear, that she was able to provide such holding for the client.

Using concepts such as counter-transference and transference within the context of supervision requires sensitivity, a light touch and a high level of supervisory skill. Identifying such a process within the room can be challenging and thought-provoking, and it is the view of the authors that there needs to be an explicit contract between the supervisor and supervisee about the 'theory-in-use' or the therapeutic model which informs the supervisory process. Creativity and depth can emerge from the supervisory use of these therapeutic processes. However, if the making of such connections is poorly executed, disruption and disconnection between the supervisor and supervisee are likely to result.

Exploration of attitudes, beliefs and values

Attitudes, beliefs and values are learned through assimilation from groups to whom individuals belong, beginning with the family of origin and extending through schooling, peer groups, work and other social groupings. These are constantly revised to accommodate the beliefs of significant others and in response to life events and experiences. Certain events, such as becoming a parent, promote revision of values through being faced with far-reaching decisions as to what should guide approaches to the upbringing of a child. The repercussions are highly significant for the future of the child and for the future of the parental relationship in which parental family histories are brought together and differences brought into focus.

In supervision, the identification of the tenets underlying the supervisee's responses to others can help to bring greater flexibility and curiosity to the exploration of the client's difficulties. Our own underlying assumptions lead us to believe this to be of value in the work!

Mechanisms for exploring values and beliefs in supervision

Alert supervisors may notice elements of their supervisees' values and beliefs in the language they use to describe their work. What people say about their clients may be conveying at least as much about the speaker as about the subject. One option for exploring this is to audiotape a supervision session with a view to reviewing it specifically to identify the values and beliefs of *both* supervisor and supervisee. Here is a passage from a supervision session which is described in Scaife (1995). This supervisor seems happy to take control of the pace, and aspects of the direction of the supervision. The passage that follows (where S = supervisor and T = therapist) is offered as an example of a transcript of a supervisory conversation. Readers are invited to make their own judgements about the values and beliefs implicit in the conversation.

T.   Well, where shall I start to tell you about this one?
S.   Well, right, if you start, who does it involve? Let's get a genogram up.

T.   There's mum who's thirty-five, Mary. She's divorced.

S.   Did she have lots of children by this marriage?

T.   There's only two. They've been separated for about three years. Two children, Emma, seventeen, and Peter who was the identified patient, thirteen now. I have been seeing this family for nearly two years.

S.   I'd hazard a guess what your problem is.

T.   Well, yes and no. It could be that that's what's my problem. She has another partner now, Chris, who's about forty-five, and they've been together for a year, and she met him after he'd come out of prison for offences of sexual abuse against children. He previously had a long-standing relationship of about eight years.

S.   What sort of age were the children who he abused?

T.   Teens.

S.   Girls? Boys?

T.   Yes. One was his partner's daughter, one was her friend's daughter and one was a lad, and it was supposed to be . . .

S.   She had to search hard to find a suitable partner . . . [ironic comment]

T.   Right. Her ex-partner was abusive towards her.

S.   Physically?

T.   Physically.

S.   And sexually?

T.   Er, yes, I would say so, and she had been sexually abused as a child by an uncle. She had a mum and dad and an older sister.

S.   Now do you know whose brother it was?

T.   I think it was the father's brother. I think I need to put you in touch with what my main problem is now because I've worked with the family for a long time. And a lot of the work – when I met Mary she was very depressed, clinically depressed, and in the course of which she did take an overdose, but I did a lot of individual work and she's certainly not depressed any more. And I was about to discharge the family when she met up with this new partner and I got notification from Social Services that they were going to hold a case conference on Peter, and that was when I discovered that Mary was wanting to get married to Chris and if he moved in, Social Services were concerned about the children.

S.   She knew all about that?

T.   Yes. And Peter was put on the register because of that case conference.

S.   Is he still registered?

T.   No, he's just become de-registered.

S.   O.K. So you have a problem which is?

T.   As a result of the case conference, I was designated, because of the relationship that I have with Mary, to work with Chris and Mary to look at the abusing behaviour and to try, I suppose, to do two things. One would be to assess the likelihood that abuse will occur.

S. For the case conference?

T. Yes, I suppose that's one thing but that's not the one that's bothered me so much as the other one which is to work with Chris to give therapy for the abusing . . .

S. These two seem like aspects of the same thing.

T. Yes, I think they are. I actually did this latter work jointly with the probation officer and I think maybe this is where an issue comes in. I've come to realise over the course of time that probation officers and clinical psychologists have different training.

S. And different agendas possibly?

T. And different genders, yes.

S. No, agendas. Right, genders too. Now just hold on. How long ago was this case conference?

T. Not quite a year, but approximately a year.

S. Right, so there's you and there's the probation officer, who I now gather is male.

T. My current problem is not about the assessment aspect because I've stated to the case conference that I think that how Mary is and how Mary and Chris's relationship is, means that it's very unlikely that these children will be abused. As a result the child has been de-registered, but I wouldn't put any money on Chris if he were in a different context.

S. The next-door-neighbour's child or whatever. He will have a next-door-neighbour wherever he lives so that's not matter for action really, is it, unless he lives in H.M. [colloquial for prison].

T. So the thing that's been the difficulty, is the thing about 'curing' him, and what's happened is that he's come to sessions and I and the probation officer have tried to get him to complete various tasks. A particular one was to write down his cycle of arousal so that we can find the position where one would need to intervene in that in order to introduce the normal boundaries.

S. Where *he* would need to, I mean I say that deliberately.

T. Right, and he consistently says he will do that, then it's not brought to the session.

S. Can I just ask you, are we still finding out what your problem is or have we moved beyond it? Because at the moment I'm still not quite sure what your problem is.

T. No, we've moved beyond it haven't we?

S. I feared we might, yes.

T. The problem is that I think I've decided that I can't do any more work with Chris constructively. I think I've decided I can't 'therapise' his abuse, but I'm not quite satisfied with myself for deciding that, and so what I need to do is to check it out: to either make myself content with that and say, 'O.K. I can't do any more work with that', or if not, decide to pursue it further in some way. So it's making a decision about whether to drop it or carry on with an attempt to therapise Chris.

S.   So the problem is, 'Have you done everything you can?'

(Scaife, 1995: 124–128)

The authors reviewed the above extract with a view to identifying the implicit values and beliefs of the participants. These are regarded as neither particularly desirable nor undesirable values for supervisors and supervisees. The purpose of the exercise is to identify underlying beliefs and values in order to challenge them and explore their impact on the way the work is being conducted. The authors identified the following, which may coincide to varying degrees with those identified by the reader:

- That family and wider context is relevant to the work.
- That the named referred person may not be the actual client as perceived by the worker and that the worker has some right to make this decision.
- That supervision focuses on solving a problem.
- That the supervisor asking questions is an appropriate activity in supervision.
- That therapeutic work with a duration of two years could be indicative of a problem.
- That supervisees have the right to define the focus of supervision.
- That the gender of workers is material to the work.
- That in therapy the therapist does a lot of work.
- That therapy is something that is 'done' to people.
- That there are such things as 'normal boundaries' that prevent people from sexually abusing others.

It is not being suggested that these are desirable or undesirable positions, only that any such dialogue might inform practitioners about the underlying views that might be influencing their work.

Another method for attempting to access underlying beliefs and values was devised for a group, but could be adapted for individual supervision. The exercise can be used with a variety of topics. Value statements are written on individual file cards and suggestions are made below as to the nature of these. The statements are provided by the supervisor, a process which protects supervisees from the disclosure of their own values at this stage. The file cards are distributed randomly between the group members. They are asked to imagine a line on the floor that corresponds to a continuum from 'agree' to 'disagree'. Group members take it in turns to read out the statements on their cards and to place each card on the continuum, explaining their decision to place it at the selected point. Other group members then debate the placement of the card, giving reasons for their different opinion. When the issue has been explored to everyone's satisfaction, another card is selected.

The advantages of the method are that people do not have to disclose their own issues and the group facilitator can provide riskier topics than might otherwise emerge. The method also highlights the diversity of views and opinions in any group.

The following are examples of items that might be used in the above exercise. They fall into two categories – namely, beliefs about therapy and beliefs about wider issues in life.

- You can have anything if you work hard enough.
- You cannot understand how events have affected people unless you have been through it yourself.
- It is inappropriate to make jokes in work with clients.
- People who are victims need protecting.
- It's never a good idea to suppress one's emotions.
- One should always admit to not knowing.
- Children should only be raised by heterosexual couples.
- Professional helpers are responsible for the outcomes of therapy.
- Clients need to have confidence in the expertise of the therapist.
- Women who are in violent relationships should be helped to extricate themselves.
- It is wrong to feel sexually attracted to clients.
- Arranged marriages stand a much greater chance of success.
- It is unethical to offer therapy without having been in personal therapy oneself.
- Religion is for people who feel insecure.
- Shameful things should always be kept to oneself.
- When people get older they are less able to do things.
- Wealth is a sign of hard work and commitment.

Exploration of life events

Transitions in the lives of professional helpers can influence professional development and may lead to changes of orientation towards the work. Matters such as becoming a parent can lead to a reconsideration of the relative contribution of nature and nurture to a child's development, for example. Life events can have very positive effects on learning and development, helping the worker to increase empathy or to take a more open-minded approach.

However, from time to time adverse life events can have so profound an impact so as to disable practitioners for a time in their work with certain clients. For someone recently abandoned by a partner, working open-mindedly with clients who are in similar circumstances may not be feasible. A task of supervision is to help in the identification of this degree of interference and to help the supervisee to make alternative arrangements for the work to be conducted by someone else until the personal matter reaches a state of greater resolution and stability.

There are a number of ways of exploring one's own life history that can be used with clients and also by professional helpers in relation to themselves. In addition to the information obtained about self, such exercises also provide an opportunity for people to experience the perspective of clients when they are requested to carry out similar tasks.

LIFELINES

Drawing a lifeline provides an opportunity to put on paper past life events and the accompanying emotions. Large sheets of paper are called for on which the person draws a line or shape on which events can be noted. In order to get started, people often find it helpful to note dates around school changes or moves of house. Detail can include events such as birthday parties or holidays and visits. In our experience there is great variance between people in the extent of the detail that can be remembered, particularly about childhood and about unhappy events from the past. Some are shocked by how little they recall and are prompted to ask friends and relatives in order to attempt to fill in the gaps. Some can recollect in detail even early life events, recalling tastes and smells and the fine detail of everyday.

This task may be conducted as a private exercise, with the results of a secondary task brought to supervision. The secondary task is to identify how these experiences might be relevant to and might influence the way that the person carries out her or his work. For someone who has detailed recall of childhood episodes, the meaning of minimal recall by a client might be perceived as pathological, whereas for therapists with minimal recall of their own childhood, minimal recall by the client would not be expected to seem odd.

The completion of lifelines might bring forth issues for therapists which they recognise as having an adverse impact upon their life and their work. In such instances supervision is not the place for their exploration, but identification of a suitable alternative forum is an appropriate task.

DRAWING ONE'S OWN GENOGRAM

Genograms or family trees are used as a shorthand and compact way of illustrating family relationships. They may contain basic information such as gender, ages and names of family members but may be further elaborated to include identification of patterns of role-relationships and can be illustrated with family 'sayings'. This can help to elaborate the underlying values transmitted by families of origin. The following are examples of ideas that have emerged from the construction of family trees in workshops for professional helpers:

- 'Whatever else, you should always provide a good table.'
- 'Never let your neighbour starve.'
- 'A table has four sides – one for each person in a family.'
- 'You can only do your best.'
- 'Hard work is its own reward.'
- 'Some things are best left unsaid.'
- 'If you say it you will make it happen.'

What also emerge are repetitive intergenerational patterns such as number of children in a family, age of having first child, gender roles, positions of power and influence, leaving or staying at home, patterns associated with birth order, and so on. From these ideas may be constructed the family script into which the person was born. These are described by Byng-Hall (1995) as a family's shared expectations of how family roles are to be performed within various contexts. He views the family plot as scripted although the cast can change. Family scripts are revealed when repeating patterns of family interaction are either observed or described. He proposes the notions of replicative and corrective scripts in which people to some degree reproduce previous family patterns or make pacts with themselves to live their lives differently. Either kind of script will be represented in the beliefs and values that professional helpers bring both to their personal and professional lives.

IDENTIFYING A PROBLEM

It is not the task of supervision to explore the personal problems of the supervisee, and the first stage of the following exercise is therefore privately conducted. The supervisee first identifies a problem of her or his own. The problem can be at any level from seriously debilitating to the level of what to buy as a present for a friend. Whilst the latter would seemingly constitute a relatively straightforward dilemma, such a choice may be underlain by more significant dilemmas and can evoke significant personal responses.

Having identified a problem, the person then thinks about what questions they would like to be asked in exploration of the problem. It would be possible to choose the kinds of questions or an approach such as free association prescribed by a particular model of therapy or to think of questions at random. The task in supervision is to consider what the selected questions or approach reveal about the expectations of the supervisee about how therapy is conducted. The problem itself need not be disclosed. Through the exercise supervisees learn about the kind of approach that they believe they would find useful for themselves, their own orientation to how helping is carried out and some idea of the potential impact of such methods on clients.

UNDERTAKING PERSONAL THERAPY

There are a wide variety of views about therapy and its usefulness. And this is just among mental health professionals! Macran and Shapiro (1998) found that most therapists who had undergone personal therapy stressed its value, although there was limited evidence that undertaking personal therapy led to better client outcomes. For some models of therapy, receiving one's own therapy is a core requirement. For others, the receipt of one's own therapy is not seen as a necessary prerequisite for working with the distress of clients. Some practitioners make a distinction between personal therapy that is undertaken with the explicit purpose of enhancing training, and therapy undertaken in response to personal distress (Beail, 1998). Benefits for the purpose of training include both learning about self and learning first-hand about the role of the client. It may be argued that to work with people's distress on a day-to-day basis without in some way experiencing one's own therapy is at best naive and at worst hypocritical. Many mental health professionals are deeply self-neglectful and it is too easy to slip into an 'I have no needs' form of working of which one should beware.

For those who choose to embark on the course of personal therapy there are a number of publications available which are helpful in the selection of a therapist (MIND, n.d.), and, as a mental health professional, asking colleagues for the names of well-respected practitioners is also effective. It is often useful to talk to a supervisor about the process of identifying a practitioner who could meet one's needs. It is also worth considering whether you might better benefit more from 1:1 therapy or a group approach.

IDENTIFYING THE NEED TO BE AWAY FROM WORK

The exploration of emotions, values, beliefs and the impact of life history and events is part of the landscape of supervision and enables the supervisor to effect a supportive and restorative function. From time to time the impact of these factors involves supervisors in helping supervisees to decide when they should and should not be continuing to work. Professional helpers are sometimes reluctant to prioritise their own needs when ill, under stress or in a personal crisis. The supervisor can play a significant role in helping supervisees both to acknowledge the magnitude of the difficulty and to give themselves permission to take time for themselves in order to restore health and well-being. On more than one occasion in such circumstances when supervisees have been asked to 'reverse roles' and give advice were one of us to find ourself in their circumstances, they have responded by saying, 'You would be crazy to carry on working'. From this emerges a plan for self-care which in the long run is a better option for staff and ensures the welfare of clients.

The decision finally to take time out of work is often the result of a very painful and protracted decision-making process. It is the experience of the authors that the view of most mental health professionals is that it is better to struggle through, no matter what life throws at you, and no matter what emotional burdens you are bearing, than to stop. The reasons for this are complex. First, there is a sense of shame about being personally vulnerable or in need, and that such vulnerabilities are more acceptably located in the client rather than the professional. Second, stopping work is a very public way of saying that one needs time out. Individuals may hold legitimate or irrational fears that their careers or professional standing with colleagues may be irrevocably damaged if others see them as not coping. Ironically, individuals may actually find themselves the objects of envy on the part of their colleagues because they have been able to give themselves the time away from work. Third, many models of therapy disconnect self-needs from the work as a legitimate focus of exploration; that damage is 'out there' and not located in the self. Thus, if personal issues become pressing and have to be acknowledged, as opposed to being defended against or projected into clients or other individuals, there is little or no permission to address personal needs. Fourth, for clinicians in private practice the tension between needing to stop working for personal reasons and the need to continue to practice for financial reasons is evident (King and Wheeler, 1999). Finally, in periods of acute distress (something that comes to us all), one of the primary fears about stopping work may be that one will never be able to pull oneself together. Panto-pragmatism may feel safer, but is not.

In conclusion, it is our view that self and emotion play a crucial part in work. Their appearance in supervision is inevitable and desirable and supervisors can occupy a pivotal role in helping supervisees to explore these issues.

Summary

This chapter has focused on the emotional experiences and needs of supervisees, and on personal qualities and life events that can influence how their work is conducted. These factors are described at different layers of the work system from the social and economic climate to individual differences which feature in client–therapist relationships. It is argued that supervision has an important role to play in helping supervisees to identify these issues and their relevance to the work, and suggestions are made as to how they may be usefully be approached.

Chapter 4

The contracting process and the supervisory relationship

Avoiding pitfalls and problems

Supervision is an interpersonal process, the success of which owes much (some may even contend almost everything) to the quality of the relationship between the supervisor and supervisee. Alderfer and Lynch (1987: 70) state that, 'the relationship between the supervisor and supervisee has more impact on the success of the process of supervision than any other factor'.

Creating a supervisory relationship in which the participants experience mutual respect, are open about their fears, difficulties, blunders, successes and challenges, learn from each other and stay within the boundaries of the supervisory task is a tall order. Establishing such a relationship at work has been seen by some as offering a similar challenge to that of creating satisfactory and rewarding relationships in one's personal life. At work, long periods of time are spent with people who may take care of, love or hurt each other. Hillman (1983), as quoted in Hawkins and Miller (undated), states that,

> Freud said the whole business of therapy was to bring a person to love and work. It seems to me we have forgotten half of what he said. Work. We have been talking of what goes wrong with love for eighty years. But what about what goes wrong with work, where has that been discussed?

Models and frameworks proposed for aiding thinking about supervision typically include the notion of a contracting process through which the supervisor and supervisee negotiate and reach agreement about such matters as the requirements of their agency contexts, timing and frequency of contacts with each other, supervisory role-relationships and the purpose and process of supervision (Scaife, 1993a; Carroll, 1996; Page and Wosket, 1994). The agreement reached is the supervision contract, which may be formal and written or informal and not recorded. Whilst usually undertaken at the point of establishing the supervisory relationship, contracting is an ongoing process in which the initial agreement is reviewed regularly to see if matters are on course and whether the supervisory needs of supervisees have changed as their learning develops. Whilst Codes of Conduct for practitioners typically give guidance about the need for an adequate contracting process (for example the Code of Ethics and Practice for the Supervision of Counsellors, BAC, 1988), Lawton (2000), in a study of eight supervisory relationships, found that the majority of participants in her study reported a very patchy experience. Furthermore, information obtained about the nature of the relationships which then developed suggested a strong link between the rigour of the contracting process at the outset and the quality of the working alliance which subsequently evolved.

Why establish a supervisory contract?

Participants need to be clear about the different desires and expectations brought to the relationship by the different parties. Where these are implicit and unexpressed, a mismatch can lead to misunderstandings from which it can be difficult to recover a functional relationship. Where expectations are implicit they usually become apparent when an injunction or implicit rule is broken. It is also important to include the expectations of any involved agencies in the contract. For example, training institutions may specify how many or what type of cases should be seen and that case-work should be written up and submitted as coursework assignments. The host agency may require those working with its clients to undertake various procedures to ensure that it is not inadvertently liable for any errors perpetrated by the supervisee. Thus the contract needs to attend to the requirements of all involved parties, which might include the supervisor and supervisee, the host and training agencies and the clients. Different supervisory relationships may involve all or some of these parties.

The contracting process also serves to prompt supervisees to think about their needs in supervision, including their needs for support and to learn. It can help supervisees to think about how they best learn and what approaches to supervision would facilitate learning.

The contracting process can also be used to share knowledge about supervision and to establish whether a common framework can be used by the parties involved with which to structure and understand the process. Importantly, the negotiation of the contract indicates that these matters are open to debate and can be revisited in the event of any difficulty or changes in needs. The discussion sets a context of openness in which different ideas and values can be acknowledged and accommodated. There is an overt plan and purpose rather than taking a risk with a haphazard and serendipitous process.

Where the supervisee is a trainee or student with the supervisor, negotiation of a contract should also include discussion of the ideas that each has regarding the evaluation of the supervisee's work. Trainees are likely to find it helpful to know what the supervisor regards as evidence of adequate knowledge and skill and how this compares with their own assessment of their work. Similarly, the contract might include agreement regarding what the trainee might do that would be negatively evaluated by the supervisor and what would constitute evidence of failure.

Whilst flexibility to meet the needs of the supervisee is regarded as a virtue in supervisors (Bernard, 1979), the contracting process may also be used to define what the supervisor can and cannot provide. Where there is a choice of supervisor this might mean that supervisees will take the route of finding an alternative supervisor better matched to their expectations and needs. Similarly, supervisors themselves should usually be in a position to decide not to take a supervisee if they are of the view, after attempting to establish a contract, that they are not able to offer what is required.

In summary, I believe the reasons for establishing a supervisory contract to be:

- To clarify the different desires and expectations brought to the relationship by the different parties and to agree what is and is not possible.
- To set a context of openness in which processes in supervision and the supervisory relationship are matters for discussion and negotiation, rather than happening by accident.
- To set a context in which different ideas may be acknowledged and valued, choices may be made and shared responsibility for learning implied.
- To prompt supervisees to think about the conditions under which their learning might flourish.
- To facilitate a sharing of knowledge about the supervisory 'field'.
- To establish a process of negotiation and renegotiation as the relationship develops.
- To establish a pattern of giving attention to both process and content in supervision which might connect reflexively with the process and content of therapy.
- To explore the evaluative role of the supervisor and to identify what factors will influence judgements.
- To identify and explore the influences of the agency and possibly training contexts in which the supervision is set.
- To identify the responsibilities of each party in the contract to the other involved stakeholders.

Setting up a supervisory contract

The establishment of the contract should probably not take place in the initial meeting between supervisor and supervisee. First requirements are to get to know each other a little and this might best be accomplished in a fairly informal way. Information regarding professional history, how each came to work as a helper, geographical origins and the like might be discussed before focusing on the elements that might comprise a contract. Where the supervisee is joining a service, perhaps for a time-limited training placement, a number of issues can helpfully be addressed in an induction to the service which might include introductions to other staff at the base, an explanation of systems for booking rooms, keeping files and keeping a diary, car parking arrangements, access to a confidential telephone line, arrangements for coffee and refreshments, conventions of dress, case management processes, collection of statistics and audit, authorisation to work in the host agency, required attendance at meetings, and methods of accessing suitable resources such as computers and the library. A list can usefully be constructed as a reference for general use.

During this discussion which focuses on practical matters, supervisor and supervisee can feel their way with each other, paving the way for the negotiation of the supervisory contract. This is more likely to be necessary where the supervisor and supervisee have no prior knowledge of each other and particularly where the pairing has been allocated by a third party such as a university, rather than selected and requested by the supervisee.

The responsibility for instigating the contracting discussion more typically lies with the supervisor than with the supervisee. The supervisor can structure the discussion either according to the preferences of the supervisee where these can be identified, or according to a structure provided by the supervisor. A number of pre-supervision questionnaires are available that can be completed by each participant as a self-assessment exercise prior to discussion of the supervisory relationship. These can help in the identification of learning needs, the exploration of a person's typical responses to characteristics of other people, identification of strengths and points for development, and so on. An example of a questionnaire for supervisors can be found in Hawkins and Shohet (1989) and for supervisees in Appendix 1.

Topics which might be included in a supervisory contract

Ground rules

Ground rules include not only rules but the practicalities and basic conditions under which supervision will proceed. In addition to an agreement regarding the timing, frequency and location of supervision, it may be helpful to address availability in the event of an emergency between sessions, or opportunities for informal contact, particularly relevant in training placements. In private arrangements the issue of remuneration also needs to be addressed. Other ground rules include clarification of the boundaries between the personal, the personal when it affects or is affected by the work, and the professional. In the event of a pre-existing personal relationship or friendship there will need to be a discussion of the implication of the dual role-relationship for the supervision. In such circumstances it may be very difficult for a supervisor to make a wholly frank negative evaluation of a supervisee or, in the event of so doing, later to re-establish the friendship.

Ground rules also include clarity regarding the responsibility for work undertaken. In pre-qualification supervision the responsibility usually lies with the supervisor which makes a difference to how willing a supervisor may be to agree to a supervisee deviating from recommended action. Post-qualification non-managerial arrangements generally identify the supervisee as the person responsible for the work carried out. However, the responsibility of the supervisor will be to meet the needs of the supervisee as laid out in the supervision contract.

What is to be learned and how

Supervisees vary in the extent to which they are clear about what they hope to learn in the course of supervision and how this learning might be expected to take place. More experienced supervisees usually have a clearer idea than beginners, and in training placements the requirements of the training institution must also be met.

Topics for learning might include developing skills in a particular model or theoretical approach to the work, might include the number and types of cases to be seen over a specified time-scale, or be focused on supervisees learning more about their own responses to the work, where their strengths lie and the identification of and work on blind spots. Supervisees might want to learn why they are experiencing difficulties in some of their work but not across the board.

The negotiation of how the learning will take place can begin with a discussion of what supervisees have previously found helpful to their learning. Some supervisees welcome advice and information-giving, others prefer a more questioning and enquiring style, whilst at times a sympathetic listener may be required. Some of the frameworks for supervision, described in more detail in Chapter 5, can support the exploration of the role-relationship that will best support learning.

Role-relationship/supervisory alliance

Whilst there are many commonalities between the supervision processes occurring in pre-qualification training, peer supervision, managerial supervision, public service and private contexts, the role-relationship is likely to be more or less constrained by these factors, most notably where the supervisor has an evaluative role and the outcome of the evaluation has significant consequences for the future progress in training of the supervisee. Some supervisees in such a context may be of the opinion that supervision cannot meet their restorative needs, fearing that if they reveal the level of their distress or allow themselves free communication, they risk negative evaluation by the supervisor.

A purpose of the contracting process is to facilitate the establishment of a supervisory alliance. The beginning of the relationship is important as it is at this stage that anxieties can be most pronounced. Liddle (1986) argues that counsellor trainees worry about their professional adequacy, impressing their supervisors, their clients, colleagues and themselves. One response to these anxieties is that of resistance, which is defined as 'any coping behaviour by a supervisee that interferes with the learning process'. In the contracting process, the expectation of anxiety can be normalised as a feature of the process of learning new skills.

The term 'supervisory alliance' derives from the notion that successful psychotherapy takes place in the context of a working alliance between client and therapist. The contracting process aims to explore what kind of relationship would work to meet the aims of supervision. Whilst different from the role-relationship of client–therapist there are commonalities, and some of the differences (for example, in relation to the responsibilities of supervisors as against therapists) are quite subtle and difficult to define with clarity. A number of frameworks have been adapted from a therapy context to a supervision situation in order to facilitate an understanding of the working alliance in supervision. These include attachment theory (in Watkins, 1995) and the notion of 'collaboration to change' (Bordin, 1979). This latter notion was extended to encompass the supervisory relationship (Bordin, 1983) and proposes three elements: the bond between the parties, the extent to which they agree on goals, and the extent to which they agree on tasks. It is argued here that the contracting process begins the process of establishing the working alliance.

Heading off problems

Whilst it is probably not desirable in establishing a contract to dwell for too long on potential problems that might develop in a supervisory relationship, it is probably better to have undertaken some exploration of how these might be handled at the outset. In the event of problems developing, the prior discussion has already indicated that these are matters for exploration and resolution through talking. A relatively brief discussion in the contracting process may be revisited when the supervisor and supervisee have developed greater familiarity with each other, ideally nipping problems in the bud before they develop. Some of the more common problems are discussed below.

Evaluation and review

Review of the contract and reciprocal feedback can ensure that the supervision stays on track. Typically people encounter some anxiety in giving and/or receiving evaluative comments and can feel very hurt, particularly if they feel problematised in the process. Supervisors who fear to hurt feelings will tend to make bland statements if asked to comment on the work of the supervisee. Supervisees who are repeatedly told that their work is 'fine' tend to feel insecure about their competence and often prefer more specific information about what was evaluated as a strength and what could be further developed. A different way for the supervisor to give feedback without risking injury to the supervisee is to offer a range of alternative meanings or approaches whilst showing honest (not affected) acceptance of the approach used by the supervisee.

The issue of evaluation and feedback is dealt with in more detail in Chapter 13. However, in order to help supervisees to begin to take responsibility for letting the supervisor know how things are going it may be helpful early in the relationship for supervisors to indicate that they will be inviting an evaluation of what they themselves are trying to achieve. A general invitation may be too nebulous and unboundaried to invite anything other than a neutral response from the supervisee. One way round this is to give the supervisee a questionnaire or rating scale with headings on which to rate the supervision. (Examples are listed in Appendix 2.) It is probably also helpful to note that it is the supervision rather than the supervisor that is being evaluated. Questionnaires or rating scales can be used in a variety of ways, and, in addition to helping supervisees to think about the evaluation of their own work, the process of inviting structured comments also provides information to the supervisee about what the supervisor values and gives the message that these matters are negotiable.

Another way in which the potential negative effects of the evaluative role may be ameliorated is by the supervisor or supervisee raising the issue as to how the supervisor might react were the supervisee to reveal actions about which criticism is feared. Hypothetical examples can be presented by the supervisee and hypothetical responses given by the supervisor. In this way, the underlying values and beliefs about what is important in the work can be explored. Most typically, supervisors value openness, disclosure and willingness to learn in their supervisees significantly more highly than exemplary performances, and open expression of this in the contracting process may make it more possible in the longer term for supervisees to disclose the work which they themselves evaluate negatively.

The disinterested or busy supervisor

Particularly in training placements with senior clinicians, workload constraints may limit the amount of time that is available for supervision and the supervisor may be distracted by seemingly more important concerns. One of the most difficult tasks for supervisees is to raise this with the supervisor as they also typically perceive other concerns to be of greater importance and may feel guilty about raising the primacy of their own needs with the supervisor. This may again be addressed in the contracting process before the problem arises by supervisees asking what course of action they should take in the event of feeling that their needs are not being met. This could be attributed either to their apparently excessive needs in comparison with other supervisees or to the other roles and demands on the supervisor.

To raise these issues from the position of supervisee is usually experienced as more tricky than from the position of supervisor and busy supervisors may suggest to supervisees how best to approach them in circumstances where they feel that the supervisor's lack of attention to supervision is by default rather than design. It is easier for supervisees to raise such issues if given advance permission and strategies than in the later event of their occurrence.

The following is a somewhat extreme example of a supervisee raising this problem with a supervisor having tried and failed in all other approaches to get their needs met. It occurred in the context of a workshop in supervision and is a role-played exchange set up with a supervisor who fails to respond to more usual appeals. The role-play (where *S'ee.* = supervisee and *S.* = supervisor) is well underway at this point with no progress having been achieved in relation to the issue.

S'ee.   I know that it is difficult to meet with me for more than half an hour a week with all your other work commitments at the moment. I understand that, but I do seem to need more than that to feel confident that what I am doing is OK and safe for the clients.

S.   I have a lot of confidence in you and you make very good use of supervision. I think it's more to do with how you feel about your work than what you really need.

S'ee.   Yes, but look, I haven't told you this before because what happened didn't feel just right, but last week Mr X suggested that we have our session in the pub because he feels embarrassed about coming to the office. He made a very good case for it and I agreed to meet him next Wednesday. He thought it would be much more helpful to him because he'd be more relaxed and comfortable.

S.   [Looks startled] I don't think that's a very good idea. What about confidentiality and how will you feel about raising issues that might have a powerful emotional impact. Don't you think it would be a bit public?

S'ee.   Well, since it was his idea I thought that he would have thought about all that.

S.   Might his suggesting meeting in the pub have other meanings – I was wondering how he sees his relationship with you?

S'ee.   Actually, I didn't really agree to meet a client in the pub. I was just making that up. [*S.* looks even more surprised and confused] You see, I know that that wouldn't be OK in this service although I know some of the people who work with AIDS sufferers do go to pubs to try to help clients to connect with their service. The problem is that I might be doing other things that you could help me to see were not very useful or even harmful, but I don't know that. You have a lot of experience and I'd really value being able to draw on that to help me with issues where I don't even know that there's an issue or other ways of thinking about things. That would help me to feel safe.

S.   Let me think about it. We'll make a time for next week and put it on the agenda for then.

In this case it seemed that the only recourse for the supervisee was to frighten the supervisor who was responsible for the case-work into giving the supervision greater priority. In the contracting process it is helpful if the supervisor is clear about how much time can be devoted to supervision, with a view to keeping to the agreed arrangement. This can be particularly difficult for senior clinicians. If the issue has been fully explored at the beginning of the supervisory arrangement it is then legitimate for either party to revisit the matter should problems occur. Whilst the example given above identifies the problem as being experienced by the supervisee, the boundary issues of time-keeping, non-interruption of sessions, and so on, might just as well be experienced by the supervisor in relation to the supervisee and can also be included in the contracting discussions.

Differences of opinion

One of the anxieties that is frequently cited by supervisees is that of having to deal with different styles and approaches to the work and to supervision adopted by tutors and supervisors. An anxiety for supervisors is dealing with unsatisfactory work, which could also be viewed as an example of a difference of opinion between supervisor and supervisee. The above were some of the difficulties listed by Pomerantz, Leydon, Lunt, Osborne, Powell and Ronaldson (1987) in a survey of trainees, university tutors and field-work supervisors who participated in an educational psychology training programme.

Resolving differences of opinion in a satisfactory manner may be more difficult for supervisory dyads than in other relationships, and one explanation for this is proffered by Doehrman (1976) from the perspective of a psychodynamic framework. She contends that supervisees (in training relationships) typically experience intense emotional reactions towards supervisors because the development of professional identity is closely linked with personal identity, and changes to professional self can therefore be experienced as threatening. She also argues that supervisors may experience powerful counter-transference reactions to supervisees which result from the position of authority and their ideas being challenged.

The contracting process can include consideration of how the participants might approach a difference of opinion. This will depend on the context of the relationship as training, managerial and/or peer supervision. Discussion might focus on what would elicit the most positive response from each party in the event of a disagreement, what each person's most typical defensive response might be, and what approaches to this are generally more successful in progressing the discussion. In establishing a contract, it is possible to discuss these matters hypothetically before actual content has contaminated the relationship. Agreeing to notice the process of a potential disagreement, placing the process outside the individuals, together analysing the process, and returning later to the content if necessary, offer more channels for successful resolution of differences of opinion than hoping that they will not occur in the first place.

Ethical dilemmas

Dealing with practice that might have damaging consequences for clients is usually an infrequent occurrence. For this reason alone it can be particularly challenging for supervisors when it occurs. In addition it may involve the need to take actions that are likely to be experienced as distressing for both supervisor and supervisee and in consequence is sometimes avoided in supervision. Where the supervisor has a formal evaluative role, to fail someone's training may be experienced as having such profound consequences for her or his subsequent career as to make its contemplation unbearable. The supervisor is then faced with the prospect of passing someone's work, in the knowledge that he or she may go on to cause further damage.

In any supervisory arrangement it is possible for the supervisor to face ethical and moral dilemmas regarding the supervisee's practice. The supervisor has responsibilities to clients and to employing organisations and/or professional bodies with which the supervisee is registered. Within the contracting process, these potential dilemmas and potential responses of the supervisor can be discussed, much as the limits of confidentiality might be raised with a client. In the rare event of the supervisor later developing concerns, such prior discussion has indicated that these are matters to be addressed, and the supervisee will already have a sense of the approach that the supervisor is likely to take.

Discussion of potential problems and how to respond to them sets a context which gives the message that these matters are subject to some negotiation within the boundaries of ethical practice. That they might arise is perceived as normal rather than pathological. The inclusion of these matters in contracting does not require an undue dwelling on potential problems, but rather a concise discussion that sets the scene for later negotiation should the need arise.

Characteristics of participants

Each of the participants in a supervisory relationship brings some qualities by accident rather than by design. These include personal features such as ethnicity, cultural history, gender, age, years of experience, and the specific experiences of working with different clients, in different models and in different services. Some of these characteristics may be purposely selected by supervisees and supervisors, but inevitably some of them will arise through happenstance. During one supervisor training course, delegates were asked carefully to select someone to work with whom they perceived on the surface to be very different from themselves. The feedback suggested that this selection for difference opened up greater learning opportunities than had people selected someone who on the surface was perceived as more similar.

Identifying personal characteristics and discussing the potential influence of these may form part of the contracting process. A young supervisor paired with an older supervisee might respond with a feeling of not having anything to offer, as in the following example in which two experienced senior nurses retrained as specialist mental health nurses:

> What they felt happened was that the people who were training them had their defences up, presumably because of their lack of confidence about these two experienced people being around, and basically it was, 'The less you bother me and the further away from me you are, the happier I will be. Just keep out of the way and I'm sure you both know how to do it anyway and that'll be O.K.' What they both said they wanted more than anything early on was somebody who was prepared to be totally open with them and reveal their own feelings and thoughts and incompetencies and to just accept them as they were at that stage of training. I think that was how they found each other.
>
> (Scaife, 1995: 75)

Difference in age and experience can also affect how people feel about working with different client groups. Not infrequently, younger workers express anxiety about how they will be perceived and received by older adults or by people who are parents when they themselves are childless. It is important that an open mind be kept for explanations for what happens in therapy and supervision that take account of these factors without them proving unduly dominant.

The characteristics and values that each party holds, and their ideas and fantasies about the other people in the supervisory relationship, might usefully be explored in the contracting process. Such exploration might inform future events that develop both in supervision and in therapy. Sometimes awareness of personal characteristics, values and beliefs does not emerge until bumping up against difference – for example, views about domestic violence when faced with the different perspectives of the parties involved. Including them in the contracting process indicates that they are appropriate material for supervision. Not only is permission granted to address them, but also each party will have gained an idea of how best to go about raising them in the context of understanding something of the values held by the other party.

Supervisor preferences and capabilities

Whilst much of the discussion regarding the contract is likely to be led by the supervisor asking questions of the supervisee, the contracting process also provides an opportunity for supervisors to state their own needs and preferences. This is also a useful skill in other circumstances; for example, in dealing with the unsatisfactory performance of a supervisee. In contracting, the supervisee might identify a need or wish that the supervisor cannot or prefers not to meet. Supervisors then need to be clear in their statement that this will not be part of the contract. Similarly, supervisors may have requirements of their own and these need to be clearly stated at the outset. For example, 'When I am supervising people in training, it is my belief that I need to see the work being carried out if I am to be properly responsible to my clients. Before I see your work I would like you to see mine and we will work out a way of doing this together that is as comfortable for us both as we can make it. What are your thoughts about this?'

This statement makes it clear that the supervisor has certain requirements and in addition indicates the purpose of the requirement and invites the supervisee to join with the supervisor in deciding *how* but not *whether* to meet the requirement. It also provides an opportunity, whilst the supervisory arrangement is elective, for the supervisee to decide against making a contract with this particular supervisor, rather than this emerging at a later stage when it may be more difficult to withdraw.

The ongoing supervisory relationship

Contracting is part of the process of establishing a supervisory alliance. Social influence theory (Egan, 1994: 58–61) suggests that the more trusting an interpersonal relationship, the greater the potential influence of one person upon the other. Trustworthiness of the supervisor was found to relate significantly to measures of supervisees' judgements of supervision, and accounted for larger proportions of variance than did expertness and attractiveness in a study by Carey, Williams and Wells (1988). Trustworthiness of the supervisor has also been found to relate to trainee performance in counselling (Carey,

Williams and Wells, 1988; Dodenhoff, 1981; Heppner and Handley, 1982; Friedlander and Snyder, 1983).

Building trust takes time and is facilitated by an attitude of openness and authenticity whereby supervisors show evidence of having knowledge of their own foibles and blind spots and a continuing interest in developing this knowledge further. Genuine respect for the views and circumstances of the other is also important, as is a flexible and curious approach to the work. The supervisor's awareness of the potential vulnerabilities of supervisees should encourage a structuring of supervision sessions such that they do not create a degree of disclosure that goes beyond the needs of the work. This is facilitated by the supervisor ensuring adherence to agreed boundaries by always having in mind the relevance of what is taking place in supervision to the work.

In a qualitative study (Worthen and McNeill, 1996) which employed in-depth interviews of eight experienced therapists, effective supervisors were characterised by an empathic attitude, a non-judgemental stance towards the supervisee, the conveying of a sense of validation or affirmation, and encouragement to explore and experiment. These qualities are illustrated in the following comments from one of the participants.

> And what was so great, was that my supervisor was really affirming of and validating of my ability to speak clearly. I felt very much understood by her and I felt also like she appreciated those abilities that I had taken pride in the past and which I had felt, I just hadn't felt were being recognized at all, at any level.
>
> (Stoltenberg, McNeill and Delworth, 1998: 113)

When sessions 'go wrong' or do not turn out as expected – for example, where clients leave the session before the planned ending, express anger or dissatisfaction with the therapy or therapist, state that they feel worse than before, and so on – the therapist can feel responsible, blamed and shamed. When feeling vulnerable in this way, one reaction is to hide this from the supervisor and to present a façade of competence rather than seek to learn from the experience (Yourman and Farber, 1997; Ladany, Hill, Corbett and Nutt, 1996). It is particularly helpful in these situations if a position of curiosity and open-mindedness is adopted by the supervisor in which the attribution of the explanation for the difficulty can be to multiple sources. In the following example, it is helpful that the supervising team is familiar with the work of the therapist and is able to state that the pattern of interaction is atypical of the therapist's usual approach. Multiple hypotheses are proposed to explain the events in the session and the therapist reaches her own conclusions about her options in future.

A family was referred to the family therapy service by a head teacher who was concerned that there had been significant deterioration in the behaviour of all three children since the acrimonious separation and divorce of the parents within the previous year. The referral noted that the children spent alternate days with each parent and that the mother had remarried and was expecting a baby. The initial appointment was attended by both birth parents and the three children. The therapist introduced herself, explained the method of work which involved a live supervising team and the interview proceeded as follows:

Th.	Could I be introduced to the people who are here?
Child	[points to youngest child] He'll tell you.
Father	[Names each person present by their first names.]
Th.	Could you tell me what brought you to our service?
Father	It's him [points to youngest child], his behaviour at school.
Th.	Are there any other things that concern you?
Mother	No [assertively], just his behaviour at school.
Th.	Are there any difficulties at home?
Father	No [loudly], just his behaviour at school.
Th.	I'm afraid that we don't deal here with problems in school. You need a different service for that.
Father	[aggressively] We've waited twelve weeks for this appointment and now you tell us that this is the wrong place.
Th.	I'm very sorry. We know that that is a problem.
Father	What do we do then about the problems at school?
Th.	I'm very sorry but the school thought that there were some difficulties at home as well.
Father	What sort of difficulties?
Th.	They mentioned that you had separated and that the children spend some time with each of you and that might be difficult for them. But as you say the problems are at school and I can tell you how to get help there.
Father	[stands up and says to family] Come on then, we're off. [Father strides out and rest of family follows]

The therapist then joined the supervising team and concern was expressed that the children might have lost an opportunity to talk about the effects on them of the separation and divorce. There was exploration of why this session might have ended so quickly and why it had not been possible to move the family on to a wider discussion as might more typically happen (*S.* = supervisor and *Th.* = therapist).

S.	Wow, that was the shortest session I've ever seen you do. I was wondering how the family might have organised you into finishing so much more quickly than you usually do.
Th.	I don't know. They really surprised me. It felt as if they really didn't

want to be here. Even when they got up though, I was still expecting them to carry on.

S.   What did it feel like in there? Did the father seem like he might be violent?

Th.   No, I don't think it was that. I felt safe. It was just that they seemed like they didn't want to be here.

S.   Was that just the father?

Th.   No, the mother as well.

S.   I noticed them in the car park on my way in – just the mother and the boys and they looked a bit uncomfortable then. What happened in reception?

Th.   Well, I didn't know the mother's new married name to invite her down and when I asked, they said she wasn't remarried and they didn't know what I was talking about.

S.   I wondered if they didn't like the idea of the screen and team, but they'd had the leaflet explaining that it would be this way.

Th.   I don't think it was that.

S.   When they insisted the problem was just at school, sometimes you would have chosen to carry on exploring that and then other things might have emerged. What was it that made you choose to say it was the wrong service?

Th.   I think it was the change in my job – I have to be very careful about not taking on anything that doesn't fit with what I'm supposed to do. Yes, and it's to do with being in the allocation meeting. I'm very aware that we have a long waiting list and recently there's been a change so that instead of accepting everything we have been turning a lot more away.

S.   So that we work with those who can most benefit?

Th.   Yes. But now I think maybe I could have chosen to talk for longer about the school problems, but I didn't think it was appropriate at the time.

The team members commented that they had been very successful in fitting the new referral criteria. Further consideration was given to the possible loss of an opportunity for the boys to talk about the effects on them of the separation and residence arrangements, and how other opportunities might be provided; to the context of the school which has been designated as 'failing' and made many referrals to the service; how referrals might contain misinformation; and to what extent the therapist might reveal the concerns of the referrer to the family.

Creating a context of safety

In my experience, one of the most important factors that contributes to sustaining a functional working relationship is the creation and maintenance of safety for all the parties involved in the helping enterprise. Whilst the conditions of warmth and empathy may help, they may not be necessary or sufficient, and without other factors may contribute to a superficial 'feel-good' relationship designed to make both supervisor and supervisee feel good because they want to be liked. This may work well when the going is easy but may come unstuck in the event of problems.

The following dos and don'ts for supervisors are offered for consideration:

- Don't ask the supervisee to do anything that you are not prepared to do first.
- Show your own work to the supervisee openly, either live, on tape or by modelling.
- Retain the main focus on the client and draw everything back to this in the end.
- Always take a respectful approach to clients and colleagues so that supervisees know that you will not 'bad mouth' them behind their backs.
- Don't break confidences.
- Don't say one thing and act in a different way.
- Discuss how the supervisee can 'manage' you should they find their security threatened.
- Make sure that challenges are specific and related to the work.
- Comment on areas where you yourself are unsure, don't know, or feel you have made an error, and talk about what can be done next.
- Where relevant, talk about your own training experiences and how you may differ now from then.
- Don't show off your knowledge in the service of your own ego.
- Be prepared to take responsibility and give instructions where client safety is at issue. Let supervisees know that they will not be allowed to act outside the boundaries that keep the system safe.
- Share some personal information in a way that you might not with clients, in order to allow your humanness to show through your professional demeanour.
- Show interest in the supervisee as a person as well as a professional.
- Notice the supervisee's knowledge and skills.

Inskipp and Proctor (1995) use the term 'under-standing' to highlight the central role-relationship of supervision, rather than the supervisor being blinded by anxiety into privileging the role-relationship as 'super-vision' (i.e. overseeing). Whilst both may be necessary, it is understanding that supports the establishment and maintenance of the supervisory alliance. The contracting process can set the scene for the manner in which the participants will relate to each other in the longer term.

Mini-contracting for specific supervision sessions

Being prepared for supervision can take a variety of forms. The process of negotiating a supervisory contract acts as one form of preparation. In addition, it is helpful if the supervisor and supervisee have thought beforehand about what they wish to be on the agenda for this particular supervision. This mini-contracting helps to stop supervision from becoming routine, predictable and boring! Needs of supervisees are likely to change over time and this can be readily accommodated when each session begins by addressing the supervisory focus and process for today. In each party's mind, the questions in this regard might be, 'What do you/I wish to accomplish as a result of today's supervision?' and 'How shall we go about accomplishing that?' Whilst being prepared is generally useful, from time to time supervisees might use the supervision to explore why they are having difficulty in clarifying what they wish to achieve in supervision. This can arise from their current home or work context in which the intensity of their emotions obscures clear thinking, or where high levels of stress and workload have evoked a pattern of disorganisation and rushing from pillar to post. In such a case the supervisee may need time to relax into the supervision before being able to identify and explore work issues. The following is an extract from a supervision session (where *S'ee.* = supervisee and *S.* = supervisor) in which the supervisee's stress level prevents her from being able to think about her work until she has had an opportunity to let off steam (Inskipp and Proctor, 1988).

S'ee.   I feel so tired, I don't know where to start. I had a terrible weekend on top of a bad week. My boyfriend had to go to the Continent and didn't get in touch when I expected him to. I found, it turned out that he had a minor accident – he's OK now. I was so worried over the weekend and then had to go straight back to work only to find that there were two staff short. I really haven't had any time to think about supervision.

S.   It sounds as if you've had a really tough time, and you're feeling like that – what would you like to do now at the moment?

S'ee.   I'd just like to sit quietly for a few minutes and relax. I really feel like having a good cry [voice becomes tearful] [deep sigh].

S.   That feels better.

S'ee.   That feels good. I think this is the first quiet time I've had all week [deep sigh].

S.   'Long and deep sighs', my yoga teacher says. It reminds me of a sea where we go to camp in Ireland and you can hear it coming in and out with a big sigh.

S'ee.   It reminds me of the sea at home but I bet that's a lot hotter than Ireland.

S.   Yes.

S'ee.   God, I could do with some sun now. I feel so cold. Just thinking about that sun makes me feel warm and alive.

Inskipp and Proctor note that this supervisee was lucky in that her supervisor noticed and responded to her need to let off steam and relax.

In a training context in which the supervisor carries responsibility for the clients, the supervisor, particularly early on, may need to know what is happening with every client. Likewise, the supervisee's needs are likely to focus on what to do rather than on a deep exploration of the interpersonal dynamics. As the supervisee gains in confidence and experience, the conversation may focus on a particular client or a particular technique, the application of particular theory or the dynamics of the therapeutic relationship. When the supervisee is prepared in advance, time is not wasted in identifying a supervisory focus during supervision itself. This is not to say that identifying the focus during supervision is not appropriate, but only that so doing as a consequence of a lack of preparation may not make the best use of time.

The initial contract is a statement of intent and the process of its construction defines the issues that the participants in supervision can expect to discuss as their relationship develops. It is probably helpful to have a written summary of the central topics, although the discussion in and of itself is key.

Summary

This chapter has explored the reasons why a contract for supervision can contribute to the establishment of a good working alliance. Topics for inclusion in the contract have been suggested. Central to a good supervisory relationship is the establishment of trust, and this takes time. Ways in which the supervisor might act to foster a trusting relationship are proposed. The chapter ends by focusing on contracting for individual supervision sessions, and it is suggested that preparation for supervision will facilitate good use of time. Further ideas about contracting may be obtained from Inskipp and Proctor (1993), Borders and Ledick (1987), Page and Wosket (1994), Bradley (1989) and Carroll (1996).

Chapter 5

Frameworks for supervision

It seems to me that there is a limited amount of theory that has been constructed specifically to explain the processes of supervision. The field is far from atheoretical, however, because much psychological theory developed in other contexts is applicable. Some of this has been explored in Chapter 2, in which the tenets of knowledge acquisition and learning were applied to the process of supervision. Since supervision occurs in the context of interpersonal relationships, theories that attempt to explain relationships are also of relevance, and it is in this arena that the tasks of supervision and therapy might be perceived to have common elements and be informed by similar ideas. The notion of the supervisory alliance, for example, derives from that of the therapeutic alliance. Psychodynamic theory can be utilised in attempting to explain what happens between the client, therapist and supervisor through the notion of 'parallel process' (Doehrman, 1976) wherein ideas about transference and counter-transference are applied to the triadic relationship.

Developmental theories have also been applied to supervision, and these draw on the idea of stages of development in order to explain what might happen in supervision, and how the supervisor might be helpful to the supervisee's learning in different ways at different stages of development (Stoltenberg, McNeill and Delworth, 1998).

Where supervision takes place in a group, ideas based on theories about groups and theories about systems are of relevance. For example, the processes through which groups form, develop a functional working relationship and eventually terminate are described by Tuckman and Jensen (1977), group dynamics are addressed by Bion ([1961], 1974), and systems theory by Tomm (1984).

Leaving aside explanatory concepts, several authors have produced models or frameworks within which to conceptualise the purposes and processes of supervision. The advantage of such frameworks is that they enable participants in supervision to organise their ideas about what is happening, thus maintaining their role as a participant in the process at the same time as being able to take the position of observer, thinking about what is happening within a preferred framework or structure or drawing on several. It is helpful for supervisor and supervisee to share their understandings of supervision frameworks with each other. If a common underlying framework is adopted this can be used to explore the events of supervision and the feelings evoked through the process. As in therapy, ideas may be drawn principally from a single structure or from many.

This chapter draws the attention of readers to a number of frameworks that have been devised in order to help participants to organise their experiences in supervision or to carry out research about the process. The selection is based on those that have been found helpful by the author and is by no means exhaustive. The choice of a particular framework is probably of less importance than the decision to educate oneself about them in order to facilitate reflection and review.

Frameworks have been dedicated to describing the purposes of supervision, to facilitating understanding of the processes taking place in supervisory relationships, and to the practicalities of how to use these ideas to facilitate the work with the client.

Of the models described in this chapter, that of Proctor and Inskipp addresses the question, 'Why are we doing this?' Hawkins and Shohet's model addresses the question, 'What are my experiences in supervision telling me about the work?' Page and Wosket (1994) focus on the structure of the supervisory session in order to ensure that it meets the identified supervisory goals. Scaife and Scaife (1996) provide a framework to address the question of what to do in supervision and with what materials. Developmental models aid the supervisory partnership in thinking about the needs of individual supervisees and how these might differ from one supervisee to another. Whilst these are the central aspects of the models described, each of the authors addresses much wider issues beyond the exposition of the specific model. They are summarised here; interested readers might wish to consult the original sources for further information.

A model addressing the purposes of supervision (Inskipp and Proctor, 1993)

There is no common agreement about the purpose of supervision, although a number of propositions have been made. Purpose is likely to differ depending on the role-relationship of the participants. In training supervision, the learning and development of the supervisee has a place at centre stage. Keeping Inskipp and Proctor's (1993) model in mind helps the supervisor to stay on track with the aims of the supervision as agreed within the contracting process. The model was developed in the context of counsellor supervision conducted independently of an employing or training institution. The contract was a private arrangement which included negotiation of a fee.

Inskipp and Proctor propose three categories of purpose in supervision:

'formative', 'normative', and 'restorative'. Supervision in any one session might include all of these aims either explicitly or implicitly.

Formative

When the supervision aims to be formative, it is the supervisee's learning and development that is the focus. No particular approach to the learning is implied and the supervisor might employ a range of methods designed to further the supervisee's knowledge or skills.

Normative

The normative function of supervision derives from the supervisor's managerial and ethical responsibilities. Whilst the extent to which this is relevant will vary between settings, the supervisor will always have some responsibility to ensure client welfare. In a training setting, the managerial role is likely to be extensive and may include having responsibility for the supervisee's casework and ensuring that the supervisee complies with the rules and norms of the organisations in which the work is carried out. Where the contract for supervision is made within an employing organisation, it is necessary to negotiate the constraints that this might impose. For example, if the employer requires that the therapist work with a certain minimum number of clients at any one time and through supervision it is concluded that this is adversely affecting the work being done, what is the responsibility of the supervisor to either help the therapist to comply with the organisational requirement, or to help the therapist to challenge the requirements? In essence, the supervisor is contracting both with the funding body and with the supervisee and needs to be clear about her or his contractual duties to each of these parties.

When supervision is arranged independently of an employer and the individual makes a personal financial arrangement, the normative function of supervision may be less to the fore. However, the supervisor will still have moral and ethical responsibilities with regard to the clients that are discussed. Should the supervisor consider that the therapist cannot meet client needs because of ill health, for example, or if the supervisor perceives abuse of a client, action must be taken. Whatever form this takes, the supervisor should seek to act sensitively and with regard to the welfare of all parties. Where other parties (such as a professional body) need to be informed, this should be done with the knowledge, and ideally with the consent, but if necessary without the agreement, of the supervisee. As with many other aspects of the supervisory process, taking action in such circumstances is facilitated if discussion of the possibility has taken place in the contracting process. Holding in mind a framework in which the normative function is identified enables supervisors to monitor and review what they are doing and why when faced with such dilemmas.

Restorative

The restorative function acknowledges the emotional effects on the individual of work, and in particular of work with people in distress. These effects were explored in more detail in Chapter 3. Within the institutions in which people work there are social, political and economic forces that can have a significant impact on the employees. Links have been suggested between the emotional experiences of employees and organisational process and structure (Czander, 1993). In addition to the potential impact of structural features, people have relationships with colleagues at work and these relationships can have at least as profound an impact as those with clients. People have relationships outside of work and the events occurring in these have an impact on self in work. Thus the potential sources of emotional arousal at work are multiple, arising from the organisational process and structure, relationships with colleagues, relationships with clients, and relationships and life events outside work. It might be agreed that any of these are a relevant and appropriate focus of supervision, the aim of the supervision being to explore the level and sources of arousal and their impact specifically upon the work.

In relation to what happens between the therapist and the client, Mollon (1989) identifies the negative emotional experiences of people learning to be therapists as 'narcissistic insults'. Typically these are experienced as shameful in that they include feeling hostile towards or sexually aroused by the people that one is supposing to help. A not unusual response to the feeling of shame is reticence and concealment. When supervision is acknowledged to have a restorative function, revelation of such feelings is legitimate. The supervisor's role is to provide support, facilitate understanding and enable the supervisee to learn by using these feelings to inform the work. Failing to reveal these feelings can lead clients and therapists into liaisons that may prove a danger to both.

Inskipp and Proctor use the analogy of miners obtaining agreement from the employer to wash off the dust of their labours in the employer's time to elaborate this function of supervision. Supervisees in training may find it difficult to believe that supervision can be used for this purpose without adversely affecting the supervisor's evaluation. The research evidence suggests that hiding things from the supervisor is a very widespread practice (Ladany, Hill, Corbett and Nutt, 1996). Supervisors typically take the view that they would prefer to know about the messes made by supervisees and are more concerned positively to evaluate openness in supervision and progress through learning from mistakes. Nevertheless, this function of supervision may need particular attention in training relationships.

Because the focus of the restorative function can be wide-ranging, including organisational issues, relationships with colleagues and clients, or the impact of life events, it is essential that respect is paid to relevant boundaries.

Where difficulties are being experienced with a colleague shared in common between supervisor and supervisee, or where personal issues in the wider life of the supervisee need attention, alternative mechanisms than supervision may need to be invoked. One of the tasks of the supervisor in carrying out this function is to monitor the level of intrusiveness into personal issues and how necessary this is for the task in hand.

Sessions that have a substantial restorative function may be experienced as less structured than others. They sometimes begin with the supervisee not knowing what issues to address and the supervisor listening attentively while the supervisee presents a confused picture that might include a vague awareness of not feeling 'right'. The supervisor listens for openings as to what may be happening for the supervisee and may use her or his counselling skills in order to try and connect. If a trusting relationship has been constructed, the supervisee will be able to give voice to frustrations, upsets and disappointments which may in itself be sufficient in order to move on. Without the restorative function the difficulties of the day are likely to be taken home and explored or enacted with family and friends (McElfresh and McElfresh, 1998).

Models addressing the process and content of supervision

General Supervision Framework (Scaife and Scaife, 1996, and Scaife, 1993b)

The framework comprises the three dimensions of supervisor role, supervision focus and the medium that is used to provide data for supervision. The model owes much to the work of Bernard (1979, 1981) and Levine and Tilker (1974). Since its original publication, the ideas of the authors have developed further and the version presented here is modified accordingly. Whilst the dimensions are categorised under discrete headings, it is not intended that these be regarded rigidly or as the only categories possible. Like any classificatory system, it will be seen to have greater or lesser fit for the purpose of understanding supervision by different people and for different material. It is intended to provide a mechanism by which to simplify the process of supervision as an aid both to conceptualisation in practice and to research. Each of the dimensions of the model is elaborated below.

Supervisor role-behaviour

In the General Supervision Framework (GSF) emphasis is placed upon what the supervisor does in the relationship with the supervisee. Whilst the spotlight in this case is on the supervisor, it is acknowledged that alternative focuses on either the supervisee or on the relationship between the

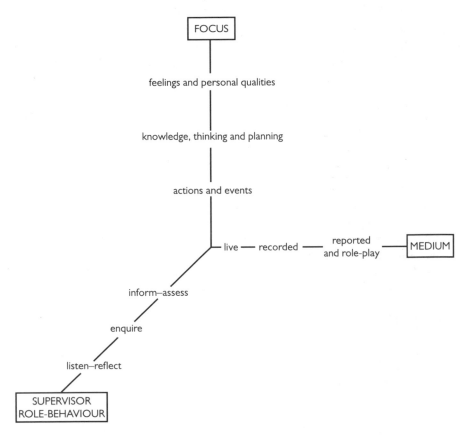

Figure 5.1 The general supervision framework

participants are also feasible. It is proposed that supervisor role-behaviour be categorised under the three discrete headings of Inform–Assess, Enquire, and Listen–Reflect. Inform–Assess role-behaviour tends to emphasise complementarity in the supervisory relationship in which there is the informer and the informed. The role-behaviours of Enquire and Listen–Reflect can lead to the experiencing of greater reciprocity. Bernard argues, in relation to pre-registration counsellor training, that the approach that the supervisor uses or the role adopted should represent a deliberate choice based on the needs of individuals at different stages of learning. However, it is also important to recognise that supervisee role-behaviour can evoke particular responses from the supervisor and that this can be very difficult to resist, even when recognised, and deemed to be not particularly helpful to learning. A commonly encountered example is where the supervisee invites Inform–Assess role-behaviour by asking the supervisor for her or his views and opinions. The three categories of supervisor role-behaviour are described further below.

INFORM–ASSESS

This category of role-behaviour involves making observations and judgements of supervisee performance, offering positive and negative critical comments and 'telling' things to the supervisee. Supervisors take responsibility for their own expertise and there is an assumption that supervisors have some knowledge and insights not available to the supervisee. It is when occupying this role-relationship that supervisors carry out the tasks of gate-keeping admission to a profession and discharging their ethical responsibilities to clients. The balancing of responsibility to clients with responsibility to the supervisee was ranked second in a list of issues which are difficult to deal with in supervision by the Educational and Child Psychology Division (DECP) of the British Psychological Society survey of educational psychologists (Pomerantz et al., 1987). This accords with Doehrman's (1976) finding that supervisors generally have a preference for a more collegial role than this category of role-behaviour exemplifies. It is usually helpful for the supervisee and supervisor to negotiate in which circumstances such role-behaviours might be chosen. These role-behaviours might also be adopted by supervisees in providing information to the supervisor about what is proving most helpful to their learning. Negotiation and agreement about how and when to adopt Assess–Inform role-behaviours can avoid the dilemmas posed by wholesale adoption of a partnership or collegial relationship in which supervisors may feel constrained about evaluating the work of the supervisee or suggesting agenda items for supervision.

Inexperienced supervisees or those new to a particular specialism may be the most likely to prefer the Inform–Assess approach. At this stage supervisors might suggest relevant reading material, describe some of their own case-work, point out key issues and dilemmas that might arise in the work, or conduct mini-seminars exploring such issues. This is not to say that the role-behaviour is no longer relevant in the case of greater experience as in peer supervisory relationships. Supervisees can continue to find it helpful to hear about the supervisor's approach and to obtain feedback on their work. However, it is likely that the balance will change with the development and experience of the supervisee.

ENQUIRE

When the supervisor adopts Enquire role-behaviour, the supervisee is likely to experience reciprocity in the supervisory relationship. This role is often preferred by supervisors (Pomerantz et al., 1987). In this role supervisors primarily ask questions but may also share their own experiences with trainees. The spirit of the role is of enquiry from a position of curiosity and exploration rather than of interrogation. Contrary to this role-behaviour, asking a question to which the supervisor has a preconceived notion of the 'right' answer would exemplify veiled Inform–Assess role-behaviour and in such circumstances it is usually better to 'come clean' rather than to expect the supervisee to read the supervisor's mind. Enquirer role equates with that described in partnership supervision (Rudduck and Sigsworth, 1985) and is also a significant feature of the Interpersonal Process Recall (IPR) model of Kagan (1984) and Kagan and Kagan (1991). A description of IPR appears in Chapter 8.

LISTEN–REFLECT

The supervisor using this category of role-behaviour is usually placing a premium on the supervisee's personal needs in the professional context. The role involves attentive listening and reflection of what has been said in such a way as to provide illumination of the issues raised. The process of reflection may introduce a development and overview of the supervisee's own ideas. The focus of this role is often on the needs and issues of the supervisee, which may include the feelings generated by the work. Alternatively, the focus may be on helping supervisees to clarify their thoughts about the professional task in which they are engaged. For example, a supervisee may, generally speaking, exhibit well-developed skills in a particular kind of work, but may be struggling to apply the skills effectively in a particular setting or with a particular client. The supervisor in Listen–Reflect mode may help the trainee to derive her or his own explanations of the difficulties in this case. This role-behaviour exemplifies Stones' (1984) and Bernard's (1981) counsellor role in which the supervisor is sensitive and attentive to the mood and personal needs of the trainee.

In practice these three categories of role-behaviour rarely obtain in pure form. In each session these and other role-behaviours might be expressed, the aim of the supervisor being to move between roles according to need. This includes the development of the supervisee in the profession and of the supervisor in meeting the learning needs of supervisees. The pattern of role-behaviours represents the result of the dance between participants in terms of what is unconsciously evoked and what is deliberately chosen. The extract below (where S. = supervisor and S'ee. = supervisee) illustrates how a supervisor might respond differently within each of the categories to a particular stimulus introduced by the supervisee:

> S'ee. 'When she started to talk about how she couldn't go out anywhere because she couldn't be bothered to get ready, I wanted to challenge her about how she managed to attend the sessions with me, but she looked so fragile I was worried that she would just think that I didn't understand. I wanted her to know that I could empathise with that, particularly given her history, and that I felt upset as well. Then I started to think that what I could offer was

pretty useless and superficial given the depths of her distress. As soon as I thought that, I didn't know what to say to her.'

Supervisor using Inform–Assess role-behaviour

S.   'I think that perhaps what you were experiencing was a dilemma about whether to try deepening the empathy, which you might do by saying something like, "You feel so depressed that nothing seems worthwhile anymore?" or making a distinction on a difference by drawing her attention to the exception to what she was describing – the evidence that maybe she can do more than she thinks she can because she is able to attend her sessions with you.'

Supervisor using Enquire role-behaviour

S.   'If you were to have followed your inclination to point out that she had managed to attend the session with you, can you think now about how you might have said that without risking her thinking that you didn't understand?'

S.   'When you focused on your empathy with her feelings of sadness, was that the point at which you started to feel that you had nothing to offer?'

Supervisor using Listen–Reflect role-behaviour

S.   'So it sounds as if you're saying that there was a dilemma for you about making a choice of direction and that when that happened, you kind of got stuck and lost your confidence.'

These role-behaviours may be selected by the supervisor to suit the specific occasion or to suit the supervisee, might reflect a preferred *modus operandi*, or the supervisor might also be invited into a particular response by the supervisee role-behaviour. This can be more or less explicit. Supervisees who have expectations that they are to begin a session by describing their previous meeting with the client often invite the supervisor into Listen–Reflect role-behaviour for the first few minutes of the supervision. Alternatively, as part of the agenda setting for supervision the supervisee might explicitly invite Enquire role-behaviour, saying, 'I have a number of conflicting ideas about the work with this client and I would like you to help me to think through which to use at this point in the work.'

Supervision focus

Supervision focus is the topic or topics to be explored in supervision. The focus is that which will be looked at and discussed, rather than how or why it will be addressed. The focus of supervision may be proposed by either or both of the parties involved. In some models of supervision – for example, clinical supervision (Sullivan, 1980; Goldhammer, Anderson and Krajewski, 1980) – the focus is primarily oriented towards skill development. When the responsibility for the selection of supervisory focus rests with supervisees, as in partnership models, it has been found that they are likely to select a focus on feelings generated within the relationship between the professional worker and the client. In the work of Rudduck and Sigsworth (1985) in the context of learning to teach, supervisees tended to select items such as whether the difficulties encountered emanated from the student teacher's youthful appearance, another supervisee querying whether she was being consistently nicer to some children than to others.

Bernard proposes that supervisors are likely to have preferred focus areas, often based on their own special interests. There is also likely to be a relationship between preferred focus and preferred model of therapy. A behavioural approach is likely to emphasise observable behaviour; a cognitive approach, thinking processes; and a psychodynamic approach the feelings and unconscious dynamics occurring in the relationships of client/therapist and therapist/supervisor.

Bernard (1979) proposes the categorisation of focus under three discrete headings. Adopting a similar structure, Scaife and Scaife have labelled the categories of focus as 'Actions, Events and Responses', 'Knowledge, Thinking and Planning' and 'Feelings and Personal Qualities'.

ACTIONS, EVENTS AND RESPONSES

This category of focus is behaviour and skills oriented. It includes supervisors asking questions about what was said and done during therapy by client and/or supervisee. The supervisor might also make observations about events that took place during the work. It could include supervisees asking questions about events and responses that they have observed in the supervisor's work. Descriptions or demonstrations of technique would exemplify this focus. It might also involve noticing a pattern or process in the session; for example, the client responding by giving information about a medical condition whenever invited to discuss feelings.

KNOWLEDGE, THINKING AND PLANNING

Knowledge, thinking and planning can either be raised directly as a focus, or might be inferred as a result of observations made. This focus would be exemplified in supervision by the reading of case-relevant literature followed by a discussion of how these theoretical ideas could be used in the work with a particular client. Supervisees in training often value this approach to supervision in helping them to link what is being taught in the academic context with their experiences of being with clients. It is within this category that understanding and conceptualising of the client's difficulties and the process of formulation are located.

FEELINGS AND PERSONAL QUALITIES

This focus addresses the expression of individual style and the use of personal qualities in the work. It can range from reflection upon a person's values, expectations, and prejudices, to the impact of life events on self in work. Examples might include identifying a tendency for the supervisee to care for and look after clients. In adopting this as a supervisory focus the supervisee might be helped to learn how this might be of help or a hindrance in the work. Other examples might be to focus on how feeling the need as the professional to take actions which produce symptom change in the client may help or hinder the client's progress, or how a recent or past bereavement in the life of the worker may be affecting the work. Within this framework, specific personal qualities and the experience or lack of experience of particular life events are not seen as having particularly positive or negative value. The focus is on self in the professional role and when these issues are explored it is important to keep in mind the relevance of the exploration for the work. Where issues go beyond work, the role of the supervisor is to ensure that these can be addressed in other more appropriate relationships – for example, with a mentor or in personal therapy.

This focus is also addressed to the ways in which the work affects the mood and feelings of the supervisee and how these in turn affect the work. Ashforth and Humphrey (1995: 98) go so far as to argue that the 'experience of work is saturated with feeling'. Mood at work can be affected by both clients and colleagues and the initial contract for supervision can be used to determine to what extent the focus can include issues that go beyond direct case-work. Different models of therapy use different language to identify the dynamics of the client–therapist relationship. The notions of transference and counter-transference (Hawkins and Shohet, 1989: 63) are helpful here, as is the idea that feelings will inevitably be evoked by the work, and the task of the therapist is not to deny their existence but rather to make meaning of them in order most usefully to employ them in the service of the client.

Adoption of this focus does not necessarily imply a need for 'support', but rather is a legitimate focus of development in what is referred to by Goffman (1968) as 'people-work'. Supervisees might thus choose agenda items for supervision such as, 'How can I use my liking for this client positively in the work?' 'How can I understand my reluctance to take on the ideas proposed by my social work colleague?' 'How can I deal with my anxiety about the session getting out of control if I allow people to shout?' 'Why do I find myself feeling angry with Mr Smith?' Questions may be addressed to the supervisor by the supervisee; for example, 'What strategies do you adopt to help you to cope with the distress that this work generates?'

In workshops described by Bernard (1981) and Scaife and Scaife (1996) supervisors and trainees respectively were found to differ significantly according to preferred focus, although this may vary according to the nature of the work being undertaken. There is also likely to be a relationship between focus and model of therapy and focus and stage of development of the supervisee, the choice of focus changing according to the stage of professional development. Shared knowledge of the framework can facilitate negotiation of focus to optimise use of supervision.

As with supervisor role, the above categorisation of focus is adopted for convenience and simplicity when studying the supervisory process. During the course of a supervision session, participants would most often move between focuses according to planned or unplanned agendas. Bernard promotes the idea of flexibility in order most usefully to meet learning needs.

Supervisory medium

The third dimension of the General Supervision Framework categorises the medium through which supervision takes place. As with role and focus, the selected medium of supervision is likely to relate to the theoretical model in which the supervised work is being conducted, and to reflect the preferences and experience of the parties involved. The medium of supervision is referred to by Levine and Tilker (1974) as 'stages' and by Pomerantz et al. (1987) as 'modes'. The possible options for the medium of supervision range across non-participatory observation through role-play, sitting in with the supervisor, bug in the ear, audiotaping and videotaping and verbal reporting. Survey findings suggest that retrospective reporting (mode III supervision, Pomerantz et al., 1987) is the most commonly adopted medium for supervision of pre-registration training in the professions of educational and clinical psychology in the U.K.

Scott and Spellman (1992) report that despite British Psychological Society guidelines on training, it is not uncommon to encounter trainees who, towards the end of training, have never seen their supervisors working with clients, or to find that trainees have never been observed working themselves. Pomerantz et al. (1987) reported that 32 of 57 trainees claimed that observation of their supervisors' work took place in less than 10 per cent of supervision sessions, and 41 claimed that their own work was observed in less than 10 per cent of sessions. This contrasts with teaching practice supervision in which the most commonly adopted medium is live classroom observation of the trainee by the supervisor. It has been argued that the use of reporting back as the medium of supervision implies the ability to practise with relative independence, and is therefore more appropriately employed towards the end of training. Arguments against the use of live methods tend to emphasise a fear of undermining the status of the supervisee in the eyes of the client, the potential negative side effects of raised anxiety levels, or intrusiveness into the relationship between clients and trainees.

LIVE SUPERVISION AND OBSERVATION

There are many possible ways of conducting live supervision in which either the trainee or supervisor takes the lead in relation to the work being carried out. These methods are explored in greater depth in Chapter 9. In contexts where the technology is available, a one-way viewing screen may be used. Communication between supervisor and supervisee may take place during scheduled breaks, via a 'bug in the ear' device through which the supervisor can speak directly to the supervisee as the work is carried out, by telephone, or by use of a 'reflecting team'. A reflecting team involves the supervisory team speaking to each other about their ideas in front of the client and therapist, who may choose to use those ideas in the remainder of the session (Anderson, 1997). Variants are common in family therapy approaches where a supervising team tends to be employed as a matter of course.

Reluctance on the part of supervisees to adopt live supervisory methods may arise from discomfort experienced as a result of being the subject of another's observations. There may be associated expectations that the focus of supervision will be Actions and Events selected by the supervisor and that the role-behaviour adopted by the supervisor will be Inform–Assess. Such expectations may be overcome through discussions between the supervisor and supervisee or through the adoption of methods of live supervision with which both parties feel comfortable.

RECORDED SESSIONS

Videotape and audiotape provide opportunities for 'action replay'. Some data will be lost compared with live supervision (for example, the 'feel' of the session), but tapes can be replayed several times. These media may be regarded as less intrusive than live methods, whilst providing an opportunity for indirect observation. Issues raised by the use of these media include confidentiality of the recorded material, and 'ownership' of the recording during the process of supervision. Technical considerations also apply. Written consent is usually an ethical requirement when recordings of sessions are made, and efforts to protect the material, for example using a numerical referencing system, are advisable. These issues are explored in more depth in Chapter 8.

Some methods of supervision, for example Interpersonal Process Recall

(Kagan and Kagan, 1991) and micro-counselling (Ivey, 1974) are based primarily on the use of recordings. Playback may include whole or selected sections of tape, the former being a relatively time-consuming option. Selections may be made by supervisor, supervisee or both participants in the supervisory process. Developments of the use of these media include the option of replay to the children, families or professionals with whom the work has been carried out (Kagan, Krathwohl and Miller, 1963). Recordings can be particularly valuable when the supervision discussion focuses on subtle or rapidly changing processes in a session.

For the supervisee, the use of recordings can offer a different kind of 'realism' compared with verbal accounts of practice. The opportunity to review one's practice on tape may evoke lines of thought not so readily stimulated by other media.

REPORTING

Discussion of the trainee's verbal or written reports is a popular and versatile medium through which supervision is conducted (Pomerantz *et al.*, 1987). Work may be discussed in advance at the planning stage, and/or retrospectively in debriefing a session already conducted. Whilst this medium may be perceived as less threatening than live or recorded supervision, information may be lost or forgotten, or not raised because it is considered to be too sensitive. It has been argued that supervisees in a training context find it easier to focus on the problems of the client rather than on their own experiences, interventions and responses when this medium is used (Levine and Tilker, 1974).

Reporting does imply respect for the judgements of the supervisee. One approach that the supervisor might usefully take is to encourage supervisees to explore their judgements, perhaps so as to locate them in a theoretical framework or in a practice model.

ROLE-PLAY

Role-play, role-reversal and behaviour-rehearsal may be used during supervision in order to pose a variety of hypothetical problems, to demonstrate and practise skills and techniques, and to explore difficulties arising in the work. This medium also includes an option for interviewing the 'internalised other', in which supervisees are asked questions in the first person as the 'other' with whom the work is being conducted (Burnham, 2000; Epston, 1993). (See Chapter 10 for a fuller description.) This medium can be a powerful aid to learning and offers the opportunity for exploration of relationships and for practice in a situation which is relatively safe for both therapist and client. It has been argued that in the use of role-play, the supervisor should initially take the role of therapist in order to demonstrate protocol and procedures, and in order to provide the trainee with the experience of being 'on the other side of the desk' (Levine and Tilker, 1974). Whether or not this is an appropriate starting point will depend on the nature of the supervisory relationship. Experienced therapists in supervision are less likely to require the supervisor to do this. Negotiation can lead to agreement as regards the supervisee taking the role of client, the role of therapist trying out a range of different approaches, or as another 'player' in the client's problem system.

As in relation to supervisor focus and role-behaviour, positive effects might be expected to accrue from the experiencing of a range of supervisory media. Whilst historically different contexts have tended to support different media as the norm for supervision, these assumptions may be questioned and may constitute an element for discussion in the establishment of the supervisory relationship.

The General Supervision Framework can helpfully be used during the contracting process as a support to the identification of supervisor and supervisee preferences regarding the three dimensions of Focus, Role-relationship and Medium. Whilst the majority of practitioners tend to indicate a desire for flexibility of focus and role-relationship, individual preferences tend to be more common in relation to the selection of a specific medium. The framework can be useful in reviewing the process of supervision should a relatively fixed pattern of role-relationship and focus tend to develop.

Double Matrix Model (Hawkins, 1985; Hawkins and Shohet, 1989; Hawkins and Shohet, 2000)

This model is addressed to the specific supervisory focus of the processes taking place in the relationships of the participants in therapy and supervision. It includes within its compass the quartet of the client, the supervisor, the supervisee and the work context. It uses the notions of transference and parallel process to aid the understanding of these processes and suggests that the supervisor needs to pay attention to six interlocking focuses. Inskipp and Proctor (1993) refer to this as the 'six-eyed supervisor'.

Mode 1   Focus on session content

In this mode, the focus of the supervision is on the client – what was said, how the client came to seek help, how the client looked, her or his gestures, use of language and metaphor. It is argued that the use of this focus helps the therapist to attend to the unique human qualities of each client and to stay open to the different options for making meaning of what the client brings to the session. This may be particularly helpful for supervisees early in training when anxiety may lead them to feel uncomfortable with uncertainty. To mini-mise this discomfort they may move too hastily to reach a formulation or

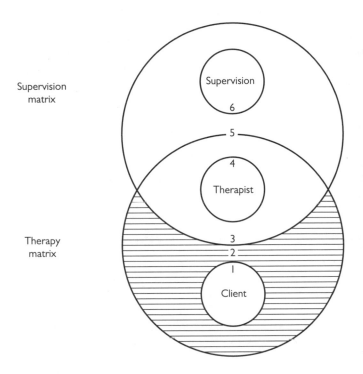

Figure 5.2 A process model of supervision

Note: Shaded area is only available to the supervision matrix through some form of reflection

explanation for the presenting problems, thus 'objectifying' (Shainberg, 1983) the client and neglecting the unique characteristics of each individual.

It is also my experience that this is often the default focus of supervision for neophyte therapists. They expect to tell the supervisor about the client and what happened in the session. Similarly, more experienced therapists often tend to focus on therapy session content as a scene-setting mechanism prior to introducing an issue or dilemma. Content has face validity as appropriate material for supervision, and may be experienced as safer than more self-focused material.

When focusing on content, the supervision may be used to make links with other content either from previous sessions or from different points in a single session, with a view to identifying patterns or gaining a deeper understanding. Content may usefully include events outside of the sessions themselves, such as the pattern of keeping, rearranging or failing appointments; between-session contacts initiated by the client; or what happened in the waiting room. The spotlight is on the client and relationships outside of the therapy itself.

Mode 2   Focus on the therapist's strategies and interventions

This focus includes both the actions and the thoughts of the supervisee, including the choices made in the session and the consideration of other alternatives. It can be pitched at the level of technique and can help supervisees to become more aware of their own actions and thoughts in sessions. Hawkins and Shohet caution against the supervisor making too many suggestions for intervention in case this acts as a brake on the supervisee's own creativity. The ideal balance between making and evoking suggestions is likely to differ according to the level of qualification and experience of the supervisee and is a matter for negotiation. It is often much easier to think of alternatives during supervision without the pressing presence of the client.

Mode 3   Focus on the process and relationship between client and therapist

Here the focus is on the transaction between therapist and client. This includes the patterns that develop, for instance of the therapist making a suggestion and the client stating that this has already been tried, of the client becoming tearful and the therapist becoming silent, of the therapist asking about feelings and the client responding with information and facts, and so on.

The supervisor helps the supervisee to stand outside the relationship with the client, taking an observer perspective on the interplay between the two. Hawkins and Shohet suggest a number of approaches that the supervisor might take in order to help the supervisee to find this view. These include creating an image or metaphor to represent the relationship, imagining how the relationship would develop were the client and therapist to be cast away on a desert island, and telling the story of the history of the relationship with the client beginning with the referral.

Supervision with this focus also explores the client's transference – what patterns the client brings to this relationship that have been learned in earlier interactions with others. This might include how the clients seem to invite the therapist to punish them, to take care of them, to flirt with them, to reject them or to fight with them. Supervision can be particularly helpful in encouraging supervisees to use their feelings as information that tells them about the client and how best to proceed.

Mode 4   Focus on the internal experience of the therapist

There is overlap between modes 3 and 4. The internal experience of the therapist is seen as having an influence on the therapy. In this mode the supervisor attends to the therapist's counter-transference – the therapist's predominantly unaware reactions to the client. They identify four different types of counter-transference:

- Feelings stirred up in the therapist which have their origin in the therapist's previous relationships.
- Feelings that arise from the therapist playing out the reciprocal role to the client's transference.
- The therapist's feelings, thoughts and actions that are used to counter the transference of the client.
- Projected material of the clients that the therapist has taken in.

Counter-transference is regarded as a response to the client that is primarily not part of conscious awareness. The task of the supervisor is to help bring this material into awareness in order that it can be used constructively rather than get in the way of the work. The supervisor attends to the gestures, images and metaphors shown by supervisees and tries to elucidate the supervisees' values and beliefs as evidenced by their choice of vocabulary, such as the adjectives that they use in referring to their client. The following extract (where *S*. = supervisor and *S'ee*. = supervisee) is used in illustration by Hawkins and Shohet:

> *S.*   Why are you allowing this staff member to drift and not confronting him?
> *S'ee.* Well, I do not want to be a punitive boss.
> *S.*   What would that be like?
> *S'ee.* As you asked that, I got the image of a little boy outside a headmaster's office.
> *S.*   So your unconscious links confronting to being a punitive head teacher. If you were this staff member's head teacher, how would you want to punish him and what would you be punishing him for?
>
> (Hawkins and Shohet, 1989: 67)

The supervision would then go on to explore whether the therapist could challenge the staff member, but in ways that would be less affected by punitive associations.

At times, the feelings evoked in the therapist towards the client can be almost overwhelming. A clue to some counter-transference reactions is to experience feelings towards the client that differ from one's typical feelings towards clients. Without supervision, these feelings can lead the therapist in dangerous directions. Bringing them to awareness offers the opportunity to use them in the service of the work.

Mode 5   Focusing on the here-and-now process between supervisor and supervisee

In modes 5 and 6 the supervisor moves away from focusing on the client and the therapist to focusing on herself or himself. In mode 5 the focus is on what is happening between the therapist and supervisor, noticing one's own reactions to the supervisee, reflecting on them and making meaning that will inform the supervision. The mechanism by which the difficulties in the therapy relationship present themselves in a similar fashion in the supervisory relationship is known as the parallel process (Searles, 1955). In a fairly straightforward example, the supervision can feel flat and hopeless when the therapy is with a profoundly depressed client.

The notion of parallel process was extended by the research of Doehrman (1976), who studied twelve cases in depth. She concluded that paralleling occurred in every client/therapist/supervisor relationship that she studied and that it could occur in either direction. In other words, aspects of the relationship between the supervisor and supervisee could be replayed in the client–therapist relationship. More recent research by a number of authors has supported the notion of parallel process (McNeill and Worthen, 1989; Williams, 1997; Raichelson, Herron, Primavera and Ramirez, 1997). Supervisors thus need to keep an eye on what they are experiencing more generally in their relationship with the supervisee, for example finding themselves frequently telling things to the supervisee when their preference is for an enquiring approach, in order to consider not only whether this is helpful in the supervision but how it might be played out in the therapy.

Mode 6   Focusing on the internal experience of the supervisor

This focus is on the 'disruptions' that are experienced out of the blue by the supervisor during supervision. This might be experiencing boredom when a particular client is being discussed, seeing spontaneous images at a particular moment in a discussion or suddenly feeling anxious or upset. This occurs in the context of the supervisor's knowledge of what he or she typically experiences when with the particular supervisee.

Supervisors can use the concept of 'immediacy' (Egan, 1994) to employ these experiences in the service of the work. Using this technique, supervisors state what they are experiencing and wonder what this might mean, as in the following example from Hawkins and Shohet:

> 'I am getting very sleepy as you go on about this client. Often when that happens to me it seems to indicate that some feeling is being shut off either to do with the therapy or right here in the supervision. Perhaps you can check what you might be holding back from saying?'
>
> (Hawkins and Shohet, 1989: 71)

Hawkins and Shohet take the view that good supervision of in-depth work with clients should involve all six focuses at some point in the work. They also suggest that the selection of focus should be linked to the learning needs of the supervisee. In my view, the complexity and challenge of using the six modes increases from mode 1 to mode 6. A focus on the client seems much safer than on the therapist or the relationship between the therapist and supervisor. In learning how to use modes 3 to 6 supervisors might benefit from role-rehearsal or exploration in their own supervision. Hawkins and Shohet's model serves usefully to highlight the range of choices and complexities of the client/therapist/supervisor relationship.

This model encourages the supervisor to keep in mind what is happening in the relationships between supervisor, therapist and client. It requires the skill of participant observation in which the supervisor experiences emotions and has spontaneous thoughts during supervision, simultaneously reflecting on these with regard to their meaning for the therapy. Hawkins and Shohet give examples of how to raise these matters with the supervisee, but the framework itself is specifically addressed to supervisory focus.

Cyclical model of supervision (Page and Wosket, 1994)

Page and Wosket's model is primarily addressed to the structure of supervision sessions. It identifies a number of stages through which each supervision session proceeds. It outlines options for what to do in supervision and can be used to help the supervision stay on track in terms of the structure of the session, ensuring that there is movement towards the goals of the session.

The supervision process is presented as a cycle of five stages proceeding from contracting through focusing, space, bridge, and review. The contracting stage has commonalities with the process described in Chapter 4, and the process is influenced by the view of Page and Wosket (1994) and of Horton (1993) that there is little place in supervision for the pupil–teacher aspects of training where the supervisee is viewed as a 'recipient' of the acquired wisdom and knowledge of the more experienced supervisor. The task of the supervisor is regarded as to help supervisees to enhance and fully utilise their knowledge, skills and attributes, bringing them to bear on work with particular clients. The factors that they list as topics to be addressed in the contracting process are duration; timing; frequency; fees; codes of ethics and practice; dealing with cancellation; boundaries between supervision, training and therapy; confidentiality; role boundaries; accountability; expectations; and the nature of the supervisory relationship. A 'mini' version of contracting may take place at the start of each supervision session.

Discussions based on expectations and relationship are viewed as crucial to the development and maintenance of an enabling and supportive relationship. It is recommended that the supervisor spend time eliciting the

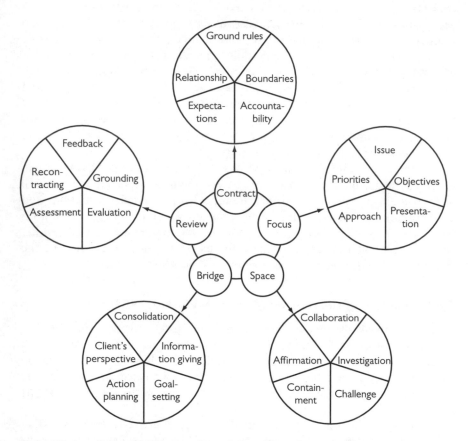

Figure 5.3 A cyclical model of supervision. Adapted from Page and Wosket (1994)

supervisee's anticipations, preferences, learning styles and learning history as an aid to planning the supervisory experience (Webb, 1983).

The next stage of the model, the focus, is the topic or issue upon which the supervisor and supervisee are directing their full attention and energy. During the focusing stage, the aim is to identify an issue, prioritising where necessary, and to identify the objectives for the session. Sometimes these can be identified through some straightforward questioning such as, 'What would you like to focus on today?' 'What would you like to happen as a result of us having this conversation?' and 'How would you like to approach this – shall I ask you questions, would you like to role-play one of the characters or would you like to tell me something first?'

It is argued that wherever possible the supervisee should take a major role in identifying the issue/s for supervision. This/these may have been prepared in advance or there may be agreement that in some sessions the supervisee will come relatively unprepared regarding supervision focus, in which case the session will begin with a process of identification.

The next step in the focusing stage is the supervisee's presentation of the issue. Most typically, presentations are verbal although they can include tapes or pictorial representations. Page and Wosket advise that supervisees prepare their presentation by already having asked themselves questions such as, 'What is my particular difficulty or problem in working with this client?', 'If I could risk telling my supervisor what really concerns me in my work, what would that be?', 'What do I need to tell or off-load to my supervisor so that I can work more freely with this client?' This can prevent supervisees from introducing important issues 'just remembered' towards the end of a session when insufficient time remains. An additional feature of the presentation is the amount of background information that is given by the supervisee. Dependent upon the objectives of the supervision session, it may be helpful to consider background at length or to pay it minimal attention. When data about the client takes centre stage, the focus is firmly on the client rather than on the therapeutic process or the dilemmas of the supervisee. When focusing on the latter, it is often helpful for the supervisor to know little of the background in order to attend to the therapist's issues and not be drawn into the role of surrogate therapist to the client.

Page and Wosket's focusing stage also includes the supervisor's approach in response to the presentation. Many factors influence supervisory style and supervision benefits when approach and style are modified to meet with the supervisee's needs during particular sessions. Rowan (1989) identified a number of styles which were regarded with varying degrees of esteem by supervisees. Valued approaches included 'insight-oriented', in which probing and questioning encouraged the supervisee to reflect upon the material, and 'feelings-oriented', also effected through enquiry specifically into the supervisee's affective experiences with clients.

Less highly regarded were the 'authoritative style', in which the supervisee's work is closely monitored and regulated, and the 'didactic-consultative' style, characterised by instruction and the giving of advice and suggestions. Also unwelcome were the 'laissez-faire style', in which supervisees are largely left to their own devices, and an 'unsupportive style', in which supervisees fear critical and unsympathetic responses to their doubts and insecurities. Least popular of all was 'therapeutic' supervision (Rosenblatt and Mayer, 1975), in which supervisees feel problematised themselves when the supervisor appears to attribute their struggles in the work to personality deficiencies in themselves.

Ensuring that features of supervisor style are a topic for open exploration in the contracting process can offset Rosenblatt and Mayer's finding that supervisees typically adopt the strategy of 'spurious compliance' when faced with an unpalatable supervisory style.

Following on from agreement regarding focus, the supervision provides an exploratory space in which to think together about the identified issue. Premature closure is avoided. This phase represents a collaborative exploration of the issue in which the supervisor may provide containment, affirmation of the supervisee's views and actions, or may challenge the approach to the work. This is regarded as the heart of the supervision process in which new ideas and understandings can develop. In the context of a collaborative relationship the supervisor can both participate in the discussion taking place and simultaneously notice her or his own reactions to the supervisee and to the material being presented. These reactions can then also be explored in what Page and Wosket deem the 'reflective alliance'. At this point in the supervision the aim is the generation of ideas rather than answers. The process of finding answers or ways forward in the work is addressed in the next stage of the model – the bridge.

The purpose of the next stage, the bridge, is to link the thinking undertaken in the space stage to proposed action. This can involve giving information, consolidating some of the ideas that emerged in the 'space', deriving action plans and goals and working out how the client might respond to the proposals. Awareness of this stage helps to keep the supervision goal-oriented and grounds the ideas considered into action. It could be regarded as time in supervision specifically devoted to making theory–practice links. It is at this point that the supervisor might give information by direct suggestion, by sharing experiences, or by introducing a new idea or technique. On the other hand the task may be to help supervisees to summarise their own emergent ideas and to explore the implications for action. Various options for action should be reviewed with regard to the anticipated response of the client. Page and Wosket suggest that one method for achieving this is the use of role switching in which the supervisee 'speaks' to the client and then changes seats, attempting to experience the intervention from the position of the client.

The final stage within the model is that of review. Mutual feedback is encouraged in order to keep in mind how the supervision is proceeding in relation to what was agreed in the supervisory contract, and how the supervision relates to the intended beneficiary – ultimately the client. The supervisory tasks of assessment and evaluation are carried out in this stage. Thinking of them in this way may help to contain them and enable greater freedom of exploration in the space.

The framework is elaborated by the identification of five steps through which each stage progresses. As with all models and frameworks, it is not intended that supervision inevitably proceed in an orderly and structured way, each stage following seamlessly from the one before. The structure is something to be kept in mind to help the process to remain useful and to effect its identified aims and purposes.

Developmental models of supervision (Stoltenberg, McNeill and Delworth, 1998; Stoltenberg and Delworth, 1987)

The notion of trainee dependency is addressed in a number of developmental approaches to supervision reported from the United States and described by Stoltenberg, McNeill and Delworth (1998) and Stoltenberg and Delworth (1987). Not infrequently, early in training, supervisees feel insecure in their role and anxious about their ability to fulfil it. Further on in training there tends to be fluctuation between dependence and autonomy, with a subsequent gradual increase in professional self-confidence and only conditional dependence on the supervisor. The process of supervision may become more collegial, with sharing and exemplification augmented by challenges to personal and professional development. Developmental models lead supervisors to expect different presentations from supervisees who are at different stages of professional development, and propose that supervisors adapt their approach according to these different presentations. Stoltenberg, McNeill and Delworth take a 'stage' approach to the description of these differences. These stages are viewed as overarching yet specific to different domains of clinical practice. Thus a supervisee might be assessed as functioning at an early developmental level in one domain whilst operating at a more advanced level in other domains. The context or environment provided by supervisors is regarded as playing a crucial role in the rate and ultimate level of supervisee development.

Stoltenberg, McNeill and Delworth identify four stages of supervisee development within three overriding structures across specific domains. The three overriding structures are defined as 'self and other awareness', 'motivation' and 'autonomy'. 'Self and other awareness' comprises both affective and cognitive components that reflect the level of the supervisee's self-preoccupation, self-awareness and awareness of the client's world. 'Motivation' describes the supervisee's interest, investment and effort expended in clinical training and practice. 'Autonomy' is a manifestation of changes in the degree and appropriateness of independence demonstrated by supervisees over time.

In stage 1, the dependency stage, the supervisee is likely to experience feelings of anxiety and insecurity whilst being highly motivated in the work. Awareness is likely to be self-focused and performance anxiety tends to prevail. Supervisees at this stage are often most concerned with surviving the session with the client. Due to the need to reflect constantly on the rules, skills, theories, and other didactic material being learned, it is viewed within the model as difficult for trainees carefully to listen to and process information provided by the client in the session.

The supervisor can help by providing safety and containment. Supervisees may benefit from having a structure for their interviews on which they can depend and to which they can revert when they feel stuck or uncertain.

Availability of brief supervision outside of a scheduled meeting is helpful and an emergency telephone number can be reassuring. Loganbill, Hardy and Delworth (1982) propose that facilitative interventions by the supervisor are possibly the most helpful for level 1 therapists. These interventions are intended to communicate support and encourage development. They include praise, reinforcement of skills and careful and attentive listening. The supervisee is likely to find it helpful to see the supervisor struggling from time to time, in order to compensate for the apparent smoothness in therapy that can sometimes be conveyed by textbooks. Positive feedback on specific supervisee contributions may be appreciated, and where the supervisor has responsibility for selecting the supervisee's case-load, screening of clients may be beneficial in order to provide a graded approach to the level of difficulty of the work.

At this stage, if the model for the work is too far removed from the skill level of supervisees, it may be difficult for them to extract the salient characteristics in order to build them into their own work.

Dependency and insecurity can be manifest in a variety of ways along a continuum from supervisees seeming to have to know everything, to seeming to know nothing. The former state can lead to avoidance in supervision and the latter can present as helplessness which may evoke more contributions to supervision from the supervisor than from the supervisee in a way that does not help learning. This interaction taking place between the two parties can be drawn to the attention of the supervisee, with both working alongside each other to look at ways to modify the process and to relieve anxiety.

Stage 2 is characterised by dependency–autonomy conflicts in which the supervisee fluctuates between over-confidence and being overwhelmed. Supervisees may experience fluctuating motivation in the work, feel out of place, and wonder, if they are in training, how they came to choose a career in professional helping. The focus in the work is likely to have moved from supervisees themselves onto the client.

At this stage supervisees are unlikely to be able both to participate in the session and to observe the process as it involves them. They tend to exhibit a principal focus on the client's perspective and level 2 therapists are regarded as capable of exhibiting a naive lack of insight regarding their counter-transference reactions to the client. Data obtained from other sources (when incompatible with the client's view) may be disregarded by supervisees at this level of development. Supervisors' attempts to increase supervisees' awareness of such reactions can be met by confusion or disbelief.

The supervisor might help by drawing attention to the fluctuating state, defining it as a normal developmental stage and not, as the supervisee may think, confined solely to her or himself. Metaphors may help, as may drawing attention to examples of over- and under-confidence. When I was learning to drive, on my second lesson as I drove down a dual carriageway, the instructor asked, 'Wouldn't you feel better if you knew how to stop?' Here humour was helpful in drawing the over-confidence to my attention.

Supervisors can provide a secure base to which the supervisee may return when feeling overwhelmed. This requires clear views and agreements regarding boundary issues as supervisees may find themselves drawn across these by the needs and demands of clients. Supervisors can provide an assertive yet warm role model through their actions in supervision.

Stage 3 is that of conditional dependency. At this stage, supervisees are developing increased self-confidence, greater insight and more consistency in their sessions with clients. They are able to focus more on process and notice what is happening to them in such a way as to inform the work with the client, even if this is not possible at the time that it is happening but occurs during session review. At this stage the supervision may benefit from being undertaken within an enquiring framework with a view to facilitating the development of ongoing self-supervision. There may be more opportunity to focus on the thinking and feeling that is informing the work and less on technique and survival strategies.

Stage 4 (or 3i) is referred to as that of 'master professional'. Here the therapist has personal autonomy, insightful awareness, and is able to confront personal and professional issues. The work is process-in-context centred. The supervisory relationship becomes increasingly collegial and the responsibility for the structure and process of supervision is largely taken by the supervisee or shared with the supervisor. The supervisee is likely to be supervising others at this stage, and might bring issues arising there to the supervision. Stoltenberg, McNeill and Delworth posit that few, if any, therapists reach this level of development across all domains of clinical practice and that the task of development is never complete.

Developmental models can also be applied to the practice of supervision and it may be helpful for supervisors to review what they see as their own stage of development in relation to this role. Stoltenberg, McNeill and Delworth argue that the effectiveness of supervisory relationships can be influenced by the relative levels of development of the participants. For example, they argue that level 1 supervisors tend to be either highly anxious or somewhat naive, focused on doing the 'right' thing and highly motivated to be successful in the role. They may find giving feedback difficult and have a preference for a relatively high degree of structure in supervisory sessions. Level 2 supervisees, in a state of conflict and confusion, are seen as an inappropriate match with level 1 supervisors and it is suggested that this particular pairing should be avoided at all costs. Similarly, therapists who are moving into level 3 functioning can lose their recently acquired consistent motivation if they are confronted with an insecure, highly structured level 1 supervisor.

Developmental models have face-validity in that most people tend to think of themselves as improving with experience. Worthington (1987) reviewed studies based on developmental models and concluded that there is some empirical support for conceptualising supervision in this way, that the behaviour of supervisors and the nature of the supervisory relationship change as supervisees become more experienced, but that supervisors do not necessarily become more competent with experience. Other examples of developmental models include those of Littrell, Lee-Borden and Lorenz (1979) and Skovholt and Ronnestad (1992).

My own experience suggests that there tends to be a noticeable change in focus as supervisees gain in experience. Beginning clinicians tend initially to focus on self, which reflects their concerns about surviving the session. It becomes possible to focus on the client as the initial anxiety level decreases, eventually moving to a focus on therapeutic process in which it is possible both to participate and simultaneously to reflect on the session. Evidence for this progression is provided by Winter and Holloway (1991) who examined the supervision focus for 56 counsellor trainees with different amounts of experience when videotape was the supervisory medium. The results indicated that counsellor experience correlated directly with the supervisee's focus on personal growth and inversely with a focus on client conceptualisation and favourable ratings of their performance.

Clinical supervision (Cogan, 1973)

The term 'clinical supervision' has been used in different ways in the supervision literature. It is used by Bernard and Goodyear (1998) to refer to supervision within the mental health professions that takes place in the context of practice but forms a bridge between campus and clinic. The title 'clinical supervision' here is used in the sense of its being a particular model of supervision that was, despite its name, developed for the purpose of supervising student *teachers*, with the word 'clinical' being chosen to emphasise a focus on professional practice in field settings rather than in the training institution. A defining feature of clinical supervision is that it rests on the conviction that performance of a skill can only be improved by direct feedback to a person on aspects of her or his practice that are of concern to that person rather than items on an evaluation form or the pet concerns of the supervisor (Reavis, 1976).

The model describes a process for the analysis of performance but also emphasises the importance of the supervisory relationship and relies on the establishment of a collegial relationship between supervisor and supervisee in which it is the responsibility of supervisees to define the supervisory focus, their strengths and weaknesses and the goals of supervision. The approach has been used in both pre-registration and post-qualification supervision.

I have conceptualised the phases of the process as follows:

1   Establishment of a collegial relationship in which a stance of openness is taken by the supervisor.

2   Planning the arrangements for data collection and observation in order to minimise the anxiety of the supervisee whilst being observed live.
3   Planning of the supervisory conference which may be undertaken by the supervisor alone or by supervisor and supervisee together.
4   The supervisor observes the practice of the supervisee.
5   Undertaking the supervisory conference in which both participants together examine what has taken place in order to develop under-standing.
6   Together, supervisor and supervisee analyse the data, focusing on critical incidents and pattern analysis and following the wishes of the supervisee.
7   Planning of a programme for subsequent change and development.

The approach is principally behaviour-focused but offers a framework from which to construct a process that could be carried out compatibly with other models described in this section.

The model was devised for a context of live supervision. It emphasises mutuality in the supervisor–supervisee relationship with the goal of develop-ing self-sufficiency and freedom to act in the supervisee. Inquiry, analysis, examination and evaluation, especially when self-initiated and self-regulated, are espoused. The person responsible for initiating the clinical supervision model is identified as the supervisee and the process is shaped to be congruent with the 'internal landscape' of the supervisee (Sullivan, 1980). This emphasis gives the model congruence with ideas about adult learning described in Chapter 2.

Other frameworks

The chapter has been by no means exhaustive in its coverage of models and frameworks of supervision. It has provided a flavour of the burgeoning litera-ture on this topic. For those who are interested to explore a wider range of such structures, works by Watkins (1997), Holloway (1995), Bartlett (1983), Friedlander and Ward (1983) and Ivey (1974) are recommended.

Summary

This chapter has described a range of frameworks within which supervision might be conceptualised. The different frameworks can aid understanding of the purposes of supervision, the content and/or process of supervision, the type of material explored and the different perspectives on how the work may be understood. The selected frameworks have the benefits of relative simplicity and utility.

The use of frameworks to conceptualise the supervision process aids think-ing about the therapy (i.e. it involves the development of meta-cognitive prac-tices, habits or repertoires for supervisors and supervisees). Frameworks can

help practitioners to organise, understand and manage the process of supervision so as to help the process of therapy.

It is argued that the use of conceptual frameworks aids the development of
a supervisory alliance and the process of connecting between supervisors and
supervisees. The identification of supervisee need is seen as an essential starting point in negotiating the relationship. Supervisee need as perceived by the
supervisee may differ sharply from what the supervisor or an institution of
higher education judges to be her or his need. The use of frameworks and
models of supervision can aid in negotiating a path which satisfies all
stakeholders.

Chapter 6

Group supervision

Brigid Proctor and Francesca Inskipp

> [G]roup supervision can offer a rich tapestry for learning and develop-
> ment with a range of possible formats and leadership roles.
>
> (Scaife, Chapter 1, p. 4)

Many supervisors run brilliant groups with unselfconscious skill. They have
learned this ability from other group leaders or have developed it naturally in
life; perhaps many more run groups which they or their participants find
unsatisfactory, uneasy or effortful. For this chapter, we are condensing what
we have done in our previous writing and training – we offer maps and some
guidance on how any reasonably skilled supervisor can set about consciously
developing the abilities that are needed for good group supervision. By good
supervision we mean supervision which is satisfying to the participants and to
supervisors and therefore enables the most effective work with clients – the
heart of the matter.

Our aim is to promote group supervision as an aid to seeing practice in a
diversity of ways – offering a tower with many windows. We value mutual cooperation in learning and development and wish to encourage readers to use
the lively and creative opportunities provided by working with a group.
Group supervision can be a restorative opportunity in a pressured, often
lonely, working life – for supervisor and supervisees. In order to make this
feasible we want to indicate the range of different kinds of supervision groups
which can be offered and to help the supervisor who has only worked with
individuals to be confident with a group. This entails furthering the abilities
of supervisors and group members as reflective practitioners. Both need to
become confident in learning publicly through 'mistakes', as well as through
success; and in learning by imitation and social influence. Supervisors
particularly have to learn what is 'good enough' group work and relinquish
any fantasies of becoming the 'perfect' group supervisor – groups are too
complex for that to be possible.

Differences from individual supervision

For the supervisee

Good group supervision demands complex roles and tasks for both super-visee and supervisor. Depending on the type of group, the supervisee may have as many as four identified professional roles in the group – supervisee, practitioner, group member and co-supervisor. Each role entails specific tasks which between them all require the development of a surprisingly wide range of skills.

Supervisors have not traditionally spelt out these roles when starting a group. Often the supervisor has not realised just what he or she may be expecting from participants. People who are ' good supervisees' may have been inducted elsewhere into 'how to do it well'. However, like the good supervisor, they may have acquired their abilities along the way and now unselfconsciously use them as part of their professional repertoire. We have come to believe, through experience, that some conscious understanding of the roles and tasks can help participants – even those who already do it well. For supervisors it is only respectful to have clarified for themselves what it is they are expecting of group members as they start the group. They can then choose to make that clear, or, on reflection, modify or change their expectations.

So what are the tasks of group supervision which follow from the four roles identified?

- *As supervisees* to learn the skills of preparing the work they wish to take for supervision in the group and then to present their work publicly, both economically and in a way that engages their colleagues.
- *As practitioners* to identify their own personal and professional develop-ment needs and to discern and communicate how the group could be a helpful learning resource.
- *As group members* to develop good 'group manners' – being aware of time and air space and becoming conscious of thoughts, feelings and communications which help or hinder the group's work.
- *As co-supervisors* to develop the skills of supervision – giving good attention to others' presentations and mutually supporting and chal-lenging each other in the work through clear feedback and thoughtful responses.

In the next section we have categorised four types of groups. These inform which skills a supervisor may need to ask participants to develop in a specific type of group. Books on supervision have usually concentrated first on the supervisor. We prefer to start from the perspective of the supervisee. If all group participants knew how to work well in a group the job of the supervisor would not be so complex. As it is, supervisors will probably need to do some training of the participants. Depending again on the type of group this may have to be one of their major roles.

For the supervisor

From the perspective of the supervisor there are also several additional roles which anyone who intends to supervise in or with a group (as opposed to an individual) has to be prepared to assume. The undertaking requires considerable management skill and encompasses at least the roles of manager of time and task, group leader, group facilitator, inductor, trainer, and group supervisor.

In the *role of supervisors* they will still have:

- normative responsibilities – managing the interface with the agency and training organisation and monitoring standards of practice;
- formative responsibilities – of inducting new practitioners or developing the reflective practice of the more experienced;
- restorative responsibilities – of supporting and encouraging hard-pressed workers.

These responsibilities will have to be exercised for several supervisees instead of for one.

In the role of *group managers* they will be responsible for:

- organisational and practical arrangements – place, time, payment, etc.;
- setting the working agreements (by negotiation or otherwise);
- ensuring sufficient adherence to the agreements or modifying them;
- monitoring that there is fair allocation of time and attention;
- introducing group reviews or appraisals.

In the role of *inductors and trainers* they will be responsible for:

- enabling participants to have the information, skills, support and challenge (Egan, 1976) they require in order to meet stated expectations of the supervisors and of other stakeholders;
- enabling supervisees to present and engage well with group supervision.

Depending on their expectations of group members, and the type of group agreement, they may be responsible for:

- modelling good 'group manners' as above;
- modelling and teaching group awareness and skills;
- modelling and teaching supervision and feedback skill.

In the role of *group facilitator*s again dependent on the group agreement, they may be responsible for:

- creating a culture conducive for this particular group to interact in a way that builds and maintains a good group alliance and when necessary repairs it;
- modelling the core qualities of respect, empathy, straightforwardness and, we would add, intentionality;
- enabling members to get to know each other well enough to create trust in the group;
- ensuring members know each others' contexts well enough to work appropriately;
- freeing the rich resources of the group in undertaking individual bits of supervision work;
- taking the lead in addressing and valuing diversity in the group;
- addressing conflict, competitiveness or other interactions, which if ignored hinder the task.

In the role of *group leaders* they have the responsibility:

- to prioritise the task or process on which it is most important to focus from moment to moment in the group.

This conscious and unconscious making of choices among a welter of responsibilities is at the heart of the job. It is useful to have ready some maps of group process, supervision tasks, and individual development needs in groups, to name a few. Such maps or frameworks (see pp. 113–118 and figure 6.1) need to find their place within an overall framework of professional ethics and personal and professional values.

The skills for making priorities and for undertaking these multifarious roles are worth considering and we will return to them later. However, since the skills will depend on the type of group being run we first want to offer a framework for categorising possibilities for different supervision groups.

Typology

We have identified four different types of supervision group. The frameworks they offer appear to have been useful to supervisors in helping to clarify with supervisees the respective roles and responsibilities that will be expected. We summarise the four types in Table 6.1 on p. 104.

Type 1 could be called *Authoritative* supervision – the supervisor, treating the group members as a more or less participative audience, supervises each member one-to-one. It can also be designated as supervision *in* a group. Type 2 we name *Participative* supervision because the supervisor negotiates

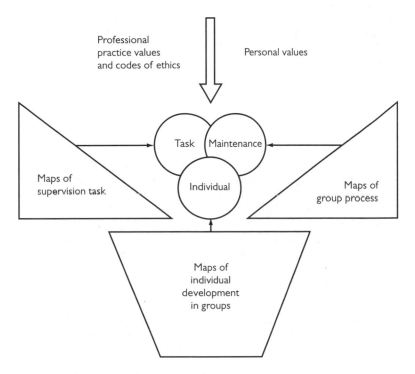

Figure 6.1 Overall map for running group supervision

with members to help them become skilled and active participants in the work of supervision – hence supervision *with* a group. Type 3, or *Co-operative* supervision is set up in such a way that the supervisor is the facilitator and wicket-keeper for the group members sharing fully in each others' supervision – hence supervision *by* a group. Type 4 is *Peer Group* supervision – members share the full responsibility of supervisor for each other, and negotiate how leadership will be shared.

These types are not discrete but can be seen as part of a continuum in which the supervisor progressively shares, with the group, the responsibilities of supervising. The framework assumes that participants will vary in their degree of ability and sophistication for working in a group. It also allows for the fact that supervisors will have varying degrees of experience, or indeed inclination, for working in a group. Those factors, together with the particular context and its working culture, will be the major determinants of which type of group the supervisor may propose.

All these types may be well or badly run and help or hinder client work. Let us suppose that consideration is being given to setting up or taking on a group. How supervisors choose which type of group to run will depend on the factors above and also what they believe about learning, self-managed or

Table 6.1 Typology of groups

Type 1   Authoritative group supervision or supervision *in* a group
Supervisor supervises individuals; members as more or less involved audience
Advantages:
> Releases supervisor to focus on the supervision
> Minimises group energy and therefore destructive interaction
> Allows freedom from responsibility for overworked practitioners
> Can be an excellent master class
> Safer for participants who distrust groups
> Easier to allocate time

Disadvantages
> Participants may be passive and resent not being involved
> Expertise stays with the supervisor and participants can feel de-skilled
> Richness of the group not utilised fully
> Can be stultifying for those who learn through interaction
> Supervisor does not develop group skills or flexibility of leadership

Type 2   Participative group supervision or supervision *with* a group
Supervisor supervises; members are taught and encouraged to participate actively
Advantages
> Develops the richness of the group
> Acts as a forum for the development of supervisory and group interaction skills
> Fosters active participation and commitment to a shared task
> Can raise self-esteem by mutual recognition of expertise
> Offers opportunities for the supervisor to develop active group skills and leadership
> Can be exciting and stimulating, therefore restorative and good for learning

Disadvantages
> Can change the focus from client/work issues to group process
> Harder to manage fair sharing of time
> Can become too busy and interfere with reflective space
> Hard work initially and more risks involved for the supervisor
> Requires skill in choosing priorities and gearing the group interaction to the task
> Can feel unsafe for supervisor or participants thereby restricting honesty of sharing

Type 3   Co-operative group supervision or supervision *by* the group
Supervisor facilitates the group in sharing responsibility for the tasks of group supervision
Advantages
> Offers a collegial experience for established practitioners
> Encourages supervision and group skill development
> Reminds participants of shared professional accountability
> Encourages creative use of self for supervisor and participants
> Can offer a variety of models of theory, style and practice
> Freer interaction allows for serendipity – parallel process, group surprises

Disadvantages
> Supervisor can lapse into a laissez-faire approach and participants feel unsafe
> Riskier – more room for destructive interaction and group process
> Requires higher level skills from supervisor and participants
> Experienced practitioners may have poor group skills and 'manners'
> Can be harder to keep the focus on client/supervision work

Type 4   Peer group supervision
Peers take shared responsibility for supervision; members negotiate structure, leadership, roles and responsibilities
Advantages and disadvantages largely as above, plus
   More economic
   Good peer groups often offer optimal safety and trust
   Can develop into a social group rather than a work group

---

otherwise, about expertise and about certainty and creative (or anarchic) chaos. Are they prepared to risk converting a group from the safety of receiving expertise to being collectively supervised by colleagues; to challenge the group members and themselves, as they join together in supervision?

Other factors which will impinge will be the composition of the group. There may be a group of eager trainees who give the supervisor permission and confidence to teach them basic skills of supervision and co-operative group work. On the other hand the group may comprise experienced mixed professionals who could possibly benefit from such teaching but who would not appreciate it! Maybe the supervisor's greatest ally in either case is taking time to declare her or his intention for the group and to give the members a chance to consider and negotiate. At this stage the supervisor may be announcing which kind of group this is *going to be* or may genuinely be *exploring* what working agreement would be most suitable for these participants, their clients, the context and her or himself. What needs to be made clear is what is negotiable and what parameters are non-negotiable.

Russian dolls: agreements and alliances

This image seems to be a useful metaphor for the interdependence of the various agreements which supervisors and supervisees need to make openly if they are to be in a fruitful working alliance. Figure 6.2 illustrates the metaphor.

The professional contract

To some extent non-negotiable parameters will be determined, as in individual supervision, by the wider professional contract. This will determine:

- what accountability is expected of the supervisors and of the participants;
- the Codes of Ethics and Codes of Practice to which all will be working;
- the conventions of confidentiality in the particular setting;
- the overall ratio of supervision to client hours;
- supervisor and supervisee rights, responsibilities and lines of

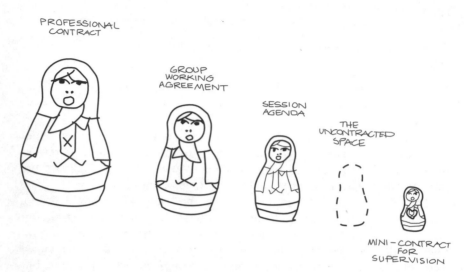

Figure 6.2 The Russian dolls: agreements and alliances

communication with all the employing organisations, agencies and training providers who may be connected with differing group members.

The first task of management is finding a way to make that professional contract clear to participants. It can be useful to let them have it in writing before the start of the group. However, whether or not this has been done, they will need time to digest and discuss the implications of that contract in practice. This process of discussing and digesting is one way in which the group members get to know each other and begin to get a feel of working in this particular group. Using the analogy of Russian dolls we call this the Large Doll because it encloses and determines the shape of any subsequent working agreement.

In Figure 6.2 we indicate what the other useful agreements are. If the agreements are well made there will be more co-operative ownership and the supervisor will not have to take so much ongoing responsibility for determining priorities and time management. Discussing and negotiating can be an exercise through which the group, led by the supervisor, overtly sets initial norms for working together and begins the forming process (Tuckman, 1965).

The group working agreement

The second doll represents the specific agreements that need to be clarified or negotiated if the group is to be enabled to forge a working alliance. We suggest that there are four major strands to this:

- The *type* of group it is going to be and consequently the specific roles and responsibilities of supervisor and supervisee.
- The *working arrangements* for the group, which include time allocation, method of presenting, pattern of sessions (time for checking in, processing, etc.) reviews, and changes of personnel.
- The *ground rules* for interacting with each other. For example, if the group is to be a Type 2 or 3 group, the ground rules might include respecting task, time and each other's opinions; clarifying what is meant before disagreeing; working to have empathic understanding of practitioner and client before advising or suggesting, and so on. Group members will each have experience as to what they find a help or hindrance when they are working in a group and they need to be encouraged to identify and share that if they are to be working participatively.
- The *individual responsibility* of participants to identify their learning needs and what help they need. For instance, one group member may want to develop the ability to be tougher and less malleable with residents in a care home while another might identify wanting to learn to be more patient and empathic.

The specific working agreement will depend on the type of group. The degree to which the features are laid down by the supervisor or negotiated with the group will depend on the type of group, and on the particular style and values of the supervisor and supervisees.

It is always an issue how and when to formulate these agreements. Some factors need to be agreed at the outset, others can be interim arrangements with the promise of review when people have experience of working together. It is a rule of thumb that participants seldom remember, let alone understand, 'agreements' made in the first session. They will always need to be revisited when participants are more able to give informed consent or feedback. A second rule of thumb is that some participants will get impatient if they are prevented from getting on and doing some supervision, while others will not want to work until they know where they stand. Therefore the process of making a working agreement allows supervisor and supervisees to become aware of the kind of culture which needs to emerge for this collection of individuals to become a working group.

Session agenda

The third doll represents agenda setting – the specific agreement at the beginning of each session. The regular pattern of the session will probably have been determined by the group working agreement. However, specific agenda items such as leftovers, reviews, requests, work on particular issues (for example, group diversity or ethical dilemmas) need to be programmed in and time allocated for them. In addition to giving the group a sense of intention, agenda building helps individuals become self-managing in using and giving time. The process of checking the agenda also allows group preoccupations to become apparent.

Doll 4 is the shadow doll – which is contained by the others but which is the area where supervisors are on their own. Before considering that, concluding the series of contracts is:

The mini-contract for a particular piece of supervision

The fifth doll brings us to the heart of the matter – what supervision is all about. It is the agreement with an individual practitioner as to what he or she wants from a piece of supervision work and perhaps how he or she would like to do it. Taking time to make a hard contract ('I want to know what to say to this client') or a soft contract ('I just want to introduce my new client and hear your responses') (Sills, 1997) serves several purposes. It focuses the supervisee and encourages the taking of responsibility for identifying the issues that need, or could benefit from, reflective space in supervision. It brings the group to attention around that reflective space. It allows supervisors to make informed choices about how to conduct themselves and the group in the best interests of practitioner and client.

Reverting to:

The shadow doll representing the uncontracted space

In the illustration, the fourth doll appears as a shadow. Managing group responses remains the responsibility of the supervisor, no matter how that role is played. In a group there are a wealth of possibilities – exponentially greater than in individual supervision. The group will, hopefully, be well held within the various agreements we have already spoken about. For instance, if an Authoritative group has been created (supervising *in* the group), the choices will have been deliberately limited. If a Participative agreement has been made, the supervisor will have undertaken to orchestrate the group responses for the most part. As a Co-operative group supervisor, the group will be more active in offering and suggesting how to carry out the work. Nevertheless, the choice – of how best to use the rich resources available at any one time – remains with the supervisor, regardless of advice or guidance from supervisee and participants. That is the supervisor's responsibility because of the overall contract with practitioner, agency and, implicitly, the clients. Later in the chapter we look at some of the possibilities and considerations involved in this.

Peer groups

In peer group supervision, the responsibility for using the group in a specific piece of work can be designated by members to one of their number, for a session or for a single presentation. At other times it can be agreed that the presenting supervisee remains responsible for how the supervision is done. In a well-working peer group, pieces of work will often 'happen' rather than being overtly 'led' – the group has become a shared improvisation group. (A warning here – this way of working needs to be honestly reviewed at regular intervals – such groups can become oppressive to less assertive members.)

Skills for supervisors

Active leadership

Leadership of a supervision group requires proactive skills and a leadership style that can manage, lead and teach without being authoritarian or bossy. Counsellors and psychotherapists can find such overt taking charge difficult. They are more used to following or subtly managing their work with clients. However, some have previously taught, or taken responsibility for a group, in more authoritarian settings and they can easily slip into being bossy. Whatever the type of group chosen, the task of the group is to enable or ensure that participants do better work with their clients. This means maintaining reflective space for practitioners and engaging them to varying extents in their own and each other's learning.

Clarity

The ability to lead requires being intentional, clear – when necessary forthright – about defining the task and how to do (or not do) it. Confidence grows with experience, but thought and preparation beforehand, both privately and with the help of supervision or consultancy, can allow supervisors to clarify their own understanding of the tasks involved and their own expectations of the group participants.

Preparation

Such preparation is particularly necessary before the initiation (or taking over of) a new group. As we have seen, the clarifying of contracts and agreements in such a way that a working alliance is forged means taking leadership both

- for *what* is to be negotiated and how, and
- for *the culture* in which the discussions and negotiations take place.

Preparation will also be essential at later stages when it may follow from pondering expected or surprising group events. What next does the group need to learn, in order for participants to continue developing as practitioners, supervisees, and group members? What sense can be made of some event? What needs to happen if the group is to learn from difficult or moving experiences? What personal/professional learning do *supervisors* need and how will that show in the next group?

Skilled use of frameworks

If supervisors become skilled at such pondering, they will have some cognitive maps or frameworks in their minds – about group development, group process, individual behaviour and development in groups, dysfunctional group behaviour, and how individual supervision work can be helped or hindered by happenings within and outside the group. The ability to have ready access to such frameworks, and to be thoughtful and creative in using and amending them through experience, is a core skill for group leaders. We suggest some hardy perennial frameworks, but they are only as useful as the skill in making them one's own, as the actual territory replaces the map or guidebook.

Purpose and preference stating

Clarity of purpose or intention has, of course, to be signalled as well as reflected upon. This calls for 'confident enough' communication. While developing confidence, words have to be chosen carefully for accuracy and impact. This entails communicating whether a statement of *intent* is just that – 'this is what I want and intend to enable or ensure'; or whether it is a statement of *preference* – 'I would prefer that . . . what do *you* want?' This distinction (Gilmore, Fraleigh and Philbrick, 1980) has been considered to be *the* most useful information in relieving the frustrations of even experienced managers. It is necessary, for instance, when parameters and boundaries are laid down in the professional contract. It is also useful if supervisors feel that a group needs 'taking in hand' at some stage of its development or when the reflective working space of an individual member is being disrupted.

Receptivity and following

For active leadership to be taken in a way that is co-operative rather than bossy or authoritarian, it has to be balanced by receptivity. This entails actively seeking feedback and opinions from the group, and listening to them with interest, curiosity, and openness – to hearing, following and even changing style or task in response! In the early stages of contract stating or negotiation it means recognising that an 'agreement' means just that. A purpose statement is non-negotiable, but a preference statement means a genuine search to find common ground for shared ground-rules or procedures, and this entails listening and hearing.

Throughout the group, receptivity shows as plenty of airspace given to participants, by listening and reflecting back or summarising to check that the supervisor has understood what is being said. In so doing, good 'group manners' and supervisor skill will be modelled to group members. At later stages of a group, it means eliciting feedback as to what is working and what is not helpful. It may entail deciding to 'go along' with what is happening even when the outcome is not clear. The supervisor may want to encourage initiative being taken by a group member, or the group as a whole being enthusiastically engaged. This active following is different from being 'pulled', reluctantly or suspiciously. When supervisors have sufficient trust in the good will and ability of the group and their own sense of overall purposes, it can lead to creative and unexpected outcomes.

Imbalance

Most supervisors have a preference (and therefore probably an ability) for either active leadership or receptivity. The latter can err towards presiding over a laissez-faire group that grows either unduly competitive for leadership, or apathetic. The former may run a tight Type 1 group, which is unlikely to evolve into a Participative or Co-operative Group. The trick is to work to develop the ability for both kinds of behaviour. It is a behaviour, not an identity, issue – not 'I'm just not like that' but 'How could I *do* that?'

Luckily (and for this framework we owe a debt to Susan Gilmore again (Gilmore, Fraleigh and Philbrick, 1980), in addition to active leadership and receptivity, there is a third category of useful behaviour for group leaders – assertion.

Assertion

In this context, assertion means simply stating, and standing by, rights and responsibilities – one's own or other people's. So if group supervisors have risked 'going along' and then become worried about, for example, time, equity, or loss of direction, they do not have to wrest themselves from receptivity to active leadership – galvanising themselves and confusing the group. They can move into assertiveness and remind the group of the time, or of responsibility for client and each other. They can query purpose or intention or just assert their presence if the group, in adolescent fervour, is busy 'disappearing' them. Like a blocked stream, the energy and initiative remains with 'the flow', but new directions have to be found.

Choosing the right fights

Assertive behaviour can reduce the likelihood of passive or active aggression from group members which active leadership can stimulate. However, like receptivity, it should not be used as a way of avoiding conflicts of interest that are interfering with good enough supervision. If a group is to grow and develop, it will almost certainly have to address differences of opinion, values, styles and ways of working, and find ways to develop through the process. Deciding which are 'the right fights' is helped by referring to maps for understanding group development and processes (Houston, 1997).

Underlying abilities

Choosing priorities

The larger the behavioural tool-kit at the supervisors' disposal, the more choices with which they are faced. The skills of active leadership, receptivity and assertion can be developed at a behavioural level. However, how and when a supervisor changes gear from one to the other appropriately depends on some complex underlying abilities. Chief among these is the ability to prioritise.

By the time practitioners become supervisors they will have developed the ability to prioritise in several contexts – managerial, therapeutic and so on. For group supervision, some of that ability has to be dismantled, furnished with fresh maps and skills and reintegrated into the ability to prioritise in group supervision. Within a group there are a myriad happenings each second. This speed of process allows little time to reflect. It may be necessary to be able to make decisions and act quickly without reacting impulsively. Supervisors need to adopt or develop frameworks of values, process and practice which assist them to be clear in their own intentions for the group, and which help them weigh and choose one value against another in an instant. Maps or frameworks are interesting in themselves to some of us, but to aid in the development of prioritising ability they need to help when asking, 'What do I do now?', 'What do I respond to?', 'How do I respond?'

In addition, group supervisors need to increase their skills in rapidly scanning their physical sensations, emotions, thoughts, and images. Sensory feedback will give them information to prioritise and act – or not act. Consciously developing physical metaphors and images can be revealing – 'in tune', 'out of hand', 'needing a touch on the reins', 'it feels like the prelude to a thunderstorm'. Often such 'physical pick-up' is more immediately 'in touch' than cognitive processing and allows the supervisor to develop spontaneity. This, in turn, can give permission to group members to risk more honest and spontaneous interaction.

Using recording, reflecting and consultation

This development of spontaneity, and even risk-taking, is balanced by the time spent in reflecting about the group. Developing appropriate ways of recording group work is useful (Sharpe, 1995). Using regular consultation is both a skill and a necessary discipline:

- for identifying what worked well and what did not;
- as an aid to reflecting;
- for exploring learning;
- for furthering skill development.

The role of facilitator: working with group process

What helps to produce a good working group? To pull together some of our earlier assertions, we suggest that it requires members:

- to feel safe enough with each other and with the supervisor to trust the group with honest disclosure of their work;
- to have clarity about the task and how this will be worked on;
- to know each other well enough as individuals;
- to accept and respect difference;
- to share sufficient values, beliefs and assumptions about human beings, professional helping and groups;
- to have 'good group manners'.

And the supervisor:

- to feel comfortable to exercise authority when necessary;
- to have some 'maps' which help the supervisor to understand and act on group process;
- to arrange opportunities for feedback on how the group members are working together.

When a group comes together and interacts the behaviour of everybody is modified by the 'forces' present – the group dynamic. The energy present can help or hinder the learning process.

There is a wide range of group dynamic theories and we give below some frameworks that we have found can help the supervisor make choices in building and maintaining a working group.

Group needs (Adair, 1983)

This framework suggests that when a group meets together there are three sorts of interlocking needs that have to be kept in balance (see Figure 6.1 on p. 103):

1   *Task needs* – usually the most apparent on the surface. The supervision task and methods by which it will be pursued, has, hopefully, been originally clarified by contracting, so that both supervisor and group members are clear. However, as the group develops this may well need further clarification and negotiation, so time will need to be allocated for this.

2   *Maintenance needs* – the need to develop and maintain good working relationships and a positive climate to work on the task. Again, by originally contracting for 'good group manners', for time to explore the 'process' of the group, and for reviews to evaluate and give feedback on how the group is working – or not working – together, some of the maintenance needs will be made explicit. However, as the group comes together and develops, the supervisor will have the main responsibility for meeting the changing needs of maintenance and possibly repair. As the group progresses, depending on the type of group, members may learn to share this responsibility.

3   *Individual needs* – members bring a range of needs such as to be recognised, to belong, to contribute, to exercise power and influence, as well as their individual supervision and learning needs. These two latter may have been made explicit in contracting, but the other needs may only emerge in different degrees in different members as the group develops. Recognising these individual needs as they emerge can help the supervisor in making choices on how to facilitate the group, and on how to work with individual members for their development.

The task of facilitating the group is greatly helped if the supervisor is aware of, and can recognise, the necessity to balance these three areas – task, maintenance and individual needs.

Developing needs (Schutz, 1967, 1989)

A second framework further explores the concept of individual needs. Within it are identified three basic needs that develop in sequence as the group comes together. As any of us become part of a new group, each of us will have progressively to recreate our own identity within that particular group:

•   *Inclusion needs* – each member will have queries about belonging to this group, and be wondering 'Who am I here?', 'Who are the others here?', 'Am I accepted?', 'Do I want to belong?' This implies that it is important for the supervisor to encourage ways for members to get to know each other as people, to create a commitment to a group that has something to offer them, and to model acceptance of each individual.

As they get to know each other they will develop:

- *Power and influence needs.* Individuals have different needs for power and influence and they need to test out with each other and with the supervisor where they stand. These preoccupations merit recognition, and, if valued, can be harnessed in the service of good work. Sometimes power struggles can hinder the task and require space and patience – and skilful interventions – to work them through. Being prepared for them – between members and as challenges to the supervisor – can help towards making the right choices of how and when to address the issues. For instance, if a member is taking up too much airspace is he or she lacking validation or a sense of belonging, or should he or she be challenged because her or his undisciplined power or inclusion needs are oppressing other members?

When a good enough accommodation has been reached (and power issues will recur as the group changes and develops) the next needs to arise are:

- *Affect needs* – the need to accept liking and disliking, tolerate or enjoy differences, and decide how to work together. If the supervisor can provide a good model of communicating empathy, respect and authenticity (straightforwardness) to individuals in the group, and can help members explore issues of conflict with each other, this will encourage the development of a facilitative climate. At best, individuals come to believe that in this group they can feel safe to 'be themselves' and deal with the consequences.

The idea that these needs arise in sequence can alert supervisors to prepare for the changing needs of individuals in the group and can help them make sense of what is happening at different times. The next framework also encompasses changes as the group develops, but concerns the group as a dynamic unit or system.

Group movement (Tuckman, 1965)

This framework describes the group, as a system in its own right, progressing through four (or five) stages:

- *Forming* – a stage of anxiety and dependence on the supervisor. What is allowed and not allowed in this group? How supportive or critical will it be? What are the norms? This stage can be helped by clarifying the task, and methods to execute it, and by helping members to communicate with, and get to know each other. It can be useful to set up simple short inclusion exercises at the beginning of a group. For example, ask each member to describe briefly something they are wearing which says something about them. Another option is to ask them to respond to sentence stems such as, 'If I were a piece of furniture I would be', or 'I am the sort of person who . . .' Negotiating the first agreements in the group, clarifying roles and type of group all help to make this a positive stage.

- *Storming* – a stage of possible resistance to the supervisor and to the task, and of conflict between members. Issues of power, influence and competition are being brought out and hopefully resolved. It requires restraint from the supervisor not to get involved with justifying, defending or attacking but to use basic skills to demonstrate acceptance of the difficulties and emotions involved in this stage and a willingness to work on them. As we have seen, it may require assertiveness – holding fast to some agreements and negotiating others. Some groups take a long time to reach this stage, some reach it early, some work through it easily. Attending to task and maintenance needs may 'soften' the storming. Recognising it as a normal and *necessary* stage if the group is to develop honesty, and safety to disagree, can perhaps help the supervisor ride it with more equanimity.

  In looking at individuals' needs for inclusion on their own terms and for power and influence, we saw that the Schutz framework could help determine what action a supervisor might take with a vociferous group member. However, Tuckman's framework offers another possibility – perhaps an individual, in addition to seeking to fulfil her or his own identity needs, might be acting as a theme setter for the group-as-system. An argumentative member, who gradually challenges the supervisor more and more and is allowed 'to get away with it' by the group, may be signalling that the group is ready to storm its way into a fuller and more realistic sense of itself, both between members and in relation to the supervisor. Now may be the time to fight the right fights, clear the decks of unspoken disagreements and reach a new accommodation – the supervisor needs to help the group express any identity with that leader, rather than treat her or him as a trying individual.

- *Norming* – the group begins to find ways to work together on the task of supervision and to enjoy feelings of mutual support, of making progress together and of accepting difference in individuals. At this stage, the supervisor may have renegotiated, or re-emphasised, roles and responsibilities during the storming phase, and the working agreement becomes more truly 'agreed'.

- *Performing* – the group members can work together, can resolve conflicts and trust each other to give feedback and support in the task of supervision. Individuals have sufficiently developed trust and 'freedom to be' – their identity needs (as above) have been sufficiently taken care of. The energy can be very exciting at this stage and it is ideal to reach it as soon as possible. However, it is not necessarily a linear process – some groups work backwards and forwards through the stages as the learning becomes more intense, emotions become high in the group, or people leave or join.

Some descriptions of this framework include a fifth stage:

- *Mourning* – the recognition that the group is ending and is going through the process of dissolution. The closer the group, and the more satisfying the work has been, the harder to finish, and supervisees may be very reluctant to acknowledge an ending. This process can offer useful learning about the difficulties of finishing a relationship with a client. It may be very important to give mourning time if a supervision group on a training course is moving to a new supervisor or groups are being reset. A supervisor taking over an existing group may find her or himself involved in a mixed stage of forming and mourning – and storming, if the group is unwilling to change supervisors.

The three frameworks above give a positive view and useful pointers on how to develop a well-working group. There is a fourth framework which can be helpful in diagnosing what is holding up the working alliance if the group seems really stuck and unable to work on the agreed supervision tasks. This is:

Bion's model of unconscious processes (Bion [1961] 1974)

This parallels Tuckman's framework of a group system's necessary developmental processes. It sets out three group processes which are dysfunctional. If they develop fully in a group it takes drastic measures to bring the group into a good functioning mode. Bion calls these processes Basic Assumptions:

- *Ba Dependence* – the group is unconsciously dominated by the belief that only a strong leader, a God, can protect the group from the insecurity and emotional stress of coming together. All communication goes to the leader; only her or his word is valid. This process can hinder groups moving from Type 1 to Type 2 and may need to be brought into awareness.
- *Ba Pairing* – the group 'allows' the interaction to be taken over by two people and somehow believes they will produce redemption or survival of the group, or solve all the supervision issues brought!
- *Ba Fight/Flight* – unexpressed emotions, especially negative ones, may cause the energy of the group to be used to fight or run away. Aggression or withdrawal becomes the norm for the group.

These are unconscious processes that a group can engage in, often when the task is not clear or too difficult, or there are underlying agendas that are not voiced. The best coping strategies are probably to bring the process into consciousness and help the group bring out and discuss unrecognised difficulties. It will almost always be necessary to revisit the professional contract and working agreement in order to ascertain if there is sufficient 'shared desire' (Randall and Southgate, 1980) for the group to do good work.

We have found the frameworks of Schutz and Tuckman to be useful in practice. What among the welter of choices is the priority at this time?: perhaps to get on with the task of supervision regardless of distractions, or to encourage the group members to express their thoughts and feelings, or to have a showdown, or to introduce an exercise to mark an ending, or to reaffirm purpose and shared interests. These, and many more options, are available for enabling the group members to work well together and a quick scan of the frameworks may help the supervisor to notice what comes to the foreground, demanding attention. We have found Bion's framework some cold comfort when a group is manifestly dysfunctional, and nothing seems to help it work well enough. Sometimes there is not sufficient 'shared desire', or willingness to trust – or indeed trustworthiness – for a working alliance to develop. 'I think I just have to accept that this is a Bion group.' In a functional group, many options present themselves when thinking about how to use group resources to undertake supervision work.

Doing group supervision

Authoritative groups and parallel process

In the supervision of an *Authoritative* group, supervision *in* the group, the method of individual supervision will be translated into a public context. It will take forethought to decide how to use the audience to supplement the work so that group members feel engaged and valuable whilst the supervisor is holding the full supervisory authority.

One method of working is to ask members to say, in turn, how they find themselves reacting to the material. This allows reactions to be understood as *parallel process* – a mirror of the thoughts and emotions which are present in the therapeutic alliance but may not have been explicitly recognised by the practitioner. Practitioners who work predominantly psychodynamically mainly use the group in this way. If supervisors draw their own conclusions from these responses – openly or covertly – the group would still fall into the category of *in* the group. If members are then invited to discuss their conclusions as a result, the group is better described as *Participative*. The supervisor will be taking greater responsibility for managing group members' reactions to their experiences and therefore have more responsibility for monitoring the *group process* engendered by the *parallel process* exercise.

For Type 2, 3 and 4 groups, there are many more ways of using the group creatively. Our personal experience is that informing the supervision issue by means of identifying parallel process is not helpful until the group has established a trusting working alliance and has quite sophisticated individual and group awareness. However, there may well be times before that when parallel process seems to be operating spontaneously. In that case, our practice is to decide if drawing attention to it is:

- helpful to the understanding of the supervisee concerned (often it can be more confusing than enlightening), or
- necessary to break through a dysfunctional process in which the group is unconsciously caught (e.g. enacting the process of 'there must be *something* you can do'), which can be as frustrating and time-consuming in the group as it is to therapist and client!

Free-flow or structure

One distinction which can help in deciding 'what to do' with a specific piece of work in supervision is that of free-flow or structure. The two are not totally distinct – even the most free discussion will require some structure; for example, time management.

Free-flow

There is an option to choose to invite or allow the group to respond in a (more or less) random fashion to a colleague's issue. In a Type 2 group, supervisors may need to make clear that, at some stages, they might choose to be quite bossy conductors of the discussion. This is necessary in order to preserve the supervisee's reflective space, and also to take on a tutoring role with regard to responses which are unclear or inappropriate. Moreover, the supervisor may, for instance, want the supervisee to hear all the responses without speaking and then choose to respond to one which seems most relevant to her or him. If time is pressing, it may be desirable to round off the session and finish the work with the supervisee individually. In order to disperse authoritative tasks it may be desirable to ask for volunteers to monitor or manage time. Inskipp and Proctor (1993, 1995) suggest guidelines for good practice in managing free-flow.

Structure

An alternative is to offer an experiential exercise, or structure, for exploring the supervisee's issue. (Experiential exercises can also be used for individual and group awareness raising and skill training, but there is not space to consider this more fully here.) By focusing attention very specifically, an exercise can bring thoughts, sensations, emotions, images, internal dialogues (and more) to the surface which may be censored or out of access in ordinary discussion.

Any medium which may be used in client work can be equally helpful in supervision; and any which can be used in individual supervision can be even more fruitful if used in a group. That includes:

- All sorts of awareness exercises and questionnaires – 'Who does this client remind you of?', 'If she were an animal what would she be?', etc.
- The use of drawing, painting, clay, contents of handbags or pockets to depict or convey the client, the therapeutic relationship or an organisation. This depiction can either be used to help the group discover 'the felt sense' of the subject; or to map out and look at a family system; a work system; the internal system of a client or of the therapeutic relationship.
- Group sculpting, music, or mime/dance used with similar intent.
- Psychodrama and socio-drama including role-playing – client, counsellor, other interested parties, etc. – the supervisee choosing who takes which part, or the group members volunteering.

Many of these can be used by supervisees working in pairs about one of their clients, followed by space for feedback and reflection in the group. At other times, one supervisee can bring client material to work on in one of these ways, to which some or all group members, for example, answer one or two questions in turn, take roles, enact a drama, or comment on a map or picture.

These exercises can result in profound insights for supervisee and group members and at the same time create strong group self-esteem. Equally, if they are not well enough set up, with clear enough intention and instructions, they can result in apathy, confusion and anger. Guidelines for good practice in using experiential exercises can be found in Inskipp and Proctor (1993, 1995) and Proctor (2000), where you will also find full descriptions of a number of exercises. We would suggest that the full resources of the group – the rich imagination and sensory perceptions of each individual and of the group system – surface most satisfyingly within a well-set-up and well-held structure.

Formats

In the previous section it was suggested that groups need not always work *as* a whole group. Much good and time-effective work can be done by breaking into co-supervising pairs or threes for some of a session. This heightens responsibility and offers opportunities for the development of supervisor skill.

In addition, groups may regularly operate as a group for only part of their supervision time. A peer group, for instance, may decide to meet as regular, or changing, pairs for half of each session, and as a group for the rest. They may meet as a peer group one fortnight and a led group the next.

Practitioners may arrange (or be given) a mix of individual and group supervision – possibly ideal but often not realistic. This takes care of the need for some individual 'safe space' in a life of responsibility for others, and also for affiliation needs.

Mixed profession and mixed orientation groups

Any of the suggestions about working agreements and choice of type of group will be particularly important where a supervisor is being asked to run an interdisciplinary group. In such groups, sufficient shared values and understanding about good practice in therapy, care and supervision; ethical codes; and group manners cannot be relied on.

It will be important to engage the group in an exercise of comparing and contrasting expectations of the supervisor and of each other. Even this may be difficult if the supervisor is not received with trust. If, in addition to a lack of goodwill on the part of group members, the supervisor feels under-confident and expects resistance or competition, it can be hard to lead with intention and determination.

In preparing for the group, it is worth remembering that members will know more about their particular setting than does the supervisor. However, the supervisor will have thought and become clearer about the purpose, roles and responsibilities in group supervision than most, if not all, of the other group members. Further, the supervisor is entrusted with the responsibility of doing the best he or she can to enable and ensure good enough service to clients, whatever that takes – and it may take surviving some quite rough or subtle testing. Discovering how to find some common concerns, interests or, indeed, passions which can unite the group in doing good work will be the first leadership challenge. Discovering how to respect and value each member and develop some empathic understanding of those who feel threatened will be the starting challenge for the supervisor both as a person and as a practitioner.

In conclusion

This chapter has been written with the assumption that if supervisors set up a group with forethought and care, taking into account:

- their own developmental stage as a group leader and supervisor,
- the context of the group – the culture and expectations of stakeholders and members,
- the developmental stage of the supervisees,
- their own values and understanding about learning, practice and living,

then there is a good chance of running a 'good enough' (Winnicott, 1965) group.

Chapter 7

Ethical dilemmas and issues in supervision

An underlying tenet of this chapter is that workers in the helping professions should seek to take a principled and ethical stance in relation to their work, not only in their direct work with clients but in all of the professional roles and tasks that they undertake. Practitioners' own individual understanding of what is 'right' or 'fitting' is likely to exert a significant influence on their practice, and such understanding is a sound starting point for taking an ethical path through the maze of work. As Baldwin and Barker (1991) state:

> Workers are accountable to their clients, their colleagues, employers and to society. Each worker has a responsibility to determine where his or her ultimate responsibility rests. Within these constraints, many workers will decide that they are, ultimately, responsible to themselves, and will operate according to a personal ethical code.
>
> (Baldwin and Barker, 1991: 195)

The ethics of work in the helping professions can also be informed by professional codes of practice, legal precedents and principles of ethics.

Supervisors can help supervisees to reflect on their personal stance on ethical issues. In addition, the role of supervisor carries responsibility for taking an ethical approach to the conducting of supervision, and supervisors have vicarious ethical responsibilities in relation to the work being carried out by the supervisee. Stoltenberg, McNeill and Delworth (1998) draw attention to the need for supervisors to be well aware of the necessity to behave as a role model for supervisees whatever their level of professional development. This chapter focuses primarily on the ethical issues pertaining to the relationship of supervision rather than on the ethical issues that arise for the practitioner. The reader is referred elsewhere (Beauchamp and Childress, 1994; Pope and Vasquez, 1991; Bond, 1993; Keith-Spiegler and Koocher, 1985; Corey, Corey and Callanan, 1993) for discussions of the latter.

Ethical principles in conducting the work

Supervisors can draw on their own knowledge of how to conduct their work in an ethically sound manner in order to foster such awareness in the supervisee. In pre-registration training this may involve drawing the supervisee's attention to relevant Codes of Practice and Legal Statutes as well as exploring examples of ethical dilemmas. Supervision can be particularly important as a space for exploration of such issues no matter what degree of experience is brought to the work by the supervisee. Even very experienced practitioners can find themselves drawn into unsound positions, and discussion in supervision can act as a safeguard. For example, when a supervisee experiences a client as seductive this can be discussed and recorded. The supervisor can then take responsibility for following this up in a later session. Knowing that someone else knows helps to introduce a boundary whereby the supervisee can be kept on track by someone more detached from the material that the client brings and the feelings that the client evokes.

Ethical dilemmas faced by supervisees

When faced with ethical dilemmas, supervisees have a choice regarding whether to handle the dilemma alone or to bring the matter to supervision. The probability of disclosure is likely to be related to the quality of the supervisory relationship. Where supervisees fear an adverse opinion or response from the supervisor, non-disclosure and unsafe practice is more likely.

In a survey by Kent and McAuley (1995) of second- and third-year trainee clinical psychologists, only 14 of 85 respondents indicated that they had not faced ethical dilemmas during training. The majority had discussed the matter with their supervisor, but in only 65 per cent of these cases had the trainee and supervisor agreed on a course of action. In twelve cases a conflict of view was not resolved and incompatible understandings prevailed. In five cases the trainee followed the supervisor's advice, but with significant misgivings, and in a further twelve cases the issue was not fully disclosed as the trainee reported having little faith in the way in which the supervisor would treat the information, or feared placement failure.

The following quotations illustrated the difficulties:

> 'I was told that I was very "sensitive" which I took to be a criticism and this soured our relationship for a while and I felt my legitimate stance had not been understood. She pathologized me, suggesting that I was making a huge fuss about nothing and my "strong views" about violence towards children were getting in the way.'

> 'I didn't trust that my supervisor would treat the information confidentially.'

> (Kent and McAuley, 1995: 29)

This study illustrates the centrality of the quality of the supervisory relationship to the effective articulation of supervisory tasks and functions.

Principles of ethics

A short history of ethics

Currently applied principles of ethics have their roots in debates about moral philosophy that took place in the eighteenth and early nineteenth centuries. (See Warburton, 1995 for an introduction.) For example, Kant (Urmson and Rée, 1989) developed the notion of 'absolute duties' and the categorical imperative, 'Act only on that maxim which you can at the same time will to become a universal law.' Kantian ethics were based on the notion of duty, emphasising the motivations of actions and not their consequences. He believed that the consequences of actions were outside our control and could therefore not be crucial to morality. A problem with Kant's theory is its failure to address conflicts of duty. Lying, for example, is always immoral for Kant, even if a predicted consequence of telling someone the truth would be to put them in danger.

A second school of thought is that exemplified in consequentialist theories. These judge the rightness or wrongness of actions on their predicted consequences. Best known amongst these theories is J.S. Mill's Utilitarianism in which 'good' is whatever brings about the greatest total happiness. Various problems have been associated with this idea, including the difficulty in calculating universal happiness and the apparent justification for adding a 'happiness' drug to the water supply! It also raises other issues such as whether the trade-off of a little unhappiness in a lot of people is justified by a lot of happiness in a few.

A third school is that of virtue theory or neo-Aristotelianism. The emphasis here is on virtuous individual traits that cannot readily be encapsulated in moral rules or principles. Virtue ethics emphasises the character of the people who perform actions and make decisions. It has been argued that the virtuous judgements of healthcare professionals result in better decisions than the following of rules, codes, or procedures (Williams, 1982: 50). A danger with this school of thought is that of circularity, in which individuals might define virtues in order to suit their preferences without reference to the more general good.

All of these traditional approaches have more recently been critiqued as failing to reflect the reasoning and methods of women. In particular, perspectives which focus on sympathy and concern for others have tended to be neglected. What is proposed is an 'ethics of care' that promotes traits such as sympathy, compassion, fidelity, discernment, love and trustworthiness in intimate personal relationships (Noddings, 1984).

General principles of ethical decision-making

Despite differences between schools of philosophy in the use of language and the starting points for generating ethical principles, there appears to be enough common ground to derive some general principles of ethical decision-making.

Principles of ethics traditionally adopted in the profession of medicine were developed during the 1920s and 1930s out of an attempt to incorporate consideration of both the morality of an action and its anticipated consequences (Ross, 1930). In defining and applying ethical principles it is implicit that the judges are members of the professional community. An attempt is made to define and apply them on behalf of the client, but clients themselves might define and apply them differently. The principles are created by the professional community to guide professional action.

The principles of ethics adopted in the medical profession have been translated to the work of professional helpers. Page and Wosket (1994) propose the use of the five principles of autonomy, beneficence, fidelity, justice and non-maleficence.

These principles offer a framework which can be used to consider the ethical dilemmas that arise in supervision. When faced with difficult decisions, supervision offers an opportunity to consider the principles in the context of the specific clinical issue, and to debate a best course of action. This process gives a degree of assurance that, whatever the actual outcomes, decisions have been taken from an ethical standpoint. Documenting the thought processes that underpin a decision can also protect the professional in the event of subsequent litigation in the light of outcomes.

Autonomy (the principle that individuals have rights to freedom of action and choice)

This is of importance in the helping professions, particularly since ways of working tend to emphasise self-actualisation and personal growth of the client as an aim of the work. Similarly, developmental models of supervision emphasise the increasing right to autonomy of supervisees as they become more experienced practitioners.

Beneficence (the principle that the actions taken should do good, using knowledge to promote human welfare)

The application of this principle needs to take account of who judges what is for the good and for whom it is judged to be good. In determining what is judged to be for the good in supervision, the participants will need to bear in mind the welfare of the supervisee, the client and involved others.

Fidelity (being faithful to promises made)

Attention to this principle helps supervisors to think carefully about what they can reasonably promise to supervisees during the contracting process with care taken not to go beyond what is possible. Confidentiality is an issue over which promises made must acknowledge the limits of the agreement. A second issue is that of clients needing to be informed that supervisees will be discussing their therapy with the supervisor. In obtaining informed consent from clients, both with regard to the therapy and to disclosure in supervision, it is important not to affect the engagement process adversely.

Justice (ensuring that people are treated fairly)

Justice is fair, equitable, and appropriate treatment in light of what is due or owed to persons (Beauchamp and Childress, 1994). Supervisors may draw on this principle to consider how to weigh the distribution of their time to different supervisees. This may be particularly challenging in the case of a neophyte practitioner who is struggling with her or his learning. The 'fair-opportunity rule' requires that this supervisee be provided with sufficient assistance to overcome any disadvantaging conditions resulting from her or his biological make-up or social context. This might mean offering a great deal more time and input than to another supervisee who is flourishing. Where time is limited, to whom is the first obligation?

Fair treatment also encapsulates the notion of equitable treatment of people irrespective of ethnicity, gender, age, class, culture, sexual orientation, disability and other individual differences.

Non-maleficence (striving to prevent harm)

In supervision, the needs of the supervisee and of clients may conflict. In training placements in which the trainee is failed by the supervisor, the principle of non-maleficence is being applied with respect to potential future clients. It could, however, be argued that the supervisees are themselves being harmed by the supervisor's refusal to sanction their joining their chosen profession.

In the application of this principle, the question of the prevention of harm to whom arises. As in the above example, the needs of one person or group are being privileged over another. In some case examples, such as child protection, the law prescribes the importance of the prevention of harm to some people over others.

In cases where the supervisee sees only one person in the system as the beneficiary, supervisors might help to create a wider perspective on the application of this principle. They might, for example, encourage supervisees to try not to cause harm to the mother and father, as well as to the child who has been the subject of abuse in a family.

Examples of conflicting ethical principles

Taken individually, the principles might lead to different courses of action and where they result in a conflict of ideas for action, consideration needs to be given to which should take precedence in specific circumstances. If we took the principle that the therapist should take whatever action he or she believes to be in the best interests of the client this would be an exemplar based on the principle of beneficence. However, if only this principle were taken into consideration, the therapist could take action in which the client's wishes were completely disregarded. In order to allow both considerations to influence the actions taken, the principle of autonomy (promoting the maximum degree of choice for all) would also need to be applied.

Below are a number of vignettes that illustrate how the ethical principles might conflict with each other in regard to the decisions and courses of action that a supervisor might take. They are offered as examples in which readers might ask themselves, 'How would I go forward from here?' One way of processing the inherent dilemmas is to identify the applicable principles of ethics, work out what follows from each principle, and then identify a course of action which might give greater weight to one principle but also takes account of the others. Sharing and documenting the process introduces additional safeguards for both supervisors and supervisees.

- *You become increasingly concerned that your supervisee has mental health difficulties. He or she comes to supervision in an agitated state and starts to tell you about what is happening for him or her, seemingly being unable to contain the material any longer. You are concerned that if you allow him or her to leave the premises he or she will be unsafe, as he or she discloses that he or she has self-harmed in the past. What principles of ethics are relevant and how might they inform your decision-making and the course of action you take?*

One of the principles at issue here is that of fidelity. Were the supervisee a client of yours, you would be unlikely to find a course of action difficult to determine. The principle of beneficence would be likely to take precedence over that of autonomy in such an instance. Actions that followed from the principle of beneficence would lie within the agreed contract with the client, and there would be no conflict with the principle of fidelity. In the case of a supervisee, taking action to ensure the supervisee's safety would be likely to violate the contract agreed regarding the supervisory role-relationship. The application of the principle of fidelity would influence whether you allow the supervisee to talk to you about personal matters more fitting to therapy than supervision. Non-maleficence to clients, were the supervisee to be practising at this time, would also be a consideration. While in this example fidelity might usually be designated a less influential role than beneficence and non-maleficence, actions taken would also aim to protect, as far as possible, the original contract for supervision.

- *You become aware that you are becoming increasingly sexually attracted to your supervisee. You take advice on this, resulting in a recommendation that you terminate the training relationship between yourself and the supervisee. You are reluctant to take this course of action as you would have to explain the unscheduled termination to the training institution.*

An anonymous survey of 464 female psychologists (Glaser and Thorpe, 1986) elicited data on experiences during postgraduate training of sexual intimacy with and sexual advances from psychology educators. The replies indicated that sexual contact is quite prevalent overall (17 per cent), greater (22 per cent) among recent doctoral recipients, and still higher among students divorcing or separating during postgraduate training (34 per cent). Sexual advances were reported by 31 per cent of respondents overall. Retrospectively these were almost invariably perceived as coercive. The survey did not address the frequency of experiencing sexual attraction, rather the frequency in which this led to sexual advances or contact. This suggests that sexual issues are likely to be more prevalent than these figures indicate.

The coercion experienced as a result of sexual advances from educators violates the principal of autonomy. The experience of sexual attraction may interfere with the supervisor's capability to adhere to the supervision contract and there is a risk of the attraction resulting in a sexual advance. Where the attraction is mutual, the pull towards a dual relationship is likely to interfere with the tasks and responsibilities of supervision.

- *You are asked to provide supervision for someone who has failed a previous practice placement. This was a result of serious concerns regarding the supervisee's high levels of anxiety which prevented adequate engagement with clients in the work. The rules of the training course are such that the student must be offered a chance to repeat the failed placement.*

The dilemma here is about consideration of balancing justice for the student with non-maleficence and beneficence for current and future potential clients. Application of the principle of justice would promote the idea of the student having a second chance. In order to ensure the welfare of clients the supervisor might introduce additional safeguards such as live supervision. The dangers are that increased vigilance on the part of the supervisor might further elevate the already high levels of anxiety of the supervisee. This dilemma itself would be fair material to raise in supervision.

- *Your supervisee is voracious for support and help to learn. Despite many hours of input from you the supervisee does not seem to progress. At what point do you decide to deny assistance in the face of her or his enthusiasm but apparent inability to learn?*

Again, the needs of the client and of the supervisee conflict. The principles of justice and beneficence applied to the supervisee might lead you to carry on trying, although it could also be argued that the supervisee would benefit from a change of career. When you have done all that you can without progress then the needs of clients are likely to take precedence. In this example there are the needs of three parties to consider since the well-being of the supervisor might be threatened by the excessive demands and needs of the supervisee.

A further example illustrates a conflict of interest in the requirements of the parties of the host training institution and the supervisor.

* *The decision that employees in your position should take part in the training programme may have been made at an institutional level. You have not been consulted but are expected to participate as supervision is a feature of your job description. The supervisee explains the requirements of the training which conflict with your views about the work. For example, the supervisee states that he or she has to complete an assignment based on the use of a theoretical model to which you do not subscribe.*

Here you are expected to show fidelity with regard to promises made on your behalf and without your consent. You cannot afford to lose your job and your employer insists that you participate. You wish to hold faith with your own beliefs about the work in order best to serve clients under the principles of non-maleficence and beneficence. Ways out might include the involvement of a colleague who works in the model prescribed by the training institution. Alternatively, a debate with your employer might refer to the principles of ethics and the bind in which you have been placed.

* *You have become aware of a blind spot of your own – you do not feel comfortable with having your work observed live or taped and therefore avoid it yourself in your own clinical practice. The supervisee has a preference to use reporting as the medium of supervision. You agree to this, enabling both of you to avoid observation of your work. The supervisor and supervisee thus find themselves colluding (possibly tacitly) in their difficulty.*

The principle of autonomy might dictate that the supervisee be responsible for the choice of supervisory medium. In post-registration supervision this would be agreeable. There may be an issue as to whether in pre-registration training it is appropriate to qualify without one's work ever having been observed. Where observation as part of training is the norm, it could be argued that some clients are dealt with inequitably because the failure to have had work observed threatens to make the supervisee's experience inadequately supervised and unacceptably narrow. In addition, if supervisors fail to take action on this developmental need of their own, then the principles of justice, beneficence and non-maleficence might be violated since their work is subject to fewer safeguards than that of other practitioners.

Codes of conduct and legal requirements

Decision-making also needs to be informed by codes of conduct which have been devised in the context of principles of ethics but which may be insufficient on their own in guiding practice. Without reference to principles of ethics, codes of conduct can become a set of rules adhered to because it is a professional requirement. Practitioners should ensure that they familiarise themselves with the codes of conduct relevant to their specific profession. However, there can be significant gaps between the practice aspired to therein and actual practice in the field. Codes of conduct are sensitive to the cultural and political context of the time. For example, in Britain the advent of the internal market in the National Health Service, increased litigation and the development of managed care networks, where information collected at one level of care is transferred to another, have influenced professional guidance on confidentiality and note-keeping. The change towards more rigorous, detailed and transferable notes has not been at the behest of clients and there is no evidence to suggest that it enhances client welfare. A survey of practitioners in the field (Scaife and Pomerantz, 1999) concluded that there was a gap between the pragmatics of actual practice and the guidance issued by the British Psychological Society (1995, 1998a) to its members on confidentiality and note-keeping. In some cases the security of notes was compromised by the absence of lockable cabinets, and files were not infrequently written up after a considerable time period had elapsed from the session being recorded. Respondents were also reluctant to record certain types of data that might compromise the position of the client – for example, the information that the client was an illegal immigrant.

Accordingly, practitioners should also apply the principles of ethics to their professional thinking and practice and strive to influence the development of codes of conduct in directions informed by consideration of client wishes and practicality.

Legal precedents are also relevant to ethical decision-making. All professionals make mistakes. What is important is that people do their best in the knowledge of principles of ethics, codes of conduct and legal precedents. Wherever there is doubt about a course of action, the approach to the ethical dilemma should be carefully thought through and the process of so doing documented. It is always advisable when in doubt to consult with another and to document the conversation that took place. When consequences can be grave this process best ensures the peace of mind and safety of all concerned.

Examples of ethical and legal issues arising in supervision

The following section introduces the position of the law on issues arising in supervision, and discusses the actions that practitioners might take to protect themselves in the event of potential litigation. However, it is important not to lose sight of the underlying drive for ethical practice: the supervisor's responsibility for the well-being of the supervisees' current and future clients.

Confidentiality

Practitioners in the helping professions owe a duty of confidentiality to clients, and this applies to information communicated directly and to that held in files such as tapes, test results, charts and notes. Any confidential communication made to the supervisor, whether directly by the client or by the supervisee, imposes the duty of confidentiality on the supervisor (Disney and Stephens, 1994). The extent to which this duty may be overridden by the courts differs according to the laws of the country in which the participants reside, but it is wise to maintain strict confidentiality unless compelled by law.

In the context of clinical supervision it is essential to inform the client that confidential communications will be shared with the supervisor, and the client's consent to this should be obtained by the supervisee. It is the supervisor's responsibility to discuss with the supervisee the ethical duty of confidentiality owed to the client. The client also needs to know the limits of confidentiality where supervision is undertaken in groups. Disney and Stephens recommend that supervisors refer to seven elements defined by Bernard and O'Laughlin (1990) as essential to the assurance of confidentiality:

- Ethical standards and canons regarding confidentiality must be identified and discussed with supervisees.
- Confidentiality of client materials must be maintained.
- Security of client materials must be maintained.
- Prohibition of non-professional discussion must be ensured.
- Prohibition of disclosure of client identity must be ensured.
- Clients must be informed of clinic policies regarding confidentiality and ethics.
- Exceptions to confidentiality and privileged communications must be identified and discussed with supervisees and clients.

Vicarious responsibility

The nature of supervision means that supervisors hear things that they cannot unknow. To know is to become to some degree responsible, although the extent of this will vary dependent upon the defined relationship. Whatever the professional responsibility, there is a personal responsibility deriving from the acquisition of knowledge.

In some cases this vicarious liability has been established through legal precedent. In particular there is a dramatic example established in USA law through the Tarasoff case (*Tarasoff* v. *Regents of the University of California*, 1974). The university psychologist warned campus police that one of his clients had threatened to kill his girlfriend. The client was questioned by police, was later released and subsequently killed his girlfriend. The university psychologist had been advised by his supervisor not to warn the victim directly as this might be regarded as a breach of confidence (Meyer, Landis and Hays, 1988). The family of the victim took legal action on the basis that university staff had been negligent because the potential victim was not warned personally. Although the case was settled out of court, it is widely regarded as having been found in favour of the victim's family. As a result several states in the USA have made the 'duty to warn' a legal standard for all mental health professionals.

The position in Britain is somewhat different and psychologists in such a case would not be expected to warn the potential victim directly. They would, however, be expected to inform the police in the case of the possibility of serious crime (Wadsborough Solicitors, 1999).

In instances such as the Tarasoff case, the supervisor may be held in part negligent for the actions of the supervisee. A supervisor and supervisee are both responsible if negligence occurs, but to differing degrees and for different reasons. The supervisor has an additional responsibility to apply experience and skill to predict and minimise the possibility of negligence (Ryan, 1991).

Responsibility to clients

A major consideration in supervision is to help safeguard the welfare of the client. The supervisor must thus address issues which call this into question. Supervisors need sufficient knowledge regarding the performance of the supervisee to be in a position to make judgements about competence to practise, particularly when acting in the role of gate-keeper to the profession. Inadequacies cannot be addressed unless they are clearly and specifically identified to or by the supervisee, and the supervisor needs to develop skills in constructive challenge and evaluation. Issues that might evoke the need for challenge and ways of approaching this are discussed further in Chapter 13.

In pre-registration training the supervisor's responsibility can include failing supervisees who are unable to meet the required standards of the profession. Of all the tasks of the supervisor this is one of the least palatable and, because it is rare, opportunities for gaining experience in how to handle failure are very limited.

Due process

'Due process' is a legal term referring to the rights and liberties of people in which any procedures to which a person is subject must be fair, considerate and equitable (Disney and Stephens, 1994). An example in relation to clients would be the taking of actions to admit someone to a mental hospital under a legal section. This must be carried out with due process. Supervisees in training also have due process rights in that the supervisor's evaluation must be fair and equitable and the supervisee must have the opportunity to appeal.

It is important that the supervisor identifies serious concerns as early as possible in order that the supervisee can be informed of their nature and have an opportunity to address them. In order to be clear and specific the word 'failure' should be used. Since supervision is about learning and development it is important that once an issue has been identified the supervisee should have a reasonable opportunity to make reparation. It is also important that the supervisee understands what is needed in order to do this. The issue of failure is explored further in Chapter 13.

Knowing about other colleagues

Whilst supervision may principally focus upon work carried out with clients, as supervisees become more experienced they may wish to discuss issues regarding their relationships with colleagues. Particularly in professions that have only a small membership, the supervisor may become party to information about the practice of a known colleague. This can pose a striking dilemma. With no formal responsibility for this colleague's work, steering a course of action may be particularly difficult. Even where the colleague is unknown to the supervisor, gross professional misconduct cannot be allowed to continue. It is not the role of the supervisor to investigate the matter or to make judgements about the case. It may be that the supervisor can best help the supervisee by identifying to whom in the colleague's organisation the information should be disclosed, and to do this with the backing of the supervisor.

Supervisor competence

Training and accreditation as a supervisor is as yet nowhere near a mandatory requirement across the helping professions. Whilst professional associations typically specify the requirements for competence to practise within the profession, the specification of standards of competence for supervisors is unusual. The issue was explored by Newman (1981: 692), who raised the following questions:

- Has the supervisor had training in the theory and practice of supervision or in the supervised practice of psychotherapy supervision?
- Do the supervisors conscientiously practise the skills they are helping their trainees to learn?
- Has the supervisor had training or experience in the assessment or treatment of the types of clinical problems and clients seen by the trainee?
- If the supervisor is not adequately qualified, has supervision by a qualified clinician been arranged or has the trainee's client been referred elsewhere?

In the absence of mandatory requirements it behoves supervisors to attend to issues regarding their own competence to practise in this role by seeking education, training and experience. The role is a responsible one, both in relation to clients and supervisees, and an ethical approach incorporates the need to attend to personal and professional development in the role.

Ethnicity, culture, gender, age, sexual orientation, disability and difference

Differences between people along the dimensions of ethnicity, culture, gender, sexual orientation, age and disability have provided a context for discrimination in favour of the dominant group throughout our cultural history. Ethical practice under the principle of justice requires that an equitable approach be made to different groups whether these involve clients and/or supervisees. The dominant group is often in the majority, but this is not necessarily the case (as, for example, in the case of South Africa under apartheid).

In this section, the specific issues of 'race', ethnicity and gender are explored. It is intended that these act as examples in which the application of broad principles is elaborated. Discrimination on the basis of age, sexual orientation and disability is no less an issue and supervisors are advised to consider their practice in relation to each of these individual differences (see, for example, Spy and Oyston, 1999; Hitchings, 1999; McCann, Gorrell, Barnes and Down, 2000).

The desirability of equity is one thing, its assurance is quite another. Cultural groups – be these at the level of society, at the level of profession membership or family – by their very nature evolve implicit rules of interaction which are difficult to discern once habitually enacted, and what is 'like me' tends to acquire the status of a norm. The assumptions of the dominant group applied to other groups generate value judgements that usually serve to affect the minority group adversely. In many of the helping professions, white middle-class values may be regarded as predominant.

An example of this is Gillborn's (1990) finding from an ethnographic study in a comprehensive school. Teachers said that they treated all the children the same. But in the case of pupils given a detention the nature of the misdemeanour differed according to their ethnicity. White pupils were more often given detentions for rule-breaking such as persistent failure to hand in homework. Detentions were more often given to black pupils on the basis of value judgements such as the way the child walked ('swaggered') down the corridor. This is an example of negative labelling derived from cultural incongruence. This example is on the one hand mundane, but on the other an illustration of the deep roots of the issue.

Analysis of longitudinal census data (Greenslade, 1991) indicated that people from an Irish background have the standardised highest mortality rates of all groups in Britain. The Irish are the only migrant group whose life expectancy decreases upon arrival in Britain. A study by Cochrane and Bal (1989) showed that people born in the Irish Republic had twice the rate of admission of English-born people and a 50 per cent higher rate than the next highest group (African-Caribbean) to psychiatric hospitals. What might account for this? Could it be racism, difference, cultural dissonance, or stress-related health problems arising from discriminatory experiences?

The above example illustrates how the assumptions of the dominant group are the basis for definitions of normality and deviance. These definitions are focused on the individual rather than the contexts in which they live. Arguments have been made that intervention to alleviate human suffering may usefully be based on an ecological analysis rather than an individually focused understanding of presenting problems (Bostock, 1998). This leads to interventions which include study groups, campaign groups and user-led services designed to help people to influence services so as better to meet their needs and to enhance their status. An ethical approach to supervision needs to include consideration of cultural and economic factors in relation to client groups, services, and the supervisor's and supervisee's own experiences.

Definition of minority

Larson (1982) suggests that the definition of majority must take account of the over-representation of white males of European descent in positions of relative power in Western society. This view leads to attribution of the term 'minority' along the dimension of power not numbers, and to the position that the central feature of being a minority is the potential of being stigmatised. Consistent with this view is the definition of the term 'racism' as incorporating the presence of both prejudice *and* power (Gill and Levidow, 1989; Gillborn, 1990). By this definition, stereotyped images of white people held by black people in Britain or the USA would not be regarded as racist because black people as a group would not be seen as having the power to alter the life experiences of white people significantly. The notion of 'institutionalised racism' has entered public debate, if not public consciousness, in the UK following the murder of Stephen Lawrence.

Acknowledgement of difference

One stage of awareness of difference is to take a stance of treating everyone the same. Smith (1981) refers to this as the 'myth of sameness' as it assumes that the skills of the helper are generic and equally applicable to individuals irrespective of their backgrounds and personal qualities. Such an approach ignores the absence of a level playing field for minority groups and leads to the application of methods devised by one group to others in which the method used is of questionable and dubious value. One example of this was the misuse of intelligence tests to assess people from cultures other than that in which the test was devised (Poortinga, 1995).

Another stage of awareness is to acknowledge difference and to attempt to redress the balance of the influence of the dominant group by positive action in favour of minority groups. This has led to the seeking of the views of minority groups regarding the approach to providing services best suited to their needs.

In the context of supervision, supervisors might overtly acknowledge difference between clients, supervisees and themselves. This might lead, for example, to carefully selecting clients for a black worker or female worker so as to protect them from experiencing rampantly racist or sexist clients. The danger here is that of the supervisor taking responsibility in such a way that might reinforce the experience of a negative power differential. It also assumes that individuals from a minority group share similar experiences whereas the use of blanket terms can mask striking variations. Of children classified as 'Asian', 17.7 per cent of Pakistani ancestry, 4.2 per cent of Bangladeshi ancestry and 26.4 per cent of Indian ancestry gained five or more 'O' level passes in 1985 in the Inner London Education Authority (Nuttall, Goldstein, Prosser and Rasbash, 1989). Lumping Asians together as a single group makes for misleading conclusions about needs and appropriate responses.

Western bias in underlying assumptions

Pederson (1987) identifies ten common assumptions that reflect a Western bias in the helping professions and which contribute to institutional racism, ageism and sexism as follows:

1   *The assumption that all people share a common idea of normality that is more or less universal.* Pederson argues that normality is culturally, politically and economically defined. A European example of this might be in

relation to the idea that children individuate from their families of origin when they reach adulthood. This is the 'normal' expectation in white middle-class families in Britain. In Crete, however, families more typically build houses which include an independent living space for their daughters whose husbands are welcomed into the daughter's family of origin upon marriage.

2 *Emphasis on the individual as opposed to emphasis on family, community and/or society.* This contrasts with the organisation and norms of some religious orders or alternative communities, exemplified by the kibbutz in Israel or Quaker communities in Britain. Pederson cites the example of teaching English as a second language in Indonesia when the students questioned him about the English-speakers' capitalisation of the first person singular 'I'. The students' view was that this represents the emphasis placed on individualism by English-speaking cultures.

3 *Fragmentation by academic discipline.* An example of such fragmentation even within one profession, that of medicine, reveals a degree of specialisation in which the different parts of the body are viewed in relative isolation from the whole person. More recently there has been a development in the West of holistic approaches to healing, many of which have their roots in Eastern philosophies.

4 *Dependency on abstraction.* Hall (1976) differentiated high-context from low-context cultures. The former require reference to a context to give a concept meaning, whereas low-context cultures are more likely to function around the notion that abstract concepts carry their own meaning with them across contexts. The use of abstract concepts tends to be more prevalent in academic contexts. Training to be a professional helper is rooted in academic institutions. There is an assumption that the abstract concepts developed in this context have general application, but their usage may disadvantage those with a less formal education.

5 *Overemphasis on independence.* This is exemplified by the cultural elevation of the individual to the position of being the unit that is supposed to function with relative independence from family and community. In contrast, Japanese culture is described as regarding dependencies as healthy and absolutely necessary (Doi, 1974).

6 *Neglect of the client's support systems.* Along with the focus on the individual comes the tendency to ignore the family and community as the 'natural' helpers of those in difficulty. In other cultures the community is seen as the expected provider of support and to fail to help a neighbour in need would be a source of significant shame. In many cultures the family, rather than therapy, is seen as the appropriate place for intimate discussion.

7 *A habit of linear thinking.* Many of the explanatory frameworks adopted in the helping professions focus on the individual as the unit of change and the unit of explanation. Explanations tend to identify a cause and an

effect. Other cultures construct explanations that owe more to the inter-connectedness of seemingly discrete events, seeing cause and effect as two aspects of the same undifferentiated reality. Even in Western Greek culture, the same word is used for 'why' and 'because'.

8 *Focus on changing the individual not the system.* Many approaches to helping are based on the assumption that it is the individual who must change to accommodate to the system. Shem (1985, 1999) articulates the potentially profound adverse effects on health and well-being that can result from patient admissions to hospitals that depend on the willingness of insurance companies to fund investigations and treatments. Voices that speak against this by suggesting that it is unethical to help people to adapt to oppressive or pathological systems (Hagan and Smail, 1997) are less-well represented in the literature and in service provision. Albee (1998) points out that no mass disorder has ever been removed by attempting to treat the affected individual!

9 *Neglect of history.* The collection of data about presenting problems may be restricted to the immediate family of the client. The disregard of the wider cultural and family histories may lead to the exclusion of explanatory concepts that include discrimination and the long-term social and economic disadvantage of some people. When women were out-performed by men in terms of educational attainment, explanations based on the inferior intellect of women as a group were postulated. As the attainments of young women at school begin to outstrip those of young men, these explanations are no longer seen to hold water (Clark and Millard, 1998). In contrast, the problem of boys' 'underachievement' has tended to be seen in cultural terms.

10 *Dangers of cultural encapsulation.* Pederson suggests that the most dangerous assumption is to think that one is aware of all of one's assumptions. He advocates the retention of a position of openness to the idea that we are relatively culturally unaware as a more useful posture in the work. This would lead to an approach emphasising enquiry rather than the making of judgements. It could be argued that in order to be a well-integrated member of Western society which is inherently sexist, racist and homophobic, there is a strong temptation to fit in, albeit unconsciously, by adopting aspects of these biases.

Supervisors have an ethical responsibility to include consideration of minorities in their work. The helping professions are 'socio-political' in nature (Katz, 1985) and tend to reflect the values and ideologies of the dominant group. All acts within the role can be seen as to a greater or lesser degree political, and work with people who belong to disadvantaged groups tends to reveal this political nature more clearly. For example, consider the question of whether to allocate a black supervisee to a black or white supervisor. Allocation of the black supervisee to the black supervisor may represent an acknowledgement of the possibility of common experiences based on membership of a minority group. However, it might also represent a tokenism and a false assumption that both parties belong to a common cultural group. Even the act to decide to consult with the supervisee about her or his preferences prior to making the allocation singles the person out if this is not the usual procedure.

Dealing with discrimination

Members of disadvantaged groups often also suffer from double or triple jeopardy in that they are, for example, both growing old and suffering additional discrimination based on their sexual orientation, gender, disability or ethnicity. The following practical ideas about how issues of minority groups might be addressed in supervision are collected under the heading of specific groups but could be adapted to also have relevance for those not specifically addressed. They are taken from the *University of Sheffield Clinical Psychology Training Course Supervisor's Handbook* (1999) and were compiled from the views of supervisors within the Trent Region of the National Health Service in the UK. First there is a definition of terms to facilitate a common understanding.

Ethnicity, 'race' and culture

Since language is socially constructed it is continually evolving. For this reason the following terms are defined for the purpose of this text in the context of the use of language at the end of the twentieth century.

'RACE'

The biologist Reiss (1993) and the population geneticist Lewontin (1982) consider the term 'race' unhelpful when applied to humans. Studies of allele (different possible forms of a gene) frequencies in humans show that the variation between any two individuals is likely to be of much greater magnitude than that between groups. Studies of the diversity of full sets of different individuals' chromosomes and evidence from palaeontology, archaeology and genetic diversity studies is consistent with an African origin of modern humans who migrated to Asia, Australia, Europe and Oceania (Cann, 1998). Attribution of 'race' is more typically made on the basis of observable characteristics (the phenotype), and the term is therefore used in inverted commas. Despite widespread agreement amongst social scientists that 'race' has no determining influence on human potential and that racial identities are socially and historically constructed (Wade, 1999), the notion of a biological basis to 'race' persists despite its roots in colonialism and imperialism.

ETHNICITY

Ethnicity refers to the perception of belonging to a group which views itself and is perceived by others as culturally distinct from other groups. Ethnic groups may be distinguished by their language, history, ancestry, religion and style of dress or adornment. These differences are learned, and distinctions have become more complex in the pluralist societies of the late twentieth century.

To illustrate the meaning of ethnicity: few people would claim that the Irish and the English are different 'races', even adopting the common, as opposed to the scientific, connotation of the word. But some would see the two as culturally and, consequently, ethnically distinct.

The distinguishing of ethnic groups may help or hinder appropriate service provision. Some consider that such definitions may implicitly enshrine them as 'strange' or 'weird'. On the other hand, the Irish community in Sheffield fought hard to win legal recognition as an ethnic minority group under the terms of the Race Relations Act, in order to benefit from the protection afforded by the legal framework.

'BLACK'

'Black' is used as a term to refer to people from a range of national, ethnic and religious backgrounds who are believed to share a common experience of white racism (Mac an Ghaill, 1988). It is also used by black people themselves.

These terms are applied in the context of a changing society. Children of families who emigrated from their birthplace earlier in this century have grown up in the context of multiple values, which present them with additional dilemmas when the beliefs of their families and those of others that they encounter at school and at work are in conflict.

Supervision might focus on the following:

- Exploration of the supervisor's, supervisee's and client's perceptions of their ethnic and cultural identities, values and beliefs, how these have developed and changed, and how they affect and are affected by the work.
- Exploration of the values associated with the role of 'helper' and 'helped' for supervisor, supervisee and in cultural and ethnic groups. This might include discussion of patterns of referral to the service.
- Examination of the basis of psychological theory and how it might be associated with the cultural and personal histories of its inventors.
- Development of skills in finding out, rather than making assumptions, about clients' values and beliefs.
- Drawing on a range of cultural and ethnic beliefs in the process of thinking about the work or challenging clients from all backgrounds. For

example, 'If you had been brought up to expect an arranged marriage, how might you have approached your relationship differently?'

- Considering the effects on clients of core socio-political issues such as poverty, discrimination, racism, deprivation and exclusion.

Approaches more specific to issues of ethnicity:

- Find out about local organisations that represent the views of ethnic groups.
- Find out how many people from different ethnic groups use the service in which the supervisee is working, how this is monitored, how it relates to the distribution of the population, and what actions are being taken by the service in regard to equity and equal opportunities generally and ethnic groups specifically.
- Find out the number of employees from minority groupings employed in the service and how this is monitored.
- Explore how beliefs and values may differ between ethnic groups by reading, visiting relevant community centres and meeting with people who have knowledge of particular groups. Discuss in supervision how applicable these findings might be to specific individuals.
- Work out a way of finding out which local professionals are from different ethnic groups and how they might inform clinical practice. Consider the need for and availability of interpreters. This is also relevant in relation to people with hearing impairments and whose disabilities include reliance on sign language.
- Consider the relevance of political issues such as immigrant or refugee status and its implications for confidentiality.
- Encourage development of awareness of population standardisation samples for any measures used in assessing clients and consider the relevance of a measure standardised on the dominant group to minority groups.

GENDER

For the purposes of this text, 'sex' is used to mean biological sex. Since misattribution of sex can occur at birth for a variety of reasons, such as incompatibility of genetic status and physical sex characteristics, 'gender' is used to refer to assigned sex. The development of gender identity as male or female is thought to be a cognitive process in humans in which assigned sex is a significant determinant (Meyer-Bahlburg, 1982; Lev-Ran, 1974).

Gender-role is a social construct which involves assigning specified social tasks, roles, norms or behaviours into the categories masculine and feminine. What are decreed as appropriate masculine and feminine characteristics in a particular society vary over time (Goodrich, Rampage, Ellman and Halstead,

1988). The feminist and men's movements have arisen from a perceived power imbalance and inequity arising from ascribed gender roles.

Gender-specific issues in professional helping   In most services there are gender differences in patterns of referral and in professional response patterns to males and females. For example, boys under the age of ten years are referred significantly more frequently than girls to child and adolescent mental health services in the UK. Women receive two-thirds of all prescriptions for psychotropic drugs (Ussher and Nicolson, 1992). Gender stereotyping plays a role in how clients might define their difficulties and what they are prepared to speak about. There may, for example, be more shame perceived in a man admitting to being hit by his female partner than in admitting to hitting her.

Supervision might focus on the following:

- Consideration of gender stereotyping in the local and wider culture and in the histories of supervisor, supervisee and client.
- Consideration of patterns of referral to the supervisee's service and service responses based on gender. Finding out how the service monitors referrals by gender.
- Consideration of how one's own and the supervisee's responses to clients, colleagues and each other are influenced by gender and how to obtain a missing masculine or feminine perspective in same-gender supervisory partnerships.
- Consideration of how the client's views of the gender of the practitioner might affect the work.
- Inclusion of a focus on the dynamics of power and responsibility as connected with gender and the presenting problem, and in the work being carried out with the client.
- Observation of and reflection upon one's own potentially differential responses to supervisees, supervisors and clients according to gender. This might include sexual attraction, arousal and sexual advances, and how these might affect the work.
- Bearing in mind that the sexual orientation of clients, supervisors and supervisees cannot be assumed.
- Encouraging the supervisee to find out about services that are organised around gender (e.g. men's groups).
- Considering the interplay of gender with other cultural issues, such as the differential experiences of a black unemployed male with learning disabilities compared with a white female solicitor.

Dual role-relationships

The potential for dual role-relationships (i.e. the supervisor having an additional role with the supervisee) is not uncommon in arrangements for supervision. These may include a line-management arrangement, a pre-existing friendship, or the development of intimacy (sexual or otherwise) during the course of the supervisory relationship which might compromise the roles of the supervisor.

Dual relationships are difficult to manage since the expectations and obligations of the different roles are sometimes divergent. An example from my own experience was of participating in a supervisory group in which one of the group members was the spouse of the supervisor. There appeared to be a dilemma around the supervisor not being seen to favour his partner, which resulted in his appearing to take an overly critical stance in relation to her work compared with that of the rest of the group. As a supervisee this was difficult to raise since the supervisor had already made the decision to accept his partner as a group member.

I take the view that whilst in some cases dual relationships are built into the nature of the supervisory task, dual relationships of any kind between supervisor and supervisee are potentially problematic. For example, supervisors may be teachers, evaluators and also facilitators of self-awareness. Kurpius, Gibson, Lewis and Corbet (1991) point out that the American Association for Counseling and Development Ethical Standards (1988: 8, H12) state, 'When the educational program offers a growth experience with an emphasis on self-disclosure or other relatively intimate or personal involvement, the member must have no administrative, supervisory or evaluating authority regarding the participant.' At the same time, the standards require that counselling trainers, 'must establish a program directed toward developing students' skills, knowledge and self-understanding' (p. 8, H3). These two standards potentially stand in conflict.

Harrar, Vandercreek and Knapp (1990) implied that all intimate relationships between a supervisor and supervisee constitute violations of professional ethics. Where intimacy develops during the course of the relationship the participants are likely to be so focused on each other as to be insulated against the outside world. It seems highly dubious that supervisors could carry out their task uninfluenced by the personal events taking place. Sometimes people who have had a social relationship with each other and then find themselves in a professional relationship agree to suspend their socialising whilst the professional relationship continues. This may serve as an adequate solution, although there is potential for the changed roles to threaten a successful return to friendship upon termination of supervision and people may prefer not to take the risk.

Line-management supervision is not uncommon in many agencies. In such arrangements, the requirements of the employing organisation may play a relatively large role in defining the relationship and the possibilities within it. For example, Morrison (1993: 1), in his book on supervision in social care, introduces the topic by stating, 'The task of the supervisor, at any level in the organisation, at its simplest is to get the organisation's job done through the staff s/he manages.' He argues that accountability is a central function of supervision and that supervision is a medium through which staff learn how the agency understands and exercises accountability and control. He points out that authority and control are often associated with punishment and punitiveness. If perceived in this way, staff are less likely to share doubts or possible mistakes as a result of which the organisation will have less control over outcomes.

Where the supervisory relationship includes line-management responsibilities, it is helpful for the participants to be clear about the restrictions that this may place on the material that the supervisee chooses to bring to supervision. Case management may occupy centre stage. Supervision may still serve the full range of functions but the roles of effecting the tasks of the employer and carrying out appraisals of the work of the supervisee inevitably play a part in supervision.

Summary

In conclusion, it is important for supervisors to be aware not only of the ethical issues underlying clinical practice but also to have considered those additional issues arising from the role of supervisor. If an ethical perspective is used as a matter of habit to view the work this not only provides a sound model for the supervisee but also serves to safeguard the well-being of clients, supervisees and supervisors themselves. Corey *et al.* (1993) propose the following cognitive process as a map to follow when an ethical dilemma arises:

- Identify the problem or dilemma.
- Identify the potential issues involved.
- Review relevant ethical guidelines.
- Discuss and consult with colleagues.
- Consider possible and probable courses of action.
- Enumerate the possible consequences of various decisions.
- Decide what appears to be the best course of action.

It is recommended that each of the above steps be documented so that in the event of negative outcomes the process of reaching a decision can be shown to have been ethically sound.

Chapter 8

Use of audio and videotapes in supervision

Historically, the most common way of conducting supervision was for the supervisee and supervisor to meet together to discuss the work in prospect or to review work carried out. This practice continues to be popular, and in clinical psychology training in the UK it is still possible, although rare, to qualify after three years of training without having one's practice seen and without having seen a supervisor working (Scott and Spellman, 1992). Although the technologies for making recordings have improved significantly in recent years, verbal recounting continues to be the most commonly used supervision format, despite supervisors rating its effectiveness lowest (Wetchler, Piercy and Sprenkle, 1989; McCarthy, Kulakowski and Kenfield, 1994).

Clinical work is a practical as well as theoretical endeavour, and the discussion of work without direct or indirect observation is atypical of methods adopted in the training of practical skills in other disciplines – for example, bricklaying, sports, culinary skills, teaching and so on, in which both supervisor and supervisee would expect their work to be viewed by the other and frequently to work alongside each other.

To adopt methods which allow supervisor and supervisee to see or hear each other's work presents a number of challenges and dilemmas but ultimately offers better safeguards to clients and enhanced development opportunities for clinicians. The use of live supervision or taped material helps to overcome the tendency towards nondisclosure reported by Yourman and Farber (1997) in which 30–40 per cent of supervisees reported that they withheld information (e.g. perceived clinical errors) at moderate to high levels of frequency. In this chapter the use of audio and videotape is discussed.

Audio or videotape

Audiotapes enable the verbal content of a session to be reviewed and in addition pauses, tonal qualities and other emotional expression can be explored. The technology of the audiotaping machine is easier to introduce into a session, is more portable, cheaper and requires less preparation than videotaping. Videotapes have the advantage of providing additional material in the visual domain and are particularly useful to therapists working with families when it can be difficult to notice the contributions of all the participants in a session. Their use enables the nuances of glances and non-verbal patterns and processes to be included in reviews of the work.

One of the dangers of introducing taping into sessions and supervision can be the fascination and complication of the technology itself. Without an operative, the camera cannot follow the movements of the client, but with an operative the film-making in and of itself can dominate. Keeping a focus on the purpose of the recording should help to avert this danger.

General issues in the use of tapes

In addition to considerations concerning the use of tapes in supervision is the issue of the use of tapes in therapy. A number of factors can present hurdles to the use of tapes in either or both contexts.

1   *The effects on empathy*. The conversations that take place between client and therapist can be very intimate and contain sensitive material which may not have been previously disclosed. The presence of a third ear or eye can be perceived as inhibiting, leading to an awkwardness and reticence on the part of either or both parties. Empathy requires that the full attention of the clinician be focused on the client, and the presence of a recording machine may distract from this. However, if the therapist is comfortable with recording it is more likely that the client will also soon forget the presence of the machine, particularly if it requires no attention during the session. It can be disruptive if the machine clicks to off at the end of one side of the tape at a particularly poignant moment in the session. Similarly, the whirr of cameras moved by operatives behind a screen can also disrupt and should be avoided in setting up recording technology.

Sometimes the presence of the machine can be palpable. For example, the client might whisper asides which are not meant for the supervisor's ears, or alternatively treats the machine as a third party to whom things must be made clear. Clients may save a particular comment or communication for the moment when the tape recorder is turned off and this may present challenges to the therapist in bringing the session to an appropriate close. Such responses can be disconcerting for the therapist at the time but also provide information about the client that can be taken to supervision and fed back into the work.

2   *Self-consciousness.* On listening to or seeing themselves on tape for the first time, people are usually critical of how they look or sound and it can take many interviews for people to become used to hearing or seeing themselves on tape. It is possible to be distracted from content and

process by perceived blemishes in presentation. Particular things said or seen can become unduly amplified in significance and can be perceived as an undermining or shameful experience. In order to avert this it is wise for practitioners who are new to taping to have experimented with recording and viewing themselves in other contexts until listening to and seeing themselves on tape becomes comfortable and familiar.

3   *Confidentiality and consent.* When working in a public service context, confidentiality can be offered to clients only within the constraints of the organisation and the law. The use of tapes can present an additional challenge to the security of information expected by the client, particularly when permission is sought for their use in supervision or teaching. Permission for recording needs to be sought in writing at the outset, and taping introduced in ways which do not subsequently undermine the work.

Aveline (1997) argues that being taped may feel abusive, in particular to clients whose sense of personal mastery and proper boundaries have been subject to coercion and abuse by powerful figures in the person's earlier life. Such clients may be unable to protest and may accede to taping against their will. He advises that careful consideration be given to the meaning of the taping for the client.

It is possible to capitalise on the increasing sense of trust in their therapist that clients typically develop over time by revisiting the issue of consent to taping at the end of every session. Occasionally clients have inaccurate ideas about the use of tapes which may be disclosed as their confidence grows. For example, Hughes and Massey (2000) reported one client to have thought that tapes of the sessions were being played to every member of the psychology department. The reminder about confidentiality and consent at the end of each session gave the client an opportunity to raise concerns about this that may otherwise have remained hidden from the therapist.

In work for public agencies written consent is essential, as is clarification as to the relationship of the tapes to the overall case record. Tapes may best be regarded as transitory records to be destroyed at the end of an episode of care, or earlier. This may need to be agreed formally with the employer.

4   *Security.* Whilst all records need to be kept securely in order to protect the confidentiality due to clients, tapes present additional challenges to this process. One method for enhancing security of tapes is to use a code letter or number on the tape itself with client identifiers recorded in a different place. Tapes may be allocated to a client and recorded over at the following session. Tapes may also be used in the work by clients taking them for their own personal review, and the client may be responsible for the ownership and disposal of taped material whilst work is underway and when completed.

5   *Technical skills.* A frequently encountered problem in the use of tapes is the poor quality of recording, particularly of sound. The person who carried out the work may be able to decipher the content of the tapes, but beyond this their use is impaired without the provision of a transcript – a time-consuming activity. There are a number of practical solutions to this difficulty, including plate microphones, lapel microphones and specially designed sound systems.

6   *The anxiety of the clinician.* Even when familiar with hearing or seeing oneself on tape, performance anxieties can remain and there may be fears of negative evaluation, which can be particularly pertinent given the nature of the work. There is potential for experiencing exposure of the self, not only of the work. Beginning counsellors and psychiatrists in training have reported that the experience of taping sessions has an inhibiting effect upon their interviewing performance (Niland, Duling, Allen and Panther, 1971; Friedmann, Yamamoto, Wolkon and Davis, 1978). Videotapes were experienced as more intrusive than audiotapes. More recently, between 61 per cent and 72 per cent of nursing students reported their experience of being videorecorded as positive and helpful in enhancing their learning of effective interpersonal skills in clinical supervision (Minardi and Ritter, 1999).

Aveline (1997) argues that playing a tape is nearly always stressful for a therapist since therapy is an intensely personal activity which confronts therapists with their strengths and limitations both as a person and as a professional. This can lead to a pattern of collusive avoidance whereby supervisees spare themselves exposure and the potential attack of a super-critical ego, and supervisors collude by becoming protective of the supervisee. While it may be explicable, one might ask whether this 'cloak of privacy' is justifiable.

Given the potential difficulties with the taping of sessions, careful consideration of practicalities and discussion of anxieties between supervisor and supervisee are best undertaken before introducing them in the work. The complexity of the process is probably best not underestimated, and it is preferable to prepare carefully rather than introduce taping hastily and be deterred by encountered difficulties.

Advantages of taping

In spite of the qualifiers above, tape recording can be highly beneficial in supervision and in therapy and may offer particular advantages over other media.

1   *Provides the opportunity for detailed review and multiple perspectives.* The potential for use in review by the client or the therapist may facilitate the

consolidation of different or new meanings or help to pick out developments made by the client or therapist over time. When tapes are reviewed
by the client, therapist and supervisor, these multiple perspectives can
generate an increased range of options for intervention and change.

2 *Removing doubts about competence.* For supervisees in pre-qualification
training, reaching the end of training rarely serves to eliminate doubts
about competence. Rather than encouraging confidence in the role, the
process of training can serve seriously to undermine it (Scaife, 1995).
Fear of being found out and of charlatanism are widespread even some
years into practice. As expressed by Mahoney (1986: 169), 'I eventually
came to recognise that I was naively (and unconsciously) assuming that
there was actually an "underground" handbook of how to be helpful that
was secretly circulated among professional counsellors after their gradu-
ate rites of passage ... I slowly began to appreciate that my expert
clinical mentors were themselves operating according to abstract and
tacit "rules" rather than concrete and explicit guidelines.'

Those in training who reach the end of the course without ever having
been observed are particularly likely to be vulnerable to such feelings.
Having one's practice thoroughly scrutinised and evaluated as competent
is likely to be much more affirming in the long run.

3 *Providing an opportunity to participate and then observe.* During interpersonal interactions, a great deal of reaction and response takes place at
such a pace that only a fraction may be given attention. Subsequent
review enables people to slow down the process, give detailed consideration to their own recalled perceptions and to reconsider the meanings in
the light of the review. Taking the position of observer may shed new
light and lead to different ways of understanding the interactions. The
use of tapes offers such opportunities for both client and practitioner. It
may be particularly helpful for practitioners in training who are enabled
to look back on their earlier work in order to review evidence of progress.

4 *Enhanced empathy.* Contrary to the idea that the introduction of taping
may result in reduced empathy, it provides an opportunity for the practitioner to give full attention to the client without the need to make notes
as an *aide-mémoire*. The taped record enables the participants to have
confidence that the material will not be lost or forgotten.

5 *Increased accountability.* The use of tapes can act as a safeguard for
clients. Doubts about how to proceed can be explored with colleagues in
the light of firsthand data. Therapists working in the knowledge that
their practice is open to direct scrutiny are less likely to find themselves
drawn into situations against their better judgement that might otherwise
be evoked by the potentially profound psychological difficulties that may
have been brought into the work with the client. The openness of practice
that is an automatic adjunct of the use of tapes thus acts as a safeguard
for both client and practitioner.

6   *Myths and mystery*. For people learning the skills of the helping professions who do not have an opportunity to observe or be observed, the process of therapy can be perceived as shrouded in mystery and uncertainty. The process of reviewing tapes enables debate, clarification and questioning, thus grounding the work in an applied knowledge base rather than its being seen as a magical and mysterious skill.

7   *Increases options for research and evaluation*. The use of tapes is probably more widespread where the process and outcome of therapy are being researched. Taped data allows for the possibility of detailed micro-analysis which expands the evidence base of professional practice.

8   *As an adjunct to therapy*. In some approaches to therapy, tapes can serve a useful role in the work with the client. For example, tapes can be given to clients to facilitate homework tasks in cognitive therapy. Whilst more controversial, feelings towards tapes as objects of projection can be explored in psychodynamic approaches.

Introducing taping to the client

Requesting consent to tape is one amongst a number of issues that are best introduced early in the first session although they may be revisited later. There is a balance to be struck between encouraging the client to understand the usefulness of such a method, whilst not offering such a laborious explanation so as to appear coercive and disengaging. Obtaining genuine informed consent is as tricky with this issue as with others such as the explanation of the limits of confidentiality. Beginners in the use of tapes may find it helpful to write out and rehearse an introduction until they feel at ease. It may also be helpful to have obtained the reactions of colleagues to a role-played introduction. Clients are likely to range from those who wish to consider such a request and its implications carefully, to those whose story cannot wait to be told. When the therapist feels comfortable with taping and relaxed about the introduction, the client may be helped to feel the same. The introduction can be repeated at a later stage should the therapist be unsure whether the client has understood the full implications of taping, and written consent gives a clearer indication of agreement from the client.

An example of a script for introducing taping to clients might read thus:

'In my work I have found it helpful to tape-record the sessions as a matter of course. This allows me to give you my full attention without worrying that I may forget something, and it helps me and my supervisor to make sure that you are getting the best possible service. If you are agreeable to taping, I will ensure that the tapes are kept confidential to you, me and my supervisor. If you wish, you may prefer to take the tape home yourself at the end of the session and if you are not happy for it to be kept then you can wipe it yourself. Later in our meeting today, when you have had more time to think about it, I will ask if you will sign a consent form. This is entirely your choice and I will be happy to work with you either way. Would you like to ask any questions now before we begin?'

In introducing taping it is easy to focus on the usefulness of the tape to the therapist, but the client may feel more positive if the introduction includes an explanation of how the taping will be of help to the client. This can be by helping the therapist to give full attention to the client during the session, and enabling review and reflection between sessions in order to produce more ideas that could be helpful to the client. Where the tapes are to be used in supervision this can also be presented to the client as a safeguard to the work, drawing on the ideas of the supervisor in addition to the therapist. Tapes may also be offered to the client for self-review. The following is an extract from a tape of a client reflecting on her review of recordings made earlier in the therapy (C. = client, Th. = therapist):

C.   I've listened to these tapes.
Th. Right.
C.   And this helped me as well. I listened to it over the weekend and made some notes and things. It was quite . . . quite a surprise to me hearing it all.
Th. What bit was surprising?
C.   Well, firstly, hearing myself on the tape I was surprised. My first thoughts were that if I didn't know this was me then I would think that this was an intelligent, friendly, lively person on there, and that's not the impression that I had I was giving.
Th. Right – what impression did you think you were giving?
C.   I thought I was dithering, stuttering and mumbling [laughs]. I'd think, 'Oh she sounds quite nice', and thinking that I sounded nice was quite a boost for me.
Th. Yeah.
C.   You know, if I can like it if it's someone else then I can like it if it's me.

Obtaining consent

In the early days of taping, clients were found generally to exhibit little resistance to the method as they moved beyond the first few sessions (Barnes and Pilowsky, 1969; Haggard, Hiken and Isaacs, 1965). Today, the climate has changed and people may be generally less trustful of professionals. The informed consent of the client to taping is essential, both in regard to paying due respect to the client's wishes and in order to protect the professional. As a first step it is often helpful to have enclosed written information with an appointment letter. The tone of this information might be to raise awareness of the possibility of taping rather than to appear coercive. The usefulness of written information may be limited by the client's disability, stage of development or familiarity with the language. At least it increases the chance that the client's expectations about the session will include the possibility of a recording being made.

If the introduction to the session proceeds in such a way that taping is presented as a normal feature of the work this can help the client to feel confident in its value. The consent form can be introduced, the session proceed, and the form be reintroduced at the end of the session when the client knows what has transpired. At this stage clients may be encouraged to give fuller consideration to how they feel about the tape and it needs to be made clear that withholding consent will in no way adversely affect the subsequent service provided. If consent is withheld, clients may be given the tape to wipe for themselves in order to have confidence that the record is expunged.

Where the session involves more than one client, consent should be obtained from all, and this will include children to the extent that they are developmentally able to understand the decision. Special care is needed with clients whose consent may be ambiguous. This is particularly the case for clients with learning disabilities whose compliance may be almost automatic, and for those who have reason to show paranoia.

Written consent

Written consent offers the best safeguards for clients and practitioners since both will then have a clear record of what has been agreed and of the undertakings of the therapist regarding confidentiality. Separate paragraphs should identify the purposes for which recordings may be used, and the approach that will be taken to storage and destruction of the recording. Clients should be able to withdraw consent at a later stage and would be advised to put this in writing. Consent forms need to be adapted to suit the clients' capacity to understand and according to their needs. A sample consent form adapted from that used by the Charles Burns Clinic in Birmingham, UK is reproduced in Appendix 3.

Tapes in supervision: issues

Once tapes have been made with the consent of the client, agreement needs to be reached between supervisor and supervisee as to how these may be used in supervision. The supervisee's work is potentially much more exposed than in reported work, with feelings of vulnerability and defensiveness likely unless a context of trust and safety has been established in the supervisory relationship. Neufeldt, Karno and Nelson (1996) identified the willingness to experience vulnerability as an essential quality necessary to the reflective process involved in the use of tapes in supervision. It may be helpful for the supervisor also to be taping her or his therapy practice, thus providing a model of willingness to experience vulnerability for the supervisee.

Bauman (1972) suggested that supervisees may claim that they are less effective when they are taped, and that any 'mistakes' are dismissed as atypical behaviours that do not need to be examined. Dodge (1982) suggested that defensive strategies include intellectualisation, rationalisation and discussion of tangential issues. Liddle (1986) suggests that when supervisees object to recording sessions because clients would find this too threatening or disruptive that what is at issue is the resistance of the supervisee. This view should be balanced against that of Aveline (1997), that some clients may experience being taped as aversive or abusive. It may be helpful for the supervisor and supervisee to identify in advance how resistance to taping might be shown and, in the event, how the supervisor might best approach this. Stoltenberg, McNeill and Delworth (1998) describe a beginning trainee whose reasons for being unable to bring a tape to supervision included forgetting to turn on the machine, poor-quality tapes, and the client's reluctance to give permission. They argue that to confront, interpret and process the dynamics around the supervisee's reluctance would only serve to exacerbate the already high levels of anxiety. Instead they suggest that the supervisor provide a clear, cogent rationale regarding taping in relation to client welfare, and issue a simple directive to have a tape ready for the following week.

Introducing taping to the supervisee

Supervisees themselves may introduce taping as a preferred medium of supervision to the supervisor. They may have used tapes in supervision previously and found them helpful to learning. In such a case, the supervisor might explore how the tapes have been used previously and discuss whether it is feasible or helpful to replicate this process or whether to try something new.

More typically, it is likely to be the supervisor who introduces the idea of taping to the supervisee. It is worth taking some time over discussion of the advantages and disadvantages of taping and to explore any preconceptions and anxieties expressed by the supervisee. Alternative review methods may be explored and the supervisor may initially review a tape of her or his own work in order to show how the process works.

When to introduce taping

It is often helpful to discuss with reluctant supervisees when, rather than if, they wish to experience taped or live observation of their work. Practitioners are unlikely to be able successfully to avoid experiencing this at some stage, and the further on in their career the more they may feel the pressure to appear 'expert'. In pre-registration supervision, trainee practitioners are usually persuaded that the earlier in their training that they practice with the

use of tapes, the less they might be expected to produce an exemplary performance. It is similarly useful to introduce taping to clients in the first session rather than once the therapy has been established. Taping is then a
natural concomitant of therapy or supervision rather than something
special – such specialness being more likely to induce feelings of vulnerability.
Initially supervisees may prefer to review their own tapes as a private exercise,
with their use in supervision programmed for a few weeks later when the
supervisee has had time to adjust to the presence of the machine in the
therapy. To start with it is probably helpful if the focus of supervision is
clearly on the client and understanding of the issues brought by the client
rather than on the performance of the supervisee. Both focuses can facilitate
learning.

Tapes may be used either in individual or group supervision, the latter
involving additional considerations regarding the type of group that is operating and the way in which group members might respond to the presentation
of tapes by individual members. These matters would be discussed during the
contracting process in which group 'rules' are established. The reader is
referred to Chapter 6 for a fuller discussion of issues associated with the
establishment and running of groups. The following sections explore the use
of tapes in individual supervision. The considerations are also applicable to
the use of tapes in groups.

Whole tape, part tape

The use of whole tapes in supervision offers some perspectives on the work
that cannot otherwise be obtained. The supervisor and supervisee can gauge
the whole session, including how it begins and ends. An overall impression as
to the flow and changes of direction, repeating patterns and themes, openings
and closing down can be obtained and discussed in the supervision. Supervisees can be sure that the entirety of their work has been indirectly observed
and might thus be more reassured as to their clinical competence.

On the other hand, listening to and discussing an entire tape in supervision
could be infinitely time-consuming. It is possible to spend an hour of supervision discussing a five-minute extract, and it is unlikely that supervisors will
be able to review whole tapes as a matter of course. During the period of
a contract of supervision or over the duration of a training placement, the
supervisor and supervisee might discuss one or two tapes in their entirety
whilst there may also be sessions focusing on extracts. Sometimes supervisors
may listen to an entire session outside supervision and then give written or
verbal comments, perhaps focusing on issues that have been identified as
points for development in advance.

Extracts may be selected in several ways. Supervisees might review tapes in
preparation for supervision, selecting particular extracts to illustrate their
development and skills in the role, or selecting points at which they felt

confused or dissatisfied with the process, seeking ideas and clarification in discussion with the supervisor. Random extracts might be reviewed, in which case seemingly insignificant moments in the work might be found to have alternative meanings. Such snapshots might also offer an overview of the process of the session.

Agreement might be reached that either party may stop the tape at any point in the replay – either to ask questions, offer interpretations, make alternative suggestions or give feedback. It is probably helpful if supervisor and supervisee agree in advance of reviewing a tape what the intent of the review is, what the review will focus on – for example, what the supervisee did, thought or felt; what the client did, thought or felt; how the supervisee was using theory or techniques to address the needs of the client; or the non-specifics of the client–therapist relationship and how the client might be experiencing the session. Multiple possibilities exist. Narrowing the focus can be experienced as less exposing since only certain aspects of the work are subject to scrutiny.

Neufeldt (1999) describes a particular method for reviewing extracts of tapes, the intention of which is to encourage supervisees to develop skills in reflecting on therapeutic process during the therapy session. For this purpose, the tape is reviewed immediately the therapy session ends in order to make the experience more immediate. The supervisee is asked to select the point in the tape at which the most puzzling interaction took place. After *each* therapist intervention the therapist is asked to describe her or his experiences *during that time*. This should include thoughts, feelings and intentions. The aim is to encourage supervisees simultaneously to attend to their own experiences and the actions of the clients whilst they are conducting the therapy.

Control of focus and feedback

The approach to the use of tapes in supervision needs to be negotiated between supervisor and supervisee. Control of the focus and feedback may be the task of either party or shared between them. In order to construct a climate of openness and safety, the review of tapes early in the relationship might be assisted by the control of the tape, the focus of the supervision and any feedback remaining exclusively within the control of the supervisee. Such an approach also pays homage to the idea that learning builds upon what the supervisee already knows. Suggestions from the supervisor might be too distant from this to be of use to the supervisee.

In cases where control of the review of tapes does lie with the supervisee, preparation for supervision could entail advance selection of a focus for the session – for example, on identifying examples of transference, responding to silences, making meaning of the client's non-verbal cues, and so on. Early on, a focus exclusively on the client might reduce supervisees' anxieties about their performance. Supervisees could also list issues on which they would appreciate feedback – 'Do you think that I would have been better to follow the client here or to introduce my own idea?' Such a process is likely to minimise surprises or shocks, although it might entail the supervisor withholding a plethora of ideas and comments. These could be noted for introduction at a later stage of supervisee development. However, supervisors managing to hold onto their own ideas in order better to help supervisees to explore their own is one of the more difficult skills of supervision.

One well-researched method for reviewing tapes that allows the supervisee to remain in control of the review process is that of Interpersonal Process Recall (IPR), which has been developed over a period of approximately 35 years by Kagan and his associates (Kagan, Krathwohl and Miller, 1963; Elliott, 1986; Bernard, 1989; Kagan-Klein and Kagan, 1997).

Interpersonal Process Recall

IPR was developed originally as a method by which people could review the interpersonal processes taking place between themselves and others. It arose when Kagan noticed that in the review of interpersonal interchanges that had taken place earlier, people were able to identify highly detailed reactions and gain insights into the communication that were not available to them during the initial interchange. This enabled them to learn more about their own reactions and also about the effects that they might be having on others.

He developed a method in which people are helped to identify their detailed reactions through the questioning of an enquirer. The role of the enquirer is precisely defined and a key feature is that enquirers do not attempt to make explicit meaning of the interchange themselves, but concentrate entirely on helping the reviewer or 'recaller' to explicate her or his own understandings. When used in supervision it can be helpful for the enquirer not to view the tape so as not to be distracted by her or his own hypotheses. The method aims to reduce the supervisee's fear of instruction and critical attack from the supervisor by putting the process explicitly in the control of the supervisee, and by encouraging the supervisor to avoid explanation, interpretation and advice (Clarke, 1997).

One of the key features of the IPR approach involves the maintenance of a separation of time-frame from the original interchange. The inquirer helps the recaller to stay focused on the there and then of the tape and not on the here and now. This is viewed as important in that it protects recallers from experiencing feelings of vulnerability or threat during the recall. They are recalling what they *did* experience – 'I may not look it but I was frightened to death' – and not what is currently being experienced. The recaller is in complete control of the playing of the tape. The recaller sets the tape running and may stop it at any point when interested to explore an aspect of the interchange. Exploration continues until the recaller wishes to move on, at which point the tape is run until the next halt brought about by the recaller. The capability that everyone has of holding vast amounts of knowledge about interpersonal processes 'on standby' is at the heart of the IPR method of enquiry. Recallers are regarded in IPR as the ultimate experts on their inner-most thoughts and feelings. The enquirer is not trying to make sense of the session being recalled. The role is to help the *recaller* to make sense of the interaction.

The enquirer's responsibility is to ask a series of open-ended questions that respond sensitively to the recaller with a view to creating freedom and open-ness of exploration. These questions are not leading or Socratic in style. Some types of questions are listed below:

Self-exploration
What thoughts were going through your mind at the time?
Any cautions on your part?
How were you feeling then?
If that sensation had a voice, what would it say?

Own behaviour
Anything you were not saying?
What keeps you from saying that?
Was there anything that got in the way of what you wanted to say or do?
What did you like about what was happening?

Perception of other
What did you think the other person was feeling?
What did you want the other person to think or feel?
How do you think the other person experienced you?
Is there anything about the client's age, sex, appearance that you were react-ing to?

Hopes and intentions
What did you want to happen next?
What effect did you want that to have on the other person?
Where did you want to end up?

Previous patterns
Have you found yourself feeling like this before?
Did you find yourself thinking about other people in your life?
What pictures or memories went through your mind?

The value of IPR in supervision and training is based on the assumption that therapists always have a wealth of information that they fail to acknow-ledge or use productively, and that sessions devoted to uncovering these clinically important impressions and making them explicit in language help supervisees to become aware of messages that they denied, ignored or had previously not perceived. The process is viewed as helping people to improve

their understanding of interpersonal processes. This might include the identification and acknowledgement of their previously unverbalised fears and
vulnerabilities in human interaction. It is Kagan's (1984) view that these
include, 'The other person will hurt me', 'I will hurt the other person', 'The
other person will engulf me', and 'I will engulf the other person'. IPR
involves a content-free enquiry that can be used to build confidence.

Another important feature of the method is that a sense of personal
responsibility for one's own behaviour is fostered in the supervisee. The
motivation to change may then be intrinsic rather than in the nature of
'jumping through hoops'. Given the chance, people are often more critical of
themselves than others would be, and criticising oneself tends not to produce
defensive reactions.

Kagan and his associates went on from their original studies of recall with
individuals to explore the idea of mutual recall in which the enquirer meets
with client and therapist who both participate in the recall. Therapist and
client each share their thoughts and feelings about a past session, paying
particular attention to how they experienced each other. This is viewed as
helping clients and therapists to become better able to talk about their experiences of each other in the present. Mutual recall is regarded as requiring self-
awareness, sensitivity to the other person and courage, but is highly effective
in producing learning. Students who have been trained in IPR appear to show
accelerated learning months after the process has been completed (Boltuch,
1975). Research suggests that client evaluation of counsellors trained in IPR
is more favourable than their evaluations of traditionally supervised counsellors (Kagan and Krathwohl, 1967). IPR is a relatively non-threatening way of
using tapes in supervision that has been adapted successfully to a range of
different contexts. It is probably a good starting method for those who wish
to use tapes to help their professional development. The skills of the enquirer
should not be underestimated, particularly as the role requires the focus to be
entirely on the thoughts and feelings of the recaller and not on those of the
supervisor.

Other methods of using recordings in supervision

The development of recording technology has made possible a range of
options for the use of tapes in supervision. These developments have accompanied the introduction of distance learning for supervisees who live a long
way from an educational establishment and for those who live in rural areas.
Miller and Crago (1989) have found audiotapes to be a useful source of
information regarding the practice of isolated therapists who live in remote
areas of Australia. Videoconferencing is also being used (Troster, Paolo,
Glatt, Hubble and Koller, 1995), and it is likely that this will develop further
and rapidly in the context of the Internet.

The use of tapes in supervision and training has a relatively short history in the helping professions, its use first being reported by Rogers (1942) and Covner (1942), but the advantages identified by Rogers continue to be of relevance today:

- Clinical trainees tended to be more directive in their interviews than they had supposed and this was only identified when they had direct access to the content of their sessions.
- Recordings have a remarkable capacity to reveal resistances, conflicts and blocks that can occur in a session.
- Recordings provide information about areas for supervisee development, in addition to abilities and strengths.

Summary

The use of tapes in supervision provides the opportunity for careful analysis of a therapist's work and can contribute to safeguarding the welfare of clients. The introduction of tapes benefits from careful consideration and planning since there are many factors to be taken into consideration, both regarding their use with clients and in supervision. Discussion regarding how tapes might be used in supervision is appropriate material for the contracting process when a new supervisory relationship is proposed.

Chapter 9

Live supervision and observation

Particularly in training contexts, supervisors and supervisees readily acknowledge the theoretical advantages of seeing each other's work. For neophyte therapists, observation of the supervisor offers the opportunity to emulate behaviours and styles that they have witnessed rather than those of which they have merely heard or read. This may involve observation of a model performance but might also allow the supervisee to observe the continuing struggles encountered by even the experienced practitioner. For example, to observe the supervisor struggling to bring a session to a conclusion may enhance supervisees' views of their own performance. Learners may benefit from observation of these differing performances at different stages in their training.

For supervisors to observe or participate live in sessions led by supervisees presents a unique opportunity to obtain the maximum information upon which to base interventions towards the goals of supervision. Even recordings omit information such as the 'feel' of the emotional climate of the session. Live supervision also offers additional safeguards to clients (Levine and Tilker, 1974), as the supervisor can take the opportunity to intervene during the session rather than after the moment has passed. Levine and Tilker suggest that this approach to supervision is particularly appropriate early in training when extensive guidance may be indicated. However, caution needs to be exercised regarding supervisor interventions made during a session lest supervisees experience themselves as undermined in front of the client.

Whilst most practitioners acknowledge the theoretical importance of the supervisor and supervisee working alongside each other, opportunities to work in this way are taken less often than might be expected. Live supervision is encountered most frequently in family work where there is a rationale for ongoing live supervision encapsulated within the theory and methodology. Its limited use in other psychological therapies may emanate from the perpetuation of approaches to supervision which supervisors encountered in their own training, high levels of anxiety about being 'found out' as inadequate exponents of the work, arguments regarding the costs of more than a single worker being present in a session with a client, and concern regarding client discomfort (for example if outnumbered by the therapists). In the latter instance, it is the view of some authors that two or more therapists working together with one client is inappropriate (Jones, 1996).

A factor to be considered in opting for live supervision is the effect on anxiety levels of both supervisor and supervisee. Liddle, Breunlin and Schwartz (1988) suggest that supervisees tend to feel positive about the promise of close attention to and feedback about their clinical work but fearful of the attendant exposure of their clinical skills. Costa (1994) suggests a variety of strategies by which anxiety can be reduced; these include negotiating a clear contract for supervision, matching the method to the supervisee's developmental stage, directly addressing anxiety and fear, developing a collaborative supervisory attitude, creating a positive evaluative focus and encouraging independence. Further ideas are offered later in this chapter.

Live supervision may take place with all parties in the same room or by using a one-way screen which lends itself to one or more supervisors participating.

What can go wrong with two or more people working together?

In my own experience, several pitfalls present themselves when working live with a colleague in the room.

Probably the most commonly adopted arrangement is some kind of co-work. When the pair shares a common method and approach to the work it may be possible spontaneously to interview together. There is a risk, however, of 'de-consulting' to the other party, leading to feelings of frustration in the workers and a meandering of direction in the therapy. The following is an extract from supervision in which the supervisee takes her difficulties in joint work with a colleague to her supervisor (*S.* = supervisee, *Th.* = therapist):

> Work is being carried out with a couple, Chris and Mary. Mary was sexually abused in childhood and Chris has been imprisoned in the past for sexual offences against children. He is considered by Social Services to be a potential risk to Mary's children. The work with the couple is aimed at establishing whether the adults can keep the children safe were they to live together.

> *S.*   When you say you, when you say you do this jointly with the probation officer, are you both sitting in the room together?
> *Th.* Yes.
> *S.*   And who does the work, or how do you allocate that?
> *Th.* Well this is an issue I think, because we have discussions about that and I've made it clear that my way of working is to do this, is to go through the layers that are necessary, but I don't think that that's his way of working. I think he normally operates more on a how

things are now level rather than what used to happen in one's childhood or something.

S.   So layers for you are historical layers rather than emotional, or layers of belief or . . .

Th.   They're emotional as well, that's right, all those things. But I feel that we . . . Although I talk with the probation officer about what I'm intending to do and we agree it, when it actually comes to the session I don't feel that we're working in the same direction because he'll ask questions about other things that are current and I'll be asking questions about . . .

S.   So there's a struggle for control of the sessions? And how do you think Chris responds to that?

Th.   [Laughs] Well, I'm sure he'd much rather stay with the probation officer's agenda than with mine. Mary would go along with my agenda.

In this example the work might have been enhanced by the prior development of a greater consensus about the aims of the work, how to achieve them, and a discussion of the roles of the two workers.

Another potential problem in working live in the room, particularly when one member of the pair is in training and the other is more experienced, is the tendency either for the learner to bow to the superior knowledge of the supervisor or for the supervisor to intervene excessively, leading to the supervisee feeling undermined. One of the most difficult tasks for the supervisor in such circumstances is to help supervisees to carry out the work in their own way, rather than trying to wrestle the learner into carrying out the work in the way that would be adopted by the supervisor. This often involves supervisors in the experience of 'sitting on their hands' and requires the development of a mind-set which differs from that of being the principal therapist. The dilemma is particularly acute for the supervisor who has responsibility for the clinical work and observes what he or she construes as missed opportunities, blind alleys or even explicit errors. On the other hand, there is plenty of pedagogic potential in these for the supervisee, providing the welfare of the client is not compromised.

Before embarking on work with a colleague in the room, it is advisable to engage in a discussion in which the approach to working together is thoroughly explored, negotiated and agreed. It may not be necessary for the supervisor and supervisee to work in the same therapeutic model if the role of the supervisor is agreed as that of helping the other to carry out the work in the way that he or she wishes. What needs to be agreed is who will introduce the session, who will speak to the client, how the two workers will communicate with each other, how the process will be respectful to all parties, where the responsibility for the session lies and so on. A number of options are possible.

Supervisor and supervisee in the room together

Co-working

In instances where there is an agreed and tested commonality of approach to the work, and each party has the confidence and role-relationship which confer equivalence of status, it is likely to be possible successfully to carry out joint work without risk of 'de-consulting' to each other as outlined in the example above. Co-working might also turn out to be satisfactory under less stringent conditions. In this approach, both parties ask questions, make reflections and so on, probably meeting to plan the session and to reflect on what transpired during it both before and after the meeting with the client.

Observing role of one party

For beginners, the role of observer can be very freeing and may be preferable to co-work. In this condition, it is agreed that the observer does not actively contribute during the session. The observation may take place without constraint or the observer may be delegated a particular task – for example, to make contemporaneous process notes of the session, to focus on the non-verbal responses of the client, to notice therapeutic process and patterns, or to note her or his own feelings and thoughts as the session progresses. When the observer is the supervisee, the particular task negotiated can relate to current learning needs. The observer might focus on the client, on the therapist or on the therapeutic process, and might note down questions about the progress of the session to be addressed later in supervision. The agreement to undertake a specific task lessens the risks of boredom and of superficial unfocused gazing that can accompany an apparently passive role.

Where it is the supervisor who observes and makes notes, it may be particularly helpful to agree a focus for the supervision in advance. Notes can be descriptive (for example about the physical layout of the room and the content of the session); evaluative of the work or of the client's presentation; and/or enquiring, inviting the supervisee to reflect further on an episode in the session. Particularly in the supervision of trainees the expectation that the supervisor will take an evaluative position can dominate in the mind of the supervisee. The following example of notes made by a supervisor of a family therapy session illustrates how this expectation can be challenged by an orientation to note-making that is aimed at stimulating the thinking of the supervisee. (The numbers in the left column refer to the time.):

15.33   Family opens with tales of improvement and the episode which generated the difference.
15.35   The question, 'Who does she most take after?' follows the mother's story in a particular way. What is the over-arching purpose to the telling of the story as well as the content of the story itself?

15.39   You change to the mother's partner at this point. What was your thinking at this point? And on reflection?

15.45   You make a summary here which I would describe as a second-order statement which clarified a significant change.

The final note above offers a judgement, but as a personal view.

Where an observational role is agreed, it is enormously helpful if the learner can first experience the role of observer rather than observed. This establishes the explicit and implicit rules regarding the role of the observer and is likely to be experienced as less threatening than being observed by the supervisor. Following an observation, the supervisor might model non-defensive responses to the supervisee's questions, might illustrate how to invite feedback, and so on.

For neophyte supervisors who may never themselves have been observed during their own training, the presence of an observing supervisee might be experienced as nerve-racking, and likely to affect the approach to the work undertaken by the supervisor. Some defensive tactics for dealing with this include only allowing observation of initial sessions or particularly structured assessments. Even those experienced at being observed can find themselves inexplicably nervous in the presence of an unfamiliar observer, especially where fantasies about perceived competence or incompetence of self and other abound. In this case, other methods of working together which involve both parties might be more suitable, or, alternatively, a pre-session discussion in which the supervisor reveals her or his fantasies might evoke a more comfortable scenario. A clearly prescribed role for the observer which focuses specifically on the client rather than on the supervisor might also help.

Once the supervisee has experienced the role of observer and knows what to expect, a reversal of roles is likely to be less anxiety provoking. It is probably helpful if the supervisee feels in control both of the session and of any ensuing discussion and feedback. Careful planning of the session and discussion of contingency plans may also help. Occasionally the supervisee encounters a position of 'stuckness' in a session which can be particularly distressing in the presence of an observer. One way round this is to agree in advance that in such an instance the supervisee may introduce a break in the session in which the supervisory dyad leaves the room for a mid-session consultation. During this period it is explained to clients that they are free to take a break themselves, either remaining in the room or returning to a reception area. In this event, it is important that the client is led to expect that such a break may be scheduled by an explanation given in the introduction to the session. It is likely to be seen as logical and helpful by the client that the supervisee may wish to take advice from the supervisor during, rather than between, sessions. As in any such explanation, it is helpful for the therapists to include an explanation of the usefulness of the process for the client.

Joint participation, different roles

Under conditions in which supervisee and supervisor are relatively unfamiliar with each other and without a clearly shared and agreed approach to the work, the most successful way of working jointly may be for each party to contribute to the session, but with clearly delineated roles.

The specificity of roles would be agreed through discussion in advance. An adjunct to this option is to role-play the agreed relationship process with a third colleague in order to ensure that both parties feel relatively comfortable working together in the way proposed. It is usually helpful that one person be designated as the leader of the session. It is this person who is responsible for participative management of the session, who makes the introductions and describes the approach to joint working to the client. This person also asks any questions and speaks directly to the client. It might be agreed that the other party may also speak to the client, but in my experience this can be confusing and my own preference is that the non-leader speaks only to the leader but in the presence of the client who sees and hears the communication between the two workers. Clients in such an arrangement frequently attempt to involve the non-leader through eye contact and social reference, as would usually be the case in a social interaction. The non-leader can respond to this by eye-reference to the leader and avoiding gaze. This helps all parties to be clear about the roles and responsibilities within this arrangement.

In this arrangement the leader invites the other therapist to contribute at intervals during the session. It is best if the first invitation takes place early in the session in order to establish the pattern. The non-leader may be invited to share her or his ideas evoked during the session so far or to suggest questions that the leader may wish to ask. In such cases it is often helpful to the leader if the rationale behind the question is included in the communication. It is agreed that whilst the client hears and may respond spontaneously to the contribution of the non-leader, it is at the discretion of the leader whether to follow up the contribution or to continue along a different path of her or his own determination. In this approach there is clarity about the control of the session lying with the leading therapist. The advantages of this approach are clarity regarding who is managing the session; little risk of one party feeling undermined by the other; the ideas of both parties being transparent to the therapists and client; conveying of mutual respect and open participation; and active involvement of both supervisor and supervisee.

The contributions of the non-leader benefit from being tentative, respectful to the client and the leader, and focused on the material brought by the client rather than on feedback to the leader. Feedback of the latter kind may be offered later by arrangement but not undertaken in front of the client. Such contributions often helpfully begin with 'I noticed that . . .', 'I was wondering if . . .', 'When that happened I felt like . . .'

Responsibility for closing the session also lies with the leader. It is important that the non-leader is invited to make contributions at intervals with sufficient frequency that the comments are timely, but not so often as to effectively represent a handing over of control of the session. Offerings from the non-leader should be brief and contain only that number of ideas that could reasonably be taken on board by the leader and/or the client at one go. It should be agreeable that the non-leader may not have a comment to offer at times, in which case the leader progresses the session as he or she sees fit. This is particularly important when the non-leader is the learner. The pair may also agree that the non-leader may interrupt the session with an idea if to withhold it becomes unbearable.

Additional advantages of this approach lie in its flexibility, the safeguarding of the welfare of the client since the supervisor is able to intervene respectfully during the work, and the availability of ideas to supervisees should they experience 'stuckness' in the session. (On respectful approaches to the work also see Hoffman, 1991; Anderson, 1997.)

As in other forms of live working, offering supervisees an initial opportunity to take the role of non-leader provides a relatively safe context in which to become familiar with the approach. It also provides an active role in which they can make a valuable contribution to the work without taking undue responsibility. Role reversal can be agreed once learners indicate that they have sufficient confidence to proceed. Further details of this approach to live supervision may be found in Smith and Kingston (1980) and Kingston and Smith (1983).

Shared leadership

Sometimes a structured form of shared leadership can be very helpful. An example might be where two workers of equivalent status are both reluctant to be the first to adopt the leadership role. Whilst the 'rules' of interaction described above might be applied, it could be agreed that the leadership role switches from one party to the other half way through the session. This might help the pair to overcome the initial hurdle with regard to feelings of vulnerability and exposure. Such an approach also allows both parties to use their ideas and to follow different directions where this seems helpful.

Outnumbering the client

Whilst it is acknowledged that the presence of two workers is likely to influence the dynamics of the relationship, the above methods have been used successfully by the author in work with individual clients. It has been possible to approximate the level of intimacy that is achievable with one client and one therapist, particularly when the method has been introduced at the first session and continued. Once familiar with the approach, additional possibilities reveal themselves. The therapist is less likely to be drawn into a pattern of relating that is counter-productive as there is always another present who can take more of an observer perspective. The work tends to feel safe as it is conducted in the presence of another, and an experience of shared responsibility can develop which is less frightening and distressing than lone exposure to the 'narcissistic insults' that can arise in the work (Mollon, 1989).

On the other hand, the client may feel outnumbered and less able to exert influence in the therapeutic relationship than in a one-to-one setting. This may be a hindrance, though in certain work it may be helpful; it is important to address the effects on the client of two workers together both through discussion in the supervisory pairing and explicitly with the client. Clients may experience the approach as particularly respectful and attentive to their needs, or as socially obtuse and uncomfortable. As in all therapeutic work, the needs of the client and the usefulness of the approach adopted should be kept under review.

Live supervision outside the room

One-to-one supervision

Live supervision with the supervisor outside the room can be implemented where a one-way screen or video-link is available. Typically, when such technology is available, supervision is undertaken by a team. But the arrangement is also suitable for one-to-one supervision. Berger and Dammann (1982) suggest that two effects result from the supervisor being outside the room in which the therapy is taking place. Firstly, the supervisor may more readily notice interaction patterns, being more in the role of observer than participant. When these observations are conveyed to supervisees, they may experience a sense of feeling stupid that they have not noticed these patterns themselves. Berger and Dammann suggest that supervisors should prepare supervisees for this experience. Secondly, the supervisor may not experience the full intensity of the client's affect and the supervisee may feel that the supervisor does not adequately understand the client and the process in the room. In order to take account of this issue it is proposed that contributions from the supervisor should be regarded as advisory rather than mandatory.

Research on supervision employing a one-way screen suggests that supervisees can experience high levels of vulnerability and embarrassment in anticipation of, and when first using, the approach (Gershenson and Cohen, 1978; Wong, 1997). However, they report that this initial stage is usually short-lived and is rapidly replaced by a stage in which the supervisor is perceived as a supporter rather than a critic. Feelings of vulnerability in the initial stages can be addressed by introducing the method in the manner outlined earlier in this chapter.

In a qualitative study of the views of supervisors and supervisees regarding helpful aspects of live supervision Wark (1995) identified three categories of supervisor behaviour: 'teaching/directing', 'supporting' and 'collaboration'. The 'teaching/directing' dimension was identified only by supervisors, whereas 'supporting' and 'collaboration' were identified as helpful by both groups. Collaboration was the most heavily supported dimension and was reflected in the supervisor attempting to proceed from the supervisee's position and attending to the needs of the supervisee. Wark suggests that the experience of collaboration can be fostered when, as Schwartz, Liddle and Breunlin (1988) suggest, the supervisor uses conscious restraint so that supervisees learn to monitor, trust and use their own skills.

Team supervision

Live supervision by a team of workers was developed in the context of family therapy. The rationale for the approach included the notion that multiple perspectives and hypotheses were preferable when working with a family group, the individuals within it being likely to hold different perspectives on and explanations for their difficulties. This way of working is intended to generate a range of options for change from which family members can select a route best suited to them.

Initial approaches to such team supervision tended to follow a pattern of pre-session consultation and discussion, an interview with the family by one team member, a mid-session discussion break in which the therapist consulted with the team, a second half session with the family, and a final break for consultation with the team followed by an intervention given to the family who then departed. Over time, variations in this approach have been developed with the intention of showing greater respect to clients, an increased sense of partnership with clients, and a reduction in the mystery of the team behind the screen (Hoffman, 1991; Anderson, 1987).

Team supervision can be applied when adopting other models of therapy and can be viewed as a sub-set of group supervision. This is discussed in Chapter 6, and there are many important issues to consider in establishing group supervision that are of relevance and will not be repeated here. Whilst the use of a team approach may be perceived as a costly use of resources, it can also be argued that therapy, supervision, teaching and training are being carried out simultaneously, thus representing an economy over time spent individually on these functions.

Many of the issues that apply to live supervision involving two workers are also relevant to live team work, but in addition sheer numbers can complicate matters further. Team involvement usually benefits from the use of technology in order not to overwhelm the client. The team may observe from behind a one-way screen or through a video-link, each of which needs to be introduced to the client. Clients are usually introduced to team members and invited to see the viewing arrangements. In my own work, clients sometimes prefer the team to sit in the room in which the interview is being conducted, and these preferences are always accommodated. Some authors have described the family, therapist, supervisor, learning team and video technician all sitting in the same room as a matter of course (Pegg and Manocchio, 1982).

Where the therapist and team occupy different rooms, communication between them may be effected through the use of an internal telephone, a 'bug in the ear' through which the team can speak to the therapist, or by knocking on the door to set up a consultation mid-session. It is important in such arrangements to agree how communication from the team will take place. This could be through one or several team members, and may involve a single idea or several ideas. The communication may be in the form of an instruction or an offer to the therapist. The therapist may offer the ideas to the client alongside and indistinguishably from her or his own, or specifically as those of the team. The effects of such interventions are various but often have the result of enhancing engagement between the clients and therapist who occupy the same space and who are both subject to the interventions of the team.

The use of communication devices such as the 'bug in the ear' and telephone presents its own challenge in the context of live supervision. These devices have typically been used in training contexts as a means whereby the supervisor can intervene whilst the therapy is in progress. Not only might this be regarded as of benefit to a client who is being seen by a practitioner-in-training, but there are potential advantages for the supervisee's learning. Byng-Hall (1982) regards the use of the earphone as offering a much quicker way of learning than by observing or reading about a technique and tentatively trying it out at a later date. Because the earphone can be experienced as highly intrusive, Byng-Hall recommends that it only be used once a trusting relationship between supervisor and supervisee has been established. He also suggests that the style of the supervisor's interventions should be adapted to suit the needs of individual supervisees, and that the device should initially be used in role-play until the supervisee is comfortable.

The earphone has been regarded as the most intrusive of the communication devices (Lowenstein, Reder and Clark, 1982) and the supervisee's sense of autonomy may be disrupted by the one-way communication inherent in its use. A number of difficulties can arise from this challenge to the supervisee's autonomy. For example, if the supervisor proposes a course of action that the supervisee was about to take, he or she is robbed of the opportunity to demonstrate this. On the other hand, if the supervisor proposes a plan of action contrary to the one in the supervisee's mind, the supervisee may be prevented from taking the initiative. Potential reactions to these situations include feelings of rage and/or giving up of responsibility and authority to the supervisor. Lowenstein, Reder and Clark suggest that a means of overcoming these difficulties is for the supervisee to be responsible for initiating consultation with colleagues behind the screen.

Mauzey and Erdman (1997) studied trainees' perceptions of phone-ins, focusing on how phone-ins are used, the effects on trainees, the trainees' views of the effects on clients, and the effects on the supervisor–supervisee relationship. They found that as supervisees became more familiar with the process their levels of anxiety diminished and they became more prepared to take risks and learn new skills. They argue that supervisors and supervisees benefit from preparatory training in the use of the earphone and that a good phone-in is characterised by the following features:

- Brief, clear, precise
- Less frequent, except in crisis situations
- Focused on welfare of client more than training
- Suggestive rather than directive
- Had clear instructions when a directive was necessary
- Was on track, rather than in a new direction
- Was supportive more often than challenging in initial training
- Considered current perspective of trainee
- Came from supervisor more often than from other team member
- Avoided strident tones
- Was timely
- Flowed from a trusting relationship with supervisor/team
- Helped supervisee with administrative control and tracking client
- Often came when the supervisee was confused
- Considered anxiety level of supervisee
- Considered developmental level of supervisee

More lengthy consultations with the team can take place behind the screen and be summarised to the client, or be presented by a 'reflecting team' in which the team comes into the room occupied by the client and therapist. In this arrangement team members discuss their ideas together whilst the therapist and client listen. At the end of the reflection the team retires to the other side of the screen and the client is free to respond to the team's ideas. In my service clients are offered a choice of whether the team talks behind the screen or in front of the client. Our experience over several years is that clients invariably request that the discussion take place in front of them. Team members to whom the reflecting team is a new concept have reported it as causing them to focus positively on the client rather than critically on the therapist, and as helping them to create views and opinions in positive frames to be offered to the client. When ideas are shared behind the screen a therapist might clumsily refer to a parent as 'over-protective'. When instead this is reflected to the parent it might be presented as, 'I was struck by what an affectionate and loving mum Charlotte has – she's very precious and so she's always kept very safe. I wondered if Charlotte some-times feels that she wants to learn more about how to keep herself safe.' This is the same idea offered more respectfully and with the 'blame-frame' removed.

In Anderson's (1987) description of the reflecting team, the family-interviewer system is not interrupted and the reflecting team members listen quietly behind the screen, each generating their own ideas. When the team members are invited to reflect on what they have heard, they take a speculative view. It is hypothesised that family members will select those ideas that fit and reject or ignore others. Following the reflection, the therapist invites the family members to comment on the team's reflections. In this approach the team does not offer feedback to the therapist and the therapist does not invite a discussion connected with her or his own learning needs. However, this is not precluded by the method, although it is likely to take place after the session with the family has ended.

Research by Young *et al.* (1989) and Smith, Yoshioka and Winton (1993) explored supervisee and client reactions to the reflecting team. The majority of both groups found the reflecting team to be either extremely or moderately helpful. Clients in particular reported valuing the reflecting team's ability to offer them multiple perspectives (i.e. two or more credible explanations of the same event).

Live team supervision offers options for intervention that are more difficult to reproduce under other conditions. For example, team members may offer different perspectives to the client in the form, 'My colleague Jan is of the view that . . . but John thinks . . .' This can help to separate the position from the person, thus facilitating a more reasoned debate. In addition there are options to introduce ideas based on differences of age, gender and ethnicity. Team members may also be able to offer particularly challenging ideas to the client with less risk to the therapeutic alliance than if they were to be offered by the therapist.

Establishing a supervisory team

The process of establishing a supervisory team and the range of options for models of leadership is explored in greater depth in Chapter 6. It is important that differences in hierarchy, status and professional discipline, including differential clinical and administrative responsibilities, be addressed. Methods for resolving differences of opinion are required, including who has the final say during a session when differences cannot be reconciled. Such discussions will need to be revisited from time to time and particularly at points of transition when members join or leave the group.

The focus of the supervising team can be on developing shared understandings of the client, but can also be on the developmental needs of its members. The giving and receiving of feedback or making constructive challenges usually needs careful handling and is discussed in Chapter 13. The structured group supervision model (Wilbur, Roberts-Wilbur, Hart, Morris and Betz, 1994) offers a process in which feedback is followed by a period of reflection and a response statement. In this process constructive challenge is a circular process in which all group members hear views of their contributions from team members.

Live team supervision offers the same advantages as other methods of live supervision, with the further complexities of the need to establish a functional staff group and the probable need for familiarity with the chosen technologies for communicating with the lead therapist. It is likely to continue being primarily of application in work with families or groups of clients, but can be adapted successfully in a training context in which more than one supervisee is working with a single supervisor.

Summary

This chapter has reviewed a range of different options for working with supervisor, supervisee and client in a session together. Such an approach would be the norm in many training contexts for other disciplines, including other kinds of 'people-work' such as medicine and teaching. It offers inherent safeguards for clients and practitioners, providing that there is careful attention to the way in which it is conducted.

Chapter 10

Creative approaches

This chapter is an acknowledgement of and tribute to the ideas of colleagues who over the years have developed strategies and techniques for approaching supervision that help to keep the process alive and fresh. My own profession of clinical psychology is dominated by talking as the medium of communication, and this can be a very effective way for people to connect, both in therapy and in supervision. This chapter describes techniques for using talk in different ways, and for using other materials and methods to widen the scope of the collaborative enquiry in supervision.

A purpose of using alternatives to talking is to try to access knowledge and understanding that a supervisee has about a client that is at the edge of awareness. We perceive others with a range of senses, and creative methods might help to make the most of our perceptions, gaining insight from a variety of creative conceptualisations, methods and frameworks. Such methods usually involve creating a representation of a client, problem or the problem system which is usually external to the supervisee and which can be the focus of study by each of the participants in supervision. Shared contemplation helps to create and sustain an atmosphere of collegiality.

Some of these methods can also be used when time is short since they can quickly reach the heart of the matter. For example, a supervisee might be asked to identify her or his dilemma with a client in a single sentence, to represent this pictorially or diagrammatically as quickly as possible, and then discuss the ideas that emerge from the representation. Consideration may then be given to any implications for the work and the whole episode may have taken no longer than fifteen minutes. Such a brief review of a piece of work may be appropriate when the majority of a supervision session has been given over to one client but the supervisee wishes to take away some tentative ideas about another. The use of brief periods of time also helps to create a boundary that keeps a clear focus on the needs of supervisees in respect of their work. Such brief reviews can also enable a wider perspective and clearer overview of the case.

Creative methods can also serve to lighten what is being experienced as an emotionally taxing and particularly heavy piece of work. Playfulness, so long as it is respectful to clients and their difficulties, not only can be enlightening in supervision but can also serve as a model for creative exercises that might be carried out by the supervisee with the client. The work can continue to be serious but the enjoyment of it may be enhanced.

The use of these different methods has greater or lesser appeal for supervisees, just as it will have for clients. Whilst encouragement to try something different is appropriate, particularly when the supervision or the work with the client seems stuck, alternative approaches to generating the material for supervision require the commitment of the supervisee to the process. Inskipp and Proctor (1995) regard the results of adopting creative methods as unpredictable because they can cut through surface presentation to something 'raw'. In this regard they caution against pressing supervisees to take part against their better judgement, and charge the supervisor with careful and respectful management of the process. They also propose that debriefing, a process of disengaging from the material explored, be undertaken as a way of closing down the exercise. This can be as simple as chatting or moving positions and relaxing but may involve more formal de-roling. It is also wise to ensure that there is time to reflect on what has been learned and its implications for the work with the client.

The creative methods described in the remainder of this chapter include visual and active methods of varying degrees of sophistication. Some require familiarity with and experience of a particular therapeutic approach. An example of this would be VanderMay and Peake's (1980) adaptation of psychodrama as a psychotherapy supervision technique. Other methods are less tied to a specific therapeutic model. Creative methods have in common the aim of providing new information based on images, actions and talking. As a result of this Williams (1995: 161) notes that, 'The tale trainees tell about therapy is the tale they spin; when they access the world of visual images, however, the tale spins them.'

Metaphor

It has been argued that an advantage of using metaphor is that it allows for the assembly of a complex array of information into a relatively simple conceptualisation or image (Rule, 1983). The image provides a springboard for developing further insights (Hampden-Turner, 1981). If the medium of the metaphor is visual, it offers possibilities of elaboration from the linearity of speech to a two- or three-dimensional representation (Arnheim, 1969: 232).

Metaphors often naturally occur to people and can be introduced in therapy by clients themselves. Using metaphors in supervision can lead to an exploration of the work through discussion and extension. In an example from my own practice, a child described his family as a battery with a negative and positive pole. This represented the relationship between his parents in which one was viewed as an optimist and the other as a pessimist. During the session I had asked what it was like to be in the middle of a live circuit. Later, in supervision the metaphor was extended to create an explanation about the marital relationship in that the polarity neither allowed the parents to separate nor to be intimate. This idea fitted with other information about the family and it was possible for the metaphor to be explored further in the next family session. It can be more creative to discuss the problem in the form of a metaphor as the issue becomes one removed from the actual problem and widens the thinking. This distancing effect can offer some safety (be less threatening) to explore difficult areas.

Metaphors may also be created in supervision and introduced to the client by the supervisee, or simply used to further understanding of the case. It is suggested that metaphors should be simple and new in order to engage interest or can be developed when introduced by the client (Kopp, 1995; Goncalves and Craine, 1991), thereby creating a context for opening up new ideas and directions.

Amundson (1988) describes a method for using visual metaphors as an aid to case conceptualisation in supervision. The method is flexible and responsive, both to the needs of the service context and of individual supervisees. He cautions that participation should be voluntary since some supervisees respond negatively to the use of metaphors by reason of not being 'visualisers', by lack of drawing ability, or by other feelings of insecurity.

The procedure involves four basic steps and takes place in a supervision group context. Initially, the case is summarised by the supervisee with the aid of a drawing that he or she has made in advance. The picture should illustrate, metaphorically, how the supervisee sees the client and her or his problems. Supervisees are asked to include how they see the case proceeding.

In the second stage the representation is discussed by the group. In the third step the focus of the discussion shifts to the relationship between the supervisee and the client. In the final step the focus is on how the drawing might be altered to reflect a different therapeutic orientation or approach.

Amundson argues that the impact of the case drawing method can come from the development and drawing of the metaphor, or from the case discussion, or by sharing the drawing with the client.

Writing and drawing

Amundson's method involves drawing, and, as he notes, people have a range of reactions to the proposal to use visual methods to further their understanding of the work that they are conducting. However, visual methods can range from diagrammatic representation of the formulation of a problem to more sophisticated use of artists' materials. Diagrams can provide an easy transition from talk to vision and may be a good starting point for those who feel less confident about the use of alternatives to talking.

The act of writing words onto paper or a drawing board serves to externalise some ideas so that they are no longer just in one person's head but are then 'out there' for the purpose of shared contemplation. The act of, say, drawing a family tree or genogram onto a white board can reveal a pattern not previously noted. The use of white boards to note key words and make links as supervisees talk about their cases can proceed as a natural extension of the discussion. In my experience, supervisees report finding this process a particularly helpful aid to case conceptualisation and formulation.

For those supervisees who feel at ease with a transition from diagrams to drawings, a variety of frameworks have been proposed for providing structure, two of which are described in more detail below.

Drawing the client as a fish

A useful exercise in a group context introduced to me by Inskipp and Proctor (1997) was to draw the client as a fish. The choice of the fish reflects their view that everyone is capable of drawing a fish irrespective of artistic skill. The exercise may then be experienced as less threatening for those who are less certain with the medium. Further containment was provided by boundaries to the task. The drawing was to be accomplished within five minutes and without talking. We were then asked to put ourselves as the therapist into the drawing. In small groups we contemplated each other's offerings with a view to noticing whatever struck us about the picture. The other participants were to follow the request of the 'artist' regarding what was desired from the group members. This exercise would adapt to individual supervision. Whether or not connections are subsequently made to the work with the client could be optional. In my case I produced the drawing shown in Figure 10.1.

My colleagues noticed the height afforded by the dais from which I apparently conducted the work and suggested that this level of protection seemed responsive to the illustrated threat of the large teeth! I talked of my

Figure 10.1 A drawing of the client as a fish

preference for an enquiring rather than conducting approach to the work and wondered how I might have got myself into the position that seemed to be represented in the drawing. None of this had been in my awareness prior to making the drawing, but helpfully informed my subsequent thinking.

This technique of asking the supervisee to represent some aspect of the work in a drawing was extended during a workshop led by Val Wosket (1998). She offered Ishiyama's (1988) framework for undertaking the drawing in a series of steps:

Ishiyama's framework

Ishiyama (1988) argues that Amundson's instructions for case drawing should be more specific and the procedure operationalised for practical and research purposes. Ishiyama provides a set of instructions that could help the introduction of the use of drawings into supervision for supervisors who are unfamiliar with this approach. A four-stage process is proposed, beginning with a more conventional approach to case conceptualisation. The supervisee is asked to respond to six sentence stems on a 'Cognitive Case Processing Form' with a view to clarification of present perceptions of the client, the therapeutic process and the client–therapist relationship. Sentence stems are: 'What I see as the client's main concern is . . .', 'The way the client interacted with me is . . .', 'What I was trying to do in the session is . . .', 'What I felt or thought about myself as a counsellor during this session is . . .', 'The way this session went is . . .', 'What I think the client gained from this session is . . .'

In order to encourage metaphoric thinking the supervisee then responds to a further four sentence stems, the responses to which may or may not be written down according to preference. These stems are as follows: 'The way I perceive the client with her or his concern may be characterised by a metaphor or image like . . .', 'The way the client responded to me or felt toward me during this session may be characterised by a metaphor or image like . . .', 'The way I conducted myself during this session may be characterised by a metaphor or image like . . .', 'The way this session went may be characterised by a metaphor or image like . . .'

Using large sheets of paper and coloured pens supervisees are then given instructions for case drawing that emphasise the irrelevance of artistic qualities and aesthetic factors. Symbols, words, phrases or sentences may be included in the drawing, which should include:

- Yourself as a counsellor and a person.
- The client and her or his concerns.
- Your relationship with the client (i.e. how you and the client related to each other).
- How the sessions went.
- Where the case is going.

In the final step, supervisees present their drawings and explain their thinking and the images to the supervisor and fellow supervisees. Further exploration can be encouraged by questioning, by sharing personal reactions to and impressions of the drawings, and by extending and developing the metaphors used. The supervisor's task is seen as one of facilitation.

Ishiyama illustrates the method with the example shown in Figure 10.2. The supervisee described the client as a man drowning in a glass of beer, calling for help and having available some life-preservers/lifebuoys that are within his grasp. The supervisee's experience as a counsellor in the session was as in the role of life-preserver, a role enacted by throwing a lifeline and struggling to pull it in. Reflecting on how the session proceeded, the swimmer–drowner was described as half-way home but in need of a larger life-preserver in order to complete the work.

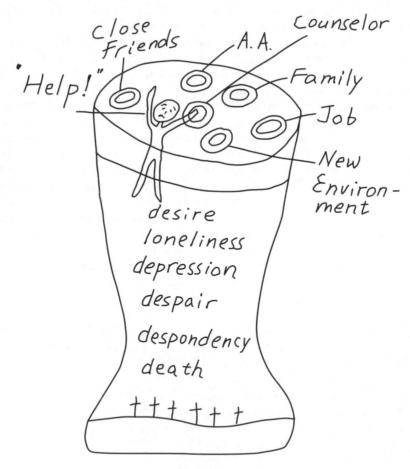

Figure 10.2 A man drowning in a glass of beer

Ishiyama describes positive reactions of supervisees to the procedure whilst cautioning that the method does not suit everyone, and that additional preparation time for supervision is needed. In addition, there is a tendency of case presenters to become more self- than client-focused when using visual methods. This can be appropriate and educational in that it enables supervisees' feelings, anxiety and self-doubt to surface and be explored. Whether or not this is helpful will depend upon multiple factors, including the objectives of the supervision and the dynamics of the relationship within the supervision group. The case conceptualisations produced are viewed as developing ideas that can inform the work and not as static and unchanging formulations.

Using objects in visual supervision

A number of authors have proposed that visualisation of a case can be aided by the symbolic use and arrangement of objects. Their use in supervision could be seen as a development and adaptation of the use of objects in therapy. The use of objects is probably more widespread in therapeutic work with children than with other client groups. Toys and play are not infrequently used as a means to enhance communication and to facilitate the expression of ideas that may not be amenable to more direct verbal expression given the developmental status of the child.

The use of objects and of play as therapy have a long tradition in the helping professions. One such method employs miniature models of people and objects which children use to construct their 'worlds' (Lowenfeld World Technique) in sand-filled trays (Lowenfeld, 1979). The method was extended to use with adults by Nourry, Samba and Bieder (1978) and by Kalff (1980).

Williams (1995) helpfully identifies differences between the use of objects for therapeutic purposes and for the purposes of supervision as follows:

- The subjects which the objects are used to represent in supervision are the therapy systems and the supervising system. The supervisee is not a client and thus not a subject of therapy or healing.
- Supervisees do not construct their personal world but rather a representation of some therapy in which they may or may not be included.
- The use of objects in supervision is not associated with a particular model of therapy.
- The supervisor takes a directive role in managing the supervisory process and gives instructions. A non-directive approach would typify therapy.
- The supervisor encourages the supervisee to make associations and interpretations as part of the supervisory process, focusing on the conceptualisation of the work.
- However the materials are used in supervision, they are dismantled by the supervisee during the session rather than being seen as completed

creations representing processes in the client and between the client and therapist. When used in therapy the creation would be preserved at the end of the session.

*   The nature of the objects and the manner in which they are used in supervision is not specified and there is room for flexibility according to circumstance and need. No standard procedure is followed as in their use in therapy.

Williams (1995) has gathered together a set of evocative objects which are attached to magnets so that they can be moved around on a marker board. In supervision these are used to represent people, roles, 'states' or relationships. He argues that the sophistication of the objects is not important provided that they can be moved around. Visual presentation enables viewing of the objects and their relationship with each other in terms of similarity, distance and continuity. In Williams's method, the objects are used by the supervisee to show or define the therapeutic system as currently perceived. The supervisor as facilitator questions the supervisee about the arrangement with a view to creating a second arrangement that is different from the original and which gives pointers for the future directions of the work. The interpretation of the arrangement is the responsibility of the supervisee. The role of the supervisor is to enquire into the positioning of the objects so that supervisees can use their imaginations to create their own interpretations.

Williams suggests a number of routines for supervisors who wish to experiment with the use of symbolic objects. The recommendations for supervisors new to this approach are as follows:

*   Clients are represented by one figure each when more than one person is included in the client system.
*   Up to four figures may be used to represent a single client, each representing different aspects or features of the client as perceived by the supervisee.
*   Typically three figures are used to represent the roles of the supervisee with the client.
*   The supervisor asks supervisees to select objects to represent their roles in the work, and to represent the client.
*   When several objects have been placed, the supervisor's usual first instruction is to, 'Move one of the figures to a place where you think it would be better employed.' The next instruction is to ask the supervisee to show on the board what happens next. These instructions are repeated until no more moves are desired by the supervisee.
*   It is often preferable that the first figure to be moved is one representing the supervisee's roles, but exceptions can be made where this seems more helpful.
*   The supervisor does not question the supervisee about why particular

figures have been selected or where they have been placed until the above moves have been completed.

- When the moves have been completed a re-run of the process may be carried out with the supervisor asking questions such as, 'What do you make of having chosen a lion to represent yourself?', 'Why do you think you have positioned yourself between the husband and wife?'

Williams has a preference for simple and naive questions. The decisions about the figures are about form rather than language. The supervisor's questions aim to help the supervisee to translate from the visual medium to articulation in speech so as to inform the direction of the work and to connect with theoretical underpinnings.

Williams describes some specific procedures for the use of objects to aid visualisation and case conceptualisation. In addition, insights may also be obtained by the use of simple materials such as buttons or stones with which to create representations of the therapeutic system through a process of sculpting (discussed on pp. 182–183).

Sociograms

Sometimes the issues that people are experiencing in their work stem from the wider context in which it is taking place. It can be helpful to identify all the elements that comprise the work system and to explore their relationship with each other and how they might be having an impact on the work. For example, an 11-year-old girl with terminal cancer for which all treatments had failed was brought as a case to supervision by a Macmillan nurse who was concerned that the child was depressed. The nurse believed that the child should take anti-depressant medication and had convinced the consultant paediatrician of the same. The family context was that the child had been raised largely by paternal grandparents after the early separation of the parents, and the child's mother had pursued a successful career. Following the mother's establishment of a new relationship and the birth of a half-sibling, the girl had moved to live with her mother and her new partner, continuing to spend weekends and holidays with grandparents. The view of the mother was that since the child had only a short life remaining, all efforts should be made to make it as enjoyable and comfortable as possible. The view of the grandparents was that the child should be treated like any other. The child's behaviour tended to conform to each of the different family circumstances. She did not complain of pain or show sadness when with the grandparents but did both when with her mother.

The child was taken to the appointment with the consultant paediatrician by her grandparents and he was persuaded that the child was well and did not require anti-depressant medication. The Macmillan nurse referred to child psychiatry as an alternative source of a diagnosis of depression. She expressed grave concern that the effects of the two strongly held views in the family were very unhelpful for the well-being of the child.

In supervision a sociogram or relationship map of the different involved parties was created and positions arranged in relation to each person's connection with the different views of the mother and the grandparents. This revealed that there was the potential for an increasing number of professionals to become 'stuck' to each side of the argument. It was agreed that this was unhelpful and that neither the mother nor the grandparents would be prepared to change their position if they perceived the source of influence to be the other side of the family. It was felt, however, that both the mother and the grandparents would listen to the child's opinion if this could be given freely to a 'neutral' party. The focus of the discussion was then on deciding who might be perceived as neutral and who would also have the skills to interview the child. It was agreed that the interview might be videotaped and shown to both sides of the family. This might allow for a decision regarding the use of anti-depressant medication to be freed from the influence of the wider context.

Through the sociogram described above, the nurse discovered that in order for her views to be influential she needed to think carefully about how to introduce them to the different family members.

The use of sociograms can be particularly helpful in exploring the wider influences on the work. Blocks to progress can be distant from the client–therapist relationship and a broader analysis can help to prevent the frustrations of trying to accomplish outcomes that are impossible in the wider scheme of things.

Sculpting

Sculpting is a method in which people or objects are placed in relation to each other to represent a person's view of a system (Lesage-Higgins, 1999; Lawson, 1989). Where people are the objects placed they can be asked to describe the experience of physically being in the system – who else they could see, whether they were physically comfortable, and so on. In individual supervision, the objects used to make a sculpt cannot be interrogated in such a fashion, but a useful alternative perspective can be created in the process of representation using objects.

In a group, the materials used for sculpting can be the group members. A supervisee is invited to think about a client in the family or social context. The supervisee then chooses two members of the family – possibly the client and a significant other, and is asked to choose two group members to represent these people. The supervisee then places these two in relationship to each other. This positioning includes the features of distance, orientation, position in space and relationship to each other. The positions may be static or moving. It is not necessary to give background to the case.

A third group member is then selected to represent another member of the client's system and he or she is placed in relation to the other two. Group members are selected until all of the people in the client's system have been represented. The supervisee may then stand back and look at the system with a view to identifying what can be seen only in the sculpt rather than attempting to make interpretations or meaning of the pictorial representation in relation to the case itself. All of the participants are then asked in turn to describe their experience of their position in the sculpt, again without making any interpretation or link to the client's family or system.

The sculpt can be repeated for a past or future time, perhaps choosing a time of transition in the system or family, such as a child leaving home or at the time of a bereavement, birth or schism. The supervisor facilitates the sculpt by a process of enquiry regarding how the people have been placed and whether this satisfies the mental picture that the supervisee has of the family.

In the absence of a group, objects such as buttons or small stones can be arranged by the supervisee to represent her or his view of the client's relationship with her or his family of origin, current social circle or therapeutic system. The objects provide for the representation of texture, colour and relative size and distance. Sculpts can be made of the past, present and future to incorporate the dimension of time. Supervisees can use an object to represent themselves in the client's system. Alternatively, the objects can be used to represent features, qualities, or roles played by the individual client.

The medium of clay can also be used to make models or representations of individuals. Because clay is malleable, it has the advantage that shapes and sizes of images can be altered as the process of moving them into different positions and relationships develops. For example, you can ask the question, 'What would it look like if this moved closer to that?'

When using such methods in individual supervision, there is a choice regarding the degree to which observations are made only of the representation, or how far each participant has permission to go further and make interpretations linked directly to what is known about the client.

The supervisor may choose to facilitate the sculpting process by prompting the supervisee with enquiries regarding whether all relevant people have been included in the sculpt. The sculpt could be completed by the supervisee trying to take the position of each of the members of the system with a view to further developing an understanding of conflicts and alliances. Many options are available. The method offers an alternative to a verbal medium and may reveal understandings not yet verbally formulated by the supervisee.

Action methods

Action methods in supervision are probably more typically employed in group than in individual contexts. But since they include role-play and role training, they can also be fruitful in individual supervision. Experimenting with taking the role of the client can be an effective way of obtaining different perspectives on the work. Working on a new technique as modelled by the supervisor, or rehearsing a strategy in supervision prior to using it with a client, can foster the development of new skills and give supervisees the confidence to proceed with new approaches to their work. Such practice also serves to help safeguard the welfare of the client.

Williams (1995: 215) advocates the introduction of an 'action culture' as early as possible if this is to be a feature of the supervision, and it would be an appropriate topic to be addressed in the contracting process.

Physical scaling

The use of rating scales is widespread in the helping professions. In addition to their use as assessment tools they can be used to evaluate progress and can be a focus of the therapeutic dialogue with the client. Williams (1995) advocates their adaptation as an action method in supervision as a gentle introduction to such methods.

An example of the use of physical scaling concerns the process of contracting about the learning needs of the supervisee. The supervisee might identify 'using Socratic questioning' as a learning need. The supervisor asks at what level of skill the supervisee evaluates her or his current performance on a scale of 1–10. The supervisee then stands on an imaginary line on the office floor and chooses, say, scale point 3. The supervisor interviews the supervisee about the meaning of a score of 3 on 'using Socratic questioning'. He or she is then asked to move to the point that will be reached after a period of time. The supervisee then moves along the line to occupy the new position and is interviewed about what he or she will be doing differently at this point.

This procedure can be used in individual or group supervision and does not have to include physical movement along an imaginary line. However, the inclusion of the physical action provides the additional experience of walking through the difference between, say, 3 and 7.

Empty chairs

Williams (1995) describes the use of empty chairs in the context of group supervision. Any method of supervision adopted in the context of a group requires careful consideration of group processes and the reader is referred to Chapter 6 for consideration of supervision in groups. Whilst the use of the empty chair in a group setting may provide a richer source of data, it is a technique that will also translate to individual supervision. Opportunities for using an empty chair arise particularly when supervisees make two statements that encapsulate two different courses of action: 'Part of me would like to . . . And another to . . .' Two empty chairs can serve to represent the two positions. The supervisee can be invited to talk to each with a view to identifying costs and benefits and potential outcomes of following the one or the other view. The effect of separating the two positions is to enable a clearer and more passionate exposition of each view. Williams (1995: 256) elaborates on a range of options for the use of the empty chair in supervision.

Role-play

Bradley (1989: 165) describes role-playing in learning contexts as, 'the exercise of behaving in a contrived experience according to a prescribed role, and by altering roles a number of learning situations can be presented'. Role-play has often been advocated as a useful method in supervision (Errek and Randolph, 1982; Meredith and Bradley, 1989; Strosahl and Jacobson, 1986) by practitioners from a range of theoretical persuasions from behaviour therapy to psychodrama.

Adopting different roles enables supervisees to move from their current perspective to explore from a different angle the knowledge that they have about the piece of work in focus. There are many roles that the supervisee might adopt, including that of the central client, of another person connected to the client, of a piece of furniture, of a part of the client, of a previous 'helper', and so on. There is also an option for the supervisee to interview the supervisor in the role of a client in order to illustrate what happened in a session or to experiment with how a particular approach might be received. The example below describes an experiment involving the kind of letter to write to a non-attending client.

The supervisor's habit was to write to clients beginning, 'I am sorry that you could not attend for your appointment today . . .' The supervisee was concerned that to write this to clients who wished to communicate something deliberate through their non-attendance might be unhelpful. She invited the supervisor to take the role of clients who did not attend for a range of reasons and experimented with how they might respond to a letter commencing in alternative ways, 'I am sorry that you did not attend for your appointment . . .', 'As you did not attend for your appointment . . .', etc.

Role-play also enables a supervisor to demonstrate a method or technique to a supervisee, and/or a supervisee to practise a technique in the relative safety of the supervision. This can range from something relatively straightforward such as how to introduce oneself to clients, to something more complex such as the use of guided imagery in relaxation training.

Occasionally, supervisees experience some difficulty in taking on the role of the other. Various techniques can help. The methods of psychodrama prescribe that protagonists are helped by being 'warmed-up' to working on their issues, and this is accomplished through the use of specifically designed exercises (Karp, Holmes and Tauvon, 1998) which could be adapted for individual use. Energy can be generated by having supervisees rearrange furniture in the room to represent the physical layout of the space in which they meet with the client. At the least it is often helpful for the supervisee to change chairs when taking another role. In order to help the supervisee to adopt the designated role, the supervisor can ask a number of 'grounding' questions prior to focusing on the identified issues for supervision. These include referring to the supervisee by the name of the person whose role they are taking and asking questions about their age, family circumstances, how they came to seek help, how long they have known the therapist, etc. When the supervisee is responding consistently in the first person rather than the third person it is probably germane to move onto more central issues.

The use of role-play can have a powerful impact through the creation of different perspectives on the work. It can also be fun and provide a diversion through lighter moments that can lift supervisees who are feeling worn down with their efforts to help. In one example of couple therapy, a supervisee role-played their clients' bed! This required the supervisor to also get down on the floor to talk with 'bed'. Once the supervisee was grounded in the role through conversation about the layout of the room and the bedcovers, the supervisor said, 'So, I bet you've seen a lot of action.' A multitude of expressions passed over the supervisee's face before the response of, 'Well, that's the problem really.'

Another important issue in the use of role-play is the need for the supervisor to ensure that the supervisee has de-roled before proceeding further to discuss the meaning of the role-play for the future work with the client, although this in itself can aid the de-roling process. Simple de-roling manoeuvres include asking supervisees to say how they are the same and how they are different from the role, or to say their name and their intentions for the rest of the supervision and for the remainder of the day. As a transition to de-roling supervisees might wish to describe their experiences in the role in general.

Role-plays should be set up with a particular intention in mind. After de-roling the discussion might focus on any insights gained and should connect back to the original purpose in having set it up.

Internalised-other interviewing

'Internalised-other' interviewing (Burnham, 2000; Epston, 1993) offers a method for exploring the relationships that people have with the various facets of their own being. Casement (1990) refers to the voices in oneself of personally influential people as one's internalised significant others. Interviews may not only be restricted to the voices of significant others. For example, an interview with a client might explore the relationship that the person has with 'having fun' or with 'excellence' or with a number of different elements that might have been mapped as relating to the presenting difficulties – 'feeling guilty', 'feeling responsible', 'feeling a failure'. In this technique the therapist speaks with the client as the selected element. The initial questions are designed to help interviewees to 'ground' themselves in the identity of the other, and subsequent ones to explore the relationship of the other with the client. For example, 'Hello, "feeling good"?', 'How old are you?', 'How big are you?', 'Do you have a particular colour or do you change colour?', 'When were you last in touch with Jane?', 'Does she contact you or do you call on her?', 'Who else comes along when you meet up?', and so on.

The stages of the internalised-other interview are identified as follows by Burnham (2000):

- Choose the person, idea, ability, problem or emotion that will be the 'other'. This choice takes place through negotiation and is best when connected with the flow of the conversation or a purpose of the interview.
- Propose the way of working as a way of fulfilling a goal of the interview.
- Explain the process as much as necessary to begin, or politely accept if the person declines the offer.
- Begin by 'grounding' the person being interviewed in the identity of the 'other'. This is accomplished by talking to the person as if meeting them for the first time and asking questions about everyday aspects of the 'other's' life.
- Continue by exploring more deeply the experience of the other in relation to the goals of the interview. These questions can be related to emotions, actions and meanings. Burnham argues that the interviewer need not be discouraged by 'don't know' responses since these are potential triggers to the curiosity of the interviewee.
- Explore the relationship between the 'other' and the person being interviewed.
- Prompt the person that this stage of the interview is ending by saying 'goodbye' to the 'other' and 'hello' to the person sitting in front of you.
- Reflect on the process and its effects on the purpose of doing the interview.

Internalised-other interviewing can be adapted for use in supervision. The supervisee might take the role of the client, or the method could be used, for example, to explore the supervisee's relationship with an element of the work such as 'stuckness' or 'despair'. The possibilities are limited only by the imaginations of the participants. The method serves to encourage the taking of a different perspective on the subject and from this an action plan can be devised.

Williams (1995: 233) describes this approach as 'interviewing for a role', a role being defined as, 'a person's functioning with one or more persons at particular times in specific situations', suggesting that people are many 'selves' in many contexts. For the use of the method in group supervision the reader is directed to Williams (1995). My own experience suggests that for effective and safe use of the method in a group setting the supervisor should be experienced in the techniques and methods of drama-based therapy that includes the use of auxiliaries, identification of the protagonist, doubling, de-roling, and so forth. These methods are described in Howells, Karp, Watson, Sprague and Moreno (1994) and Yablonsky (1992).

The use of creative methods is more typically found in those helping professions in which such methods are adopted with clients. This does not prevent their translation to those professions more typically engaged in verbal approaches and they are recommended as a way of obtaining alternative perspectives and keeping supervision fresh.

Summary

This chapter describes a range of methods for presenting work in supervision that go beyond the traditional medium of talking. It is recommended that these methods are adapted to suit the experience and confidence levels of the participants and should be used as tools to enhance the work of supervision in specific ways rather than as techniques to turn to when one doesn't know what to do next. All creative methods can tap into unconscious material and can produce unexpected results. This needs to be acknowledged by supervisors using these approaches. For readers who are interested in and wish to develop the use of metaphor and the physical representation of relationships in supervision further, original sources include Robbins and Erismann (1992) on the development of a stone sculpting workshop, Barnat (1977) on the use of metaphor in allaying supervisee anxiety, and Noucho (1983) on the use of visual imagery in training.

Chapter 11

The influence of different models of therapy and counselling on the supervisory process

Across different models of therapy and counselling there are common themes and ideas that inform both the practice and the supervision of the practice. Whatever the model of therapy, there will be differences between practitioners in style and understanding of the parameters of the model and hence much diversity of supervision within and between models. As long as half a century ago Fiedler's (1950, 1951) studies established that those who adhere to a particular therapeutic theory cannot be regarded as interchangeable units. He found that there could be more difference between two therapists who espoused the same theory than between two therapists with apparently dissimilar theories. A psychologist's espoused theory may correspond only imperfectly with what he or she does in actual practice (Goodyear, Bradley and Bartlett, 1983).

In this chapter we focus on the differences between models of therapy insofar as these are likely to influence the way in which supervision is conducted. This is against the background of differences in style and understanding between therapists of the same theoretical persuasion. The influence of the supervisor's preferred theoretical model can be a focus of discussion in the contracting process.

Differences between supervisors from different theoretical orientations were studied by Putney, Worthington and McCullough (1992). Cognitive behavioural supervisors were perceived to act in a consultant role and to focus on skills and strategies more than did humanistic, psychodynamic and existential supervisors, who were perceived as more often operating within a relationship model and in a therapist role. Supervisors were not perceived to differ with regard to their focus on growth and skill development and their focus on the supervisee.

Goodyear, Abadie and Efros (1984) used videotapes of supervision of the same piece of therapeutic work to compare approaches to supervision undertaken within Gestalt (Erving Polster), Client-Centred (Carl Rogers), Psychoanalytic (Rudolph Ekstein), and Rational–Emotive Therapy (Albert Ellis) models. Videotapes were rated along a number of dimensions by 58 experienced supervisors. Of the four supervisors, Rogers was perceived as the person most likely to favour a modelling role and Ellis as the least likely. Ekstein and Ellis were perceived to function more in the role of critic than were Polster and Rogers. Ellis was perceived as taking the role of teacher more often than Rogers, and as focusing on skills and strategies to a greater extent than the other three supervisors. Ekstein and Ellis were seen as focusing more on case conceptualisation. The authors conclude that their results confirm the findings of Miars, Tracey, Ray, Cornfeld, O'Farrell and Gelso (1983) that theoretical orientation towards therapy is related to a supervisor's manifest behaviour, roles and attitudes. Friedlander and Ward (1983) found similar results in a different study using the same stimulus materials.

The following sections of this chapter identify the features of four theoretical approaches to therapy as they might be expected to influence supervision. The selected approaches are psychodynamic, person-centred, cognitive behavioural and systemic. Each is illustrated with a transcript of supervision conducted by a supervisor who subscribes to the particular approach, cognitive behavioural being represented by a transcript undertaken by Albert Ellis whose specific approach is Rational–Emotive Therapy. The reader is invited to reflect upon the extent to which each transcript illustrates both the theoretical stance and the personal style of the supervisor.

Psychodynamic models

There are three principal elements that comprise training in a psychodynamic approach to counselling and therapy. These are a personal analysis or personal therapy, a taught theoretical component and supervised practice. This tripartite model was developed when formal psychoanalytic institutes and societies were established in the 1920s (Moldawsky, 1980).

Two schools of thought developed in relation to the roles of teacher and analyst. The Hungarian position advocated combining the roles of supervisor and analyst, whereas the Vienna position promoted the idea that the pursuit of resolution of personal conflicts through personal therapy should be undertaken with a different person than should supervised practice (Caligor, 1984; Thorbeck, 1992). Binder and Strupp (1997) argue that these two positions have become increasingly integrated over time. The supervision is centred on the therapy with the client, whilst the supervisee is simultaneously seen as unwittingly enacting with the supervisor important dynamics occurring in her or his relationship with the client. Psychodynamic training emphasises this enactment through the notion of 'parallel process' in which the interpersonal processes taking place in the dyads supervisor–supervisee and supervisee–client are seen as influencing and informing each other.

Doehrman's (1976) view of parallel process was that conflicts arising in supervision tended to be replayed in the therapy with the supervisee's client. Thus, supervisees might identify with their supervisor and act towards the client as they had experienced the supervisor acting towards them or, by counter-identification, act towards the client in the opposite fashion. Most subsequent writings emphasise the source of parallel process as being in the therapy with replay in the supervision (Binder and Strupp, 1997). For example, the supervisee is receptive to messages from the client and becomes the transmitter of these messages in supervision, evoking responses in the supervisor that were evoked in herself or himself in the therapy.

There is a degree of integration of didactic and therapeutic roles effected by the psychodynamic supervisor who applies psychodynamic clinical theories and methods usually associated with therapy to achieve the educational goals of supervision. The purpose, however, is educational. The supervisor's role is to provide theoretical and technical input and to interpret the parallel process. In psychoanalytic training independent personal analysis continues to be a requirement (Dewald, 1997). The requirement for personal therapy is also predominantly the case in psychodynamic therapy training more generally.

The theory of learning in psychoanalytic supervision is of a developmental progression that takes place through the establishment of a learning alliance. In the beginning the supervisee is seen as being heavily reliant on the supervisor and the focus is on learning technical strategies. In this stage there is explicit reliance on the guidance of the supervisor. Gradually the supervisee begins to emulate the supervisor through having internalised or introjected images and qualities of the supervisor. In this stage the supervisee is seen as developing a capacity to reflect on her or his functioning within the supervisory relationship which then generalises to the therapeutic relationship. Gradually supervisees are seen as developing the capacity to engage in the reflection process through the mechanism of their own internal supervisor (Casement, 1988). Casement argues that towards the end of training the process of supervision should develop into a dialogue between the external supervisor and the supervisee's internal supervisor.

Another feature of supervision within a psychodynamic framework is that the source of data for discussion is usually the supervisee's notes made contemporaneously or immediately following a therapy session, or the supervisee's free associations. More recently, tape recordings have been regarded as useful (Perr, 1986), whilst other supervisors maintain that recordings make an unjustified intrusion into the therapeutic relationship (Tennen, 1988).

One of the implications of these ideas is the importance of establishing a solid supervisory relationship as a platform from which to discuss the processes that are taking place in the supervision, the processes that are taking place in the therapy, and how these relate to each other.

Supervisees can also expect to bring the issue of how the work makes them feel to the supervision, using this to understand the client's transference and the therapist's counter-transference. One of the roles of the supervisor is to help the supervisee to see how he or she is being drawn into unconscious enactments with the client. These may be necessary to the work but be detrimental if they are not identified. For example, therapists may find themselves extending the boundaries of the sessions with a particular client – where, when and for how long the sessions take place – as they are drawn into a pattern of relating with its origins in the client's history. The supervisor can help the supervisee to notice such patterns. Their meaning can be explored in supervision through the notions of transference and counter-transference, and the new awareness and understanding used to facilitate the therapy with the client.

This use of feelings to inform the work is brought out in the following extract from a supervision session (where *S.* = supervisor, and *T.* = trainee) reported in Scaife (1995). The commentary was added to the transcript by the supervisor in order to highlight some features of a psychodynamic model.

S.   You've mentioned she's quite good at mothering.

T.   Watching her in the room she is good at mothering.

S.   But it's harder for her to mother herself?

T.   Yes, because she sees herself as ugly inside. That she's so ugly inside that if she goes out in the street, people will see it, and that she can't bear to go out or come and see me because people will see her absolute ugliness. That's one day, but another day . . .

S.   I'm wondering what those ugly feelings are.

T.   It's the anger and the hatred I think.

S.   That seems likely, the anger and the hate. Maybe in the sessions with you she could express them.

T.   That's been one of my themes, to get her to express that, not just in the present, but to events in the past and I've tried to do that using drama because it seems to need a fairly powerful expression, but she's very frightened of the power of those feelings.

S.   Power of them, and I wonder if she's frightened at showing *you* what they are because you might again reject her. If she shows you those ugly awful feelings, are you going to do the same as the rest and reject, abandon. She's got herself some mothering, and if she expresses those, maybe the fear would be that she's got a lot to lose.

Commentary: Fear of these primitive emotions of anger, rejection, hatred, envy, and abandonment are a typical focus of a psychodynamic model.

T.   Would it be appropriate to raise that as an idea?

S.   Yes. Certainly would, and even maybe, does she feel angry with you, or even envious. She's got a woman therapist, and I'm wondering if she also has feelings towards women. Does she know you're a mother?

T.   Yes, I would think so. It's fairly obvious.

S. It could be that there's some envy around. That she can see you are together with a good job.

T. I think there is anger towards women as well. She almost got close to a woman who she met at a course she went on, and clearly prevented the relationship developing further.

S. That could be another reason why the sessions haven't developed. It's quite dangerous for her to show those feelings, not just because they're dangerous feelings as such but also they may be towards you. This thing of her ugly feelings, can you remember what you said that you feel when she picks up the 'phone? What do you feel towards her?

T. I said I didn't feel as sympathetic.

S. What does that mean?

T. Well it's actually a slight feeling of detachment. Is it rejection? I don't know.

S. You do feel detached?

T. Well, I think I see it, when she 'phones and it's a crisis time, I see it as part of a repeating pattern. I don't get overtaken by the current crisis like I think I would do, or I'm capable of being with some other people. I think, 'Well, here's another crisis, and I know I'm not going to be able to do anything to put this right, so I don't actually need to dive in here.' I suppose with some people I would dive in and rescue them or something. It's hard to put a label on it.

S. Do you feel that in the sessions? Does she give you any other strong feeling?

T. Yes, some of the things she's described about her life have been very sad. I've felt very sad about them and I've felt very much like wanting to help her put those right as far as it's possible to do that.

S. I think what I was wondering about, I seemed to pick up something from what you said earlier which was different from, what you say, experience with your other clients, and I was trying to put that together with the case. Given the fact that in your experience of her, you've been seeing her a long time, and there hasn't been much apparent change. Putting that together with, you said you feel detached in some ways as though here's another crisis and you can't do anything. I'm wondering if that's how she feels.

Commentary: Part of the transference experience is one of the client projecting her feelings onto the therapist.

T. Helpless would be the right thing, I think, which prompted me to start writing this letter which I've decided not to send because I think it was prompted by speaking to her on the 'phone, which was a helpless letter to the G.P. basically, saying I can't do anything.

(Scaife, 1995: 121–123)

This extract shows briefly how the model and theory in which the therapy is conducted are used reflexively to inform the process of supervision. Identifying the implications of the therapeutic model for the process of supervision may constitute part of the discussion undertaken in the contracting process. This will help the supervisee to know where to look for the data to bring to supervision.

Person-centred model

In a person-centred model the focus is upon the needs of the client, not on what the therapist might want to happen. Translated into supervision, the supervisor focuses on the needs and understandings of the supervisee rather than on the supervisor's own ideas about the work. The process uses active listening in an attempt to obtain a deep understanding – the core condition of accurate empathy. The main goal of therapy is to become connected with the client rather than to specify the goals and outcomes of the work. This might also translate to supervision. The assumption is that change will emerge from the state of being connected. As in psychodynamic models, the relationship between the participants is seen as key.

The following (where *R.* = Rogers, and *H.* = Hackney[1]) is a passage from a supervision session led by Carl Rogers, as described in Bernard and Goodyear (1992).

R.   . . . it interests me that she said, 'When I make up my mind to do it, I'll go ahead and do it.'

H.   Yeah.

R.   And when you responded accurately to that . . . that threatened her . . .

H.   Uh-uh.

R.   Which I think means that that was a very important statement for her.

H.   Uh-huh.

R.   I've often noticed that if a person takes quite a positive step-uh-expresses a feeling quite positively, and you understand it accurately, God, that's almost too much for them.

H.   Huh.

R.   They tend to draw away from what they just said.

H.   Right. Right. That was the reaction I got from her when I said that.

R.   [Pause] The-uh . . . when you say she has a sort of differing type of motivation, different . . . reason for motivation each time she comes

[1]   From Janine M. Bernard and Rodney K. Goodyear, *Fundamentals of Clinical Supervision.* © 1992 by Allyn and Bacon Reprinted/adapted by permission.

in-uhm . . . that wouldn't bother me. I-I would-I would-uh . . .
go with whatever . . . shred of feeling she would let me have at the
time.

H. Uh-huh. [Pause] I'd like to be able to do that. [Laughs]

R. [Laughs] Well, I'm saying what I would do; that doesn't mean that's
necessarily what you should do.

H. Well, I don't think what I'm doing is working for me. Uh . . . and I
don't think it really is working for her either, so-uhm . . . and I think
it would be-I think I'd be better-uh . . . in this case if I-uh . . . could
feel a little bit less responsible when she comes in with less
motivation.

R. She came in of her own accord. She asked to see you.

H. That's right. That's right. And she's been very faithful-uh . . . so far
in the case.

R. Wonderful. So then anything that you do that takes any responsibility away from her is really quite unnecessary.

H. Uh-huh.

R. She did decide to come; and she comes.

H. Right.

R. [Pause] An interesting, mixed-up, modern young woman, it seems
like.

H. Yes, it is. Uh . . . and a delightful young woman, too. She really is.
Uh . . . she's the person I think I like most among the people I'm
working with.

R. OK. OK, that's important. That's one reason why you want it to go
well.

H. That's right. Right.

R. [Pause] My feeling of her is very . . . good . . . feeling, and I like that.
It means you will get somewhere, but-uh . . . [pause]. But if you like
her enough to want her to go your way, that's-that's a different
matter.

H. Yeah. Well . . . you-that's especially true because I'm not really
sure . . . what way it would be if it was going my way. And I-I'm not
clear there either, so . . .

R. Well, you were-you were somewhat clear toward the end of the
interview as to a step that you clearly thought was advisable for this
coming week.

H. Right. I had an agenda at that point; I was wanting to set up . . . an
opportunity for her and-and her husband to-uh-to have a conversation. Whether that came off or not was another matter. But part of
the sense that I was picking up at that point was that because of the
pace of their lives they never even really had the opportunity. And
then she got-uh ignored or missed-uh.

R.   Well, that's where you did feel a responsibility for helping set up something that would make that come off.

H.   Oh, I was-I was taking care of it all. Yes. [Pause] Where do you think it might go if I were to-uh . . . that-that's maybe an impossible question to ask.

R.   Uh-huh.

H.   If I were to-uh . . . to try to follow what her inclinations were-uh-as far as . . . her trying to find a moment with her husband, where do you think that might go? Do you think-do you think she would bring the initiative out of that?

R.   I haven't any idea where it would go, but to me that's the fascination of-of therapy, is not knowing; and yet-uh-connecting just as deeply as I can with the, in this case, the confusion, the-uh . . . 'Maybe I will; maybe I won't. Maybe I like Don; maybe I like John.' Uh . . . just connecting as deeply as possible with that feeling and following it wherever she leads me . . .

(Bernard and Goodyear, 1992: 322–323)

In this extract Rogers highlights the requirement of the method for the therapist to follow the client rather than his own inclinations, and resists an invitation to provide answers.

Patterson (1997) states that the supervisor offers a supervisee-centred relationship in which the qualities of genuineness, respect and empathy are key. These are viewed as the core conditions for therapeutic progress. The supervisee is identified as responsible for setting the agenda for supervision, and for choosing the material to be examined and the issues on which to focus. The requirement of the training is that supervisees work within the assumption that the core conditions are sufficient for therapeutic progress to be made, and thereby put the assumption to the test. Supervisees are not expected to depart from the agenda of creating the core conditions and are explicitly required not to try other techniques. The criterion for evaluation is effectiveness in providing the core therapeutic conditions. Supervisees evaluate themselves against this criterion and make tape recordings of their sessions from which extracts are used as the material for supervision. Self-evaluation is regarded as making a significant contribution to the establishment of a constructive supervisory relationship.

Within this approach, supervisees are expected to take major responsibility for their own learning. However, supervisors effect their responsibility to clients by recommending personal therapy for the supervisee should they perceive the supervisee's personal adjustment to be problematic. This could result where some parallel process is not being resolved or where the supervisee's personal material is persistently intruding and making it difficult for her or him to stay in the client's frame of reference. If necessary the supervisor will discontinue the practicum should it be considered that clients could be damaged. Thus, in this model as in others, ethical considerations will override all others.

The following features of person-centred supervision are noted:

- In pre-registration training the supervisor bears responsibility for the supervisee's clients, and in order to keep track the supervisee begins each supervision by reviewing each of her or his clients. The level of detail varies according to perceived need and it is recommended that one client is the subject of continuing detailed focus.
- The approach is little concerned with diagnosis and personality dynamics since the focus of the work is on the acceptance and understanding of the client as a person. Rather than diagnostic assessment, the therapist is more concerned with the 'stage in process' of the client, as in Rogers' seven stages of process, and the supervisor might need to know that the supervisee has some understanding of this with each client. Supervision nevertheless helps supervisees to identify evidence of severe disturbance or organic presentations that might warrant referral elsewhere.
- Didactic instruction by the supervisor is minimal.
- The intention of supervision is to facilitate the supervisee's development in work and the supervisor responds to the difficulties that the supervisee has in her or his relationships with clients. Because of the commonality in core conditions for the relationships supervisor–supervisee and client–therapist, and between the skills of supervision and therapy, there can be an overlap in which the line between supervision and therapy can be difficult to determine (Bonney, 1994). However, the roles and responsibilities of the supervisor and supervisee are agreed in a process described as 'structuring the relationship', and this agreement may be reviewed as the supervision proceeds.

Patterson views these features as appropriate to more generic ways of working in addition to their specificity to a client-centred approach. Whilst other elements can be added from a preferred theory, he regards these additions as inconsistent with a client-centred approach.

Cognitive behavioural models

Cognitive behavioural approaches place a primary emphasis on cognitive processes as they influence behaviour and emotions. The approaches involve the identification of underlying schemas (Padesky, 1994) or philosophies (Woods and Ellis, 1997) that play a causal role in the client's emotions and behaviour. A task of the therapist is to help the client to develop more helpful beliefs through a process of challenge and reconstruction which leads to symptom-reduction.

A number of approaches within this group of therapies have developed, for example the Cognitive Therapy (CT) of Aaron Beck (1988) and Judith Beck (1995) and the Rational–Emotive Therapy (RET) of Ellis (Ellis and Dryden, 1987). Whilst these approaches are classified here under the same umbrella, exponents of each specific method would highlight differences as well as similarities. My own understanding suggests that in RET the therapist tends to be more overtly directive, whereas in CT a process of collaborative guided discovery is the aim. In RET unhelpful thought sequences are referred to as 'irrational', whereas in CT they are described by the term 'negative automatic thoughts'. An example of such a thought in both models would be 'I am an unlovable person.'

Descriptions of supervision in both models (Woods and Ellis, 1997; Leise and Beck, 1997) emphasise the educational role of the supervisor. Training methods include reading and discussion, direct observation of therapy and opportunities for practice. In cognitive therapy the use of tapes is recommended, with a view to identifying the strengths and weaknesses of the supervisee. It is suggested that reluctance to tape be addressed by identifying the automatic thoughts (for example, 'recording will cramp my style') of the supervisee in a process similar to the one adopted with clients.

The following extract from Bernard and Goodyear (1992) is of Albert Ellis supervising within a Rational–Emotive Therapy model, and it illustrates some aspects of the RET approach. The extract begins with a brief statement from Ellis regarding the approach that he intends to take to the supervision (*E.* = Ellis, *H.* = Hackney).

E.   But I want to explain first that-uhm – I'm naturally going to supervise from my own standpoint which is Rational Emotive Therapy, and this tape was almost the opposite . . .

H.   Yes.

E.   of what RET would be. So . . . uhm – I'm going to . . . get you on points which are illegitimate to some degree, you see.

H.   That's fine because what we – our purpose is to bring out RET.

E.   Right. So I'm going to assume wrongly that you . . . were trying to do some kind of RET session . . .

H.   Good.

E.   and criticize it from that . . . standpoint, because actually I wasn't quite clear what – uhm . . . you were trying to do at points. Uh . . . sort of general psychotherapy, but I wasn't quite sure. But, as I said, I'll ignore that. Now, the first thing that I noticed from RET standpoint was . . . too much emphasis on the situation, what we call the 'A' activating event . . .

H.   Uh-huh.

E.   and then we have a 'B', a belief about it; and then a 'C', a consequence. Now – uh – a feeling in our gut. Now, I assume the consequence was . . . sort of came in along the side, that she's upset about the fact that her husband doesn't talk the way she wanted him . . .

H. Right.

E. to. But I wasn't sure what her feeling . . . was. We first make clear that it was an inappropriate feeling, because she might just be sorry and regretful . . .

H. Right.

E. about it, and that we wouldn't consider an emotional problem. So if she were depressed or anxious, or real . . . upset about it, that would be different. And I think she was.

H. That's – that's right.

E. Yeah.

H. Yes.

E. So let's assume that she's . . . anxious about that and certain other things – it was obvious – that she was anxious about. So the 'C' was fairly clear; we'll say she was depressed or anxious about his not – they've been married for quite a while, is that right? She doesn't . . .

H. Well-uh . . . not as long as it might seem. They've been married six months.

E. Oh, I see. Yeah. Because she mentioned twenty-seven years. Is he twenty-seven years of age?

H. She was saying that – yes, he was twenty-seven years of age. And – uh – his style has taken twenty years to twenty-seven years to develop.

E. Yeah.

H. That's what the reference was.

E. All right. So the first thing that came in was – uh . . . you said to her, earlier in the session, 'You had to . . . smoke him out.' And she sort of agreed to it. But we would be looking for the upsetting factor which, in my head, would be immediately, 'as you shouldn't have to.'

H. Right.

E. And now I would try to confront her: 'Are you saying that that's unfortunate, that you had to smoke him out?' which is really . . .

H. Uh-huh.

E. But she's really angry and upset because she shouldn't have to . . .

H. Right.

E. smoke him out.

H. And if she smokes him out, then she feels that she didn't get what she wanted anyhow, because it should have happened spontaneously.

E. Yes, that's right. So she's in a box there, and also she didn't get what she thinks she needs, her wants were. In RET, any want, even an unrealistic want, is not too bad.

H. Uh-huh.

E. You want a million dollars right now, as long as you say you don't need it. And then you were rightly, which is part of RET, giving her a little skill training . . .

H. Yeah.

E. which we'd go back to 'A', the activating event . . .

H. Uh-huh.

E. and show her very simple techniques of maybe handling it better. We wouldn't consider that of paramount importance, but we'd do it along with the changing of her belief system, and 'C', her consequences or feeling.

(Bernard and Goodyear, 1992: 336–337)

Ellis adopts an instructional approach in which he takes the data provided by the therapist and analyses it according to the model of therapy. There is a focus on understanding within the ABC structure, as a result of which actions and approaches to the therapy follow. These include showing the client techniques, and working towards changing her beliefs. The extract also shows Ellis instructing the therapist in the technique of analysing the data.

Liese and Beck (1997) describe the key features of cognitive therapy supervision as follows:

- First the supervisor identifies any misconceptions that the supervisee may hold about cognitive therapy. Such misconceptions are frequently associated with beliefs that the model takes no account of clients' emotions, childhood experiences, the therapeutic relationship or interpersonal factors.
- Where misconceptions are identified, the supervisor educates supervisees through direct instruction, discussion, role-play, assigned readings and direct observation of cognitive therapy in action.
- Supervisees usually undertake individual supervision with a weekly frequency for an hour per session. In addition, bi-weekly group supervision is prescribed.
- Supervision sessions follow a format akin to that of cognitive therapy, proceeding through the stages of check in, agenda setting, bridging to the previous supervision session, inquiry, review of homework, prioritisation and discussion of agenda items, new homework, brief summarising of key points, ending with the supervisee's feedback about the supervision session.
- Since the quality of the supervisory relationship is considered a central feature to the success of the enterprise, the above format is not rigidly followed.
- The main style of supervisory intervention is through direct instruction, although guided discovery is also employed.

- Role-play in which the supervisor demonstrates techniques and the supervisee plays the role of the client are considered to be helpful to learning.
- Tape recordings of therapy sessions are viewed as a useful medium for presenting the work with the client. Where supervisees are reluctant to use tapes in supervision the supervisor helps them to examine their negative automatic thoughts about tapes. Supervisees are seen as learning from their own review of tapes, this enabling identification of strengths and weaknesses. In addition, supervisors may use standardised scales such as the Cognitive Therapy Adherence and Competence Scale (Liese, Barber and Beck, 1995) to evaluate the work of the supervisee.

In both RET and CT supervision there is an understanding that difficulties in the supervisee's learning can result from the supervisee's personal issues when these are perceived to have a bearing on their work. In such instances, the approach to their solution is based on careful conceptualisation of the difficulty, which might reveal maladaptive beliefs such as, 'I need to be perfect.' This application of the model to the difficulty with the supervisee's learning demonstrates reflexivity between the model of therapy and the model of supervision.

Systemic model

A systemic model that emphasises the desirability of viewing the client in the context of their family and wider systems typically employs live team supervision. Whilst a systemic approach can be used effectively in work with individuals, most frequently it has been used with families as one approach to family therapy. The theory proposes that the client and therapist together comprise a new system and that patterns of interaction will develop that are influenced by the client's and therapist's habitual ways of relating. It is easy for the therapist to be implicitly invited to join the client's patterns, the team's presence helping to provide a more detached, different or 'meta' perspective on the therapist–client system. Systemic theory also emphasises the desirability of staying open to many and different ideas about clients and their situation. The presence of several people in the supervising team with a range of backgrounds and personal qualities helps to ensure that the therapist does not become unduly wedded to a particular way of viewing things.

Whilst the development of systemic therapy has incorporated ideas from constructivism (Von Glasersfeld, 1991), social constructionism (Gergen, 1985), post-modern narrative approaches to therapy (Anderson and Goolishian, 1988), and ideas about relationship based on feminism (Gilligan, 1982), the original tenets described by the Milan team continue to have relevance. In therapy and in supervision a position is adopted that includes a preference for openness to multiple hypotheses rather than the creation of a static explanation or diagnosis, rejection of a causal-linear way of thinking in favour of circularity and a focus on patterns of interaction, and the taking of a stance of 'neutrality', more recently developed into the notion of a position of 'curiosity' (Palazzoli, Boscolo, Cecchin and Prata, 1980; Cecchin, 1987)

The model includes the idea that the history of the client's system and transitions, such as new partnerships, the birth of children, moves of house and so on, may be important in the analysis of the problem. Problems may arise from the struggles of the system and the individuals within it to adapt to a transition. Habitual patterns of interaction may no longer fit the new circumstances. A major intervention strategy of the therapy is the use of questions – known as 'circular' (Burnham, 1986) or 'reflexive' (Tomm, 1987) – to help the client to develop new meanings or stories about themselves and their situation as a result of which the problem is seen differently and the client is enabled to experiment with actions and approaches that are different from those adopted to date. Interventions can include reframing, in which the therapist offers a new meaning for the same data, or the prescription of rituals in which the element of time is introduced with the intention of creating difference by punctuating sequences of interaction. For example, if two parents have different ideas about how to manage their child's behaviour, the therapist might prescribe that both parents follow the ideas of the mother on Mondays, Wednesdays and Fridays, and of the father on Tuesdays, Thursdays and Saturdays. The systemic approach has moved away from the therapist as expert towards a greater sense of collaboration between client, therapist and supervising team.

Translated reflexively from the model of work to the model of supervision the following are key issues in systemic supervision:

- The value of live supervision in which the ideas of the supervisor or supervising team are available during the therapy session. Tapes and reporting can also be used providing there is a focus on generating a multiplicity of ideas. Where work is reported to the supervisor, the view is taken that the segment of communication a therapist most characteristically focuses on will say more about the therapist than about the client (Hoffman, 1991).
- The value of multiple perspectives towards which a both/and, rather than an either/or, position is adopted.
- A focus of supervision being on the patterns and interchanges taking place between the client and supervisee as a source of information about how the client's habitual patterns involve others.
- The adoption of a curious and questioning stance. A major strategy used in supervision as in therapy is the use of circular or reflexive questioning.
- The intent of the supervisor to create conditions that can make a difference without necessarily prescribing the direction of the difference.

- The role of the supervisor being as participant-manager of the process of supervision.

Because the model of therapy attempts at its heart to be non-blaming of individuals and to adopt positive constructions of the actions of the individuals involved, this could pose a dilemma with regard to the evaluative role of the supervisor. As stated by Flemons, Green and Rambo (1996: 43), 'if, as postmodernists assert, there is no privileged, expert position, how can supervisors evaluate their trainees?' They conclude that evaluation can be undertaken within their family therapy doctoral training programme, but that this is in the context of collaborative relationships with students. Both supervisor and supervisee are seen as being able to learn from each other, and evaluations are made of each party by the other.

Where the work is undertaken in the context of a supervisory team, a discussion of authority and hierarchy and the implications of these factors needs to take place at the outset. Where the responsibility for the work lies with the supervisor, the status of interventions may be agreed as mandatory and issued in the form of an instruction to the supervisee: 'Ask the mother how near she thinks the father is to leaving the family.' In this example the authority of the supervisor is being brought to bear. In order to effect their gate-keeping role it may be helpful for supervisors to draw on the ideas of Lang, Little and Cronen (1990), who identify different domains of action. In the domain of explanation the focus is on understanding and the style is non-judgemental. In the domain of production the position is one of evaluation in a world of rights and wrongs. The supervisor may find it helpful to identify the domain from which he or she is operating at any particular time yet to intervene sensitively and aesthetically within Lang, Little and Cronen's domain of aesthetics, whether acting within the domain of explanation or the domain of production.

The practical issues involved in live supervisory teams are outlined by Burnham (1986):

- It is vital to clarify the differences in status, discipline and hierarchy between team members, including under what circumstances these differences would matter. The issue of responsibility benefits from being dealt with openly in order to foster the establishment and maintenance of trusting relationships.
- Rules for the resolution of disagreements should be agreed. Disagreement is viewed as usual and helpful within the model. Often a resolution of differences is not required but there may be occasions, for example in cases in which abuse is disclosed or suspected, when a course of action must be agreed and taken.
- The status of supervisory interventions as requests or commands should

be established. Commands are viewed as best kept to a minimum so that supervisees do not experience themselves as the puppets of the team.

Burnham describes the supervisor's task as that of taking a position which provides information about the interactions between clients and between clients and the supervisee. The tasks of supervision depend on what has been agreed about the role-relationship of the supervisor and supervisee. Where the relationship is one of trainer–trainee Byng-Hall (1982) states that the balance of authority lies even more with the supervisor than with other supervising techniques. However, as a general rule it is suggested that supervisors should pause before intervening since the trainee's strategy may work, the trainee often comes up with the idea that was on the tip of the supervisor's tongue, and the opportunity for both the supervisor and supervisee to discover the supervisee's potential is reduced. Montalvo (1973) suggests that the trainee be encouraged to follow her or his own ideas where they conflict with those of the supervisor unless the prefix 'must' is used in sharing a thought. The context for Byng-Hall's approach is where the supervisor has the opportunity to communicate with the supervisee during sessions by means of an earphone; an example (where $S.$ = supervisor, $T.$ = therapist, and $C.$ = client) is provided as follows:

$S.$ [earphone] Ask Dinos whether he is Greek or English.
$T.$ Do you think of yourself as Greek or English Dino?
$C.$ I am . . . I feel both at different times. When I am with my friends I am English . . .
$S.$ [earphone] Note the youngest boy talking to his father in Greek.
$C.$ . . . at home we speak Greek.
$T.$ When people all speak Greek at home it helps everybody to feel you haven't really left Crete.
$S.$ [earphone] Good.

(Byng-Hall, 1982: 51)

Byng-Hall suggests using this method of supervision to convey instructions to learners, to suggest strategies, to draw attention to something, to give an authoritative message from the team, to compliment and encourage the supervisee, or to increase or decrease the intensity of what is happening between the supervisee and client. Whatever the agreed tasks of the supervisor it is important that these are adhered to in the making of interventions. A systemic model can inform supervision carried out more conventionally in a one-to-one relationship. The transcript on pp. 43–46 provides such an illustration.

Ways of conducting live supervision are discussed at greater length in Chapter 9 and issues associated with group supervision in Chapter 6. These features can be adapted successfully to other models of therapy.

Summary

In this chapter the approach to supervision within four different models of therapy has been described. The selection of these particular models is to a degree serendipitous, although between them they illustrate some of the major differences of emphasis in approaches to therapy translated to the supervision process. Each model shows some congruence between the approach to therapy and the approach to supervision, albeit influenced by differences of style between individual supervisors. Discussion of these could be used in contracting for supervision in order to facilitate supervisors and supervisees in debating and negotiating the arrangements that they wish to make for themselves.

Chapter 12

Learning logs in supervision

Thinking and reflection

Education in schools and further education establishments does not inevitably encourage thinking. Particularly when driven by a set curriculum and examinations, the learner may act more in the manner of an information absorber and regurgitator. Apps (1982) likens this to the actions of a small child pulling a wagon around the house adding items that take her or his fancy en route. When a parent says, 'Can you give me the little red block', the child reaches into the wagon and hands the item to the parent as requested. This happens to students at examination time, and they are apt to be successful the more effective they have been at collecting and memorising the items called for. Engel (1971) goes so far as to say,

> Intellectual activity – from science to poetry – has a bad reputation in my generation. The blame falls on our so-called education system, which seems designed to prevent its victims from learning to think, while telling them that thinking is what you do when you study a textbook. Also, to learn to think, you must have a teacher who can think.
>
> (Engel, 1971: viii)

In contrast, thinking and reflecting on information and experiences can result in new knowledge and new ideas. The capacity to think is an essential element of the work of the professional helper. Each client has a unique presentation and unique problems, the task of the helper being to adapt information and skills to fit this particular circumstance. This was recognised in the work of Jung (1963):

> Naturally, a doctor must be familiar with so-called 'methods'. But he must guard against falling into any specific, routine approach. In general one must guard against theoretical assumptions. Today they may be valid, tomorrow it may be the turn of other assumptions. In my analyses they play no part. I am unsystematic very much by intention. To my

mind, in dealing with individuals, only individual understanding will do. We need different language for every patient.

(Jung, 1963: 153)

An orientation towards thinking is that of being curious – constantly probing, searching, questioning and wondering about alternatives. A practitioner who is thinking is prepared to suspend judgement and take time to consider the client's story as it emerges, without prematurely jumping to conclusions and formulaic action.

Learning new ideas and developing new skills requires time for reflection. It is possible to be excited by discussions that take place in supervision, and about information obtained from papers and books read and workshops attended, only to find that the ideas stimulated by them sink without trace unless there is an opportunity to think about their implications and their application in the workplace. Supervision can provide a space for reflection and integration of new ideas, but when supervision itself is the source of these more time may be needed.

One way of facilitating reflection and review is with the aid of a learning log or reflective diary in which ideas about the work and any implications for practice can be noted. The process of writing down thoughts, uncertainties and tentative understandings in a learning log can help in making connections between ideas that have emerged in different settings and at different times. Reflective journals have been adopted as a means to aid learning in the context of education for over a decade (Woodward, 1998) and have more recently found their way into the training of medical students (Niemi, 1997), general practitioners (Snadden, Thomas, Griffin and Hudson, 1996), and nurses (Button and Davies, 1996). Hellman (1999) describes their use in facilitating the development of reflective skills in the training of counselling supervisors.

What are learning logs and reflective diaries?

A number of terms have been used to refer to the products of reflective writing, which include 'learning logs', 'reflective journals', 'portfolios', and 'diaries'. These terms generally refer to writing carried out regularly by learners with a view to clarifying and developing their thinking about the topic being studied. They have been seen as serving a number of purposes for their authors.

* *Reconstructing knowledge*. Reflective diaries are reported as showing evidence of their authors relating ideas introduced by the teacher or supervisor to their own experience. Roberts (1989) describes the use of learning logs in the context of initial teacher training. The logs showed that student teachers developed understanding of the course by

searching for evidence which enabled them to accept or refute new ideas. They also asked themselves questions about the link between experience and information which helped in the emergence of new meanings. This process of reflection is seen as an essential element in adult learning as part of the experiential learning cycle (Kolb, 1984). The process of reconstruction draws on past experience and current events and makes links to the future. The logs that were most valuable to students in Roberts's study were those in which there was a constant looking back-wards to their authors' experience as learners, and forwards to being beginner teachers, showing a continuous attempt to make sense of new knowledge in terms of past and imagined future experiences.

- *Recording ideas that emerged in the supervisory conversation.* Supervision often leads to the identification of new ideas through the inter-subjective process taking place. Learning logs can be used as an *aide-mémoire*, and time can be set aside at the end of the session for together summarising what has emerged and making a note in a log. These can be reviewed in the process of planning the next session with the client.
- *Clarifying thinking.* The process of thinking is such that ideas often emerge spontaneously during an incubation period when the attention of the thinker has been elsewhere. Ideas arising in supervision can continue to be developed and clarified, both spontaneously and through further deliberate consideration. Sometimes logs are used when people think that there may have been a misunderstanding that needs to be cleared up later. An example from Roberts (1989: 197) is, 'I think I may have given the impression in this session that I am a raving fascist . . . I would hope this is not the case.'
- *Expressing feelings.* Logs can be a useful place to express feelings, per-haps with a view to bringing them to supervision at the next opportunity. By writing about positive emotions, supervisees can reaffirm their commitment to the work.

These are the aims of encouraging supervisees to complete learning logs for their own personal and professional development. When the logs are used for other purposes, such as evaluation of the student by professional training courses or for feedback to the supervisor or teacher, the content is likely to be affected (Snadden, Thomas, Griffin and Hudson, 1996). What is recorded has also been shown to be influenced by the degree of structure suggested and the way in which the idea of learning logs has been introduced.

Types of learning logs

Private records

Learning logs written as an aid to thinking and learning can be a private exercise carried out by supervisees for their own benefit. Their musings can be used for self-evaluation and for reviewing progress. The material included can be unbounded since no one else will see the document. When used in this way, authors need to be motivated by their viewing the exercise as useful and worthy of the time commitment involved. In their study, Snadden *et al.* (1996) found some resistance to the idea of reflective writing even though the diaries served no formal assessment purpose. The enthusiasm of trainers was essential to their being adopted by learners.

Interactive learning logs

In the training of general practitioners reflective diaries were not found to be effective for formal assessment purposes since the threat of assessment was regarded as adversely affecting the type of material collected. However, logs can still be used interactively between supervisees and supervisors. Such logs may not be assessed, but rather may be a course requirement, or maintaining a log may be agreed as a feature of the contract for supervision. The interaction between supervisor and supervisee may be through exchanged written comments, or supervisees may use their logs to inform their verbal contributions to the next supervision session.

When used interactively and when both parties write in the log, the nature of the contributions made by the supervisor and supervisee may be very influential each upon the other. Roberts (1989) reports the use of learning logs by student teachers with school children. Analysis of the entries made by the pupils showed three categories of response: 'descriptive' – statements of what had happened in the lesson; 'evaluative' – in which judgements were made about aspects of the lesson; 'reflective' – in which the pupils explored their ideas. Initial results were disappointing in that very few pupils used the latter category, rarely recorded any of their thinking and almost never used them to explore their thinking further. Possible explanatory factors for this finding included the pupils' expectations of what to write being conditioned by their previous experiences of being asked to write in school, their expectations of what to write being constrained by their interpretations of the instructions given, and their tendency to write about what they guessed the teacher wanted to read rather than what they wanted to say. An analysis of the teacher's contributions produced the categories 'evaluative positive', 'evaluative negative', 'questions', 'expressing feelings' and 'replying to an entry'. Within these categories the evaluative dominated. Following the analysis the teacher changed his contributions so that the category of 'questions' dominated. Subsequently some of the questions were answered briefly by pupils in their logs, some were discussed orally, but they were also found to encourage opening up of the pupils' thinking. From this point the logs were seen as more communicative, as including more reflection and argument, and of more use to both pupil and teacher.

When used interactively the learning of both parties may be facilitated. Reflection upon the process of supervision itself might be included and enable the supervisor to learn more about what is helpful to the supervisee and what is unhelpful. Where the supervision is carried out live by a team, written interactive logs can be particularly valuable. The focus of such supervision may rarely address the process taking place between the supervisee and the team since it tends to be focused on the process taking place between the supervisee and the client. The reflections of the supervisee about the ideas of the team and how they were communicated to her or him, the ideas that occurred to the supervisee during the session but that were not actively used in the work and the dilemmas faced by the supervisee might all provide useful material for the learning of those involved.

Obstacles to people writing reflectively include a lack of familiarity with this style of writing, fear of negative evaluation resulting from open-ended writing requirements, privacy issues, and the inequality of the role positions of supervisor and supervisee. To this end, a functional supervisory alliance and an open supervisory relationship better support the writing of interactive learning logs. Supervisors can model the process through their own preparedness to reflect, to write about their confusions and uncertainties and to ask questions about the usefulness of their interventions. Willingness and ability to reflect is affected by the developmental level of the supervisee, perception of the trustworthiness of the supervisor, clarity and nature of the expectations regarding the log and the quality of the feedback from the supervisor (Kerka, 1996).

Learning logs as assessment tools

Logs are intended as a place to record ignorance and confusion in addition to emerging ideas. When the log is to be seen by other than the author, these matters may be concealed. The content may then tend towards a description of what took place in supervision, and evaluation of the input of the supervisor. This might be of help to the supervisor but of limited value to the supervisee. There may be little evidence of reflection on the uncertain process and progress of learning. This may be even more the case when learning logs are a means of assessing the progress and performance of the supervisee.

The development of logs as an assessment procedure arose from the shift in higher education to the notion of authentic or performance assessment. This is intended to allow learners to demonstrate application of knowledge, skills and attitudes using situations that reflect or simulate actual life experience

(Woodward, 1998). Issues identified as arising from the use of learning logs for the purposes of evaluation include the following:

- The need to set criteria, goals or standards to form a framework on which to base assessment of the log. The criteria need to be broad if they are to encourage reflection.
- The importance of recognising that the assessment allows authors to demonstrate their learning but that learning also occurs for the assessor and the author as a result of engaging in the process.
- There is an assumption that authors are able to identify what they know, what and how they are learning and can demonstrate this in their logs.
- That the selection of entries and justification of meeting the assessment criteria should be in the hands of the author.
- That previously hidden learning and reflection on action has the opportunity to emerge and be assessed as a result of the reflective writing process.

When logs are used for assessment, they can serve the purposes of both formative and summative evaluation. In realising their function in relation to the development of critical thinking and reflection, supervisors have an important role in offering their own reflections as the log develops. The downside for the supervisor is the amount of additional time needed to read the logs and to undertake their own reflection on the material therein. Commitment to and enthusiasm for this is essential to the success of the venture.

An example of the successful use of learning logs as an assessment tool is described by Lee (1997). She instructs her English students during the first week of the course to set up double-entry logs: the left pages for assignments, notes and daily work, the right for more personal responses in the form of memories, realisations, explorations, extensions, associations and evaluations. The recording of this is a year-long project that will receive the same grade value as any other assignment. Each subsequent session begins with 2–4 written prompts on the board for students to answer or complete in their logs. Within the log students also make evaluations of their other course-work, including any agreements and disagreements with the grade awarded by the marker. The success of the logs may depend significantly on the attitude of genuine collaboration and interest in the students and their opinions shown by the teacher. This is illustrated in the following entry made by a student who was explaining the purpose of the self-evaluations to a researcher:

'She (the teacher) wants to know our opinion and she wants to communicate. That's what we're trying to learn this whole year – communication, and it's that meta-cognitive deal – how to think for yourself. She wants us to learn how to evaluate ourselves before we turn (work) in. She's like real independent and she wants everybody to learn how to do everything for themselves. On every assignment she lets us evaluate what we think we should get as a grade.'

(Lee, 1997: 44)

This teacher's stated intention is for the learners to develop skills in distancing themselves from their tasks in order to observe their own strategies. This idea is similar to the notion of the development of an internal supervisor (Casement, 1988), which allows for simultaneous experiencing and reflection on the experiencing. Her success in fostering a climate of open exploration is illustrated in the following entry:

'I don't think you know what you are doing. I've never been in a class like yours before. Why can't we work exercises out of a book? I don't like all this writing and thinking. You're the teacher. It's your job to tell me.'

(Lee, 1997: 42)

This student successfully completed the course and the teacher felt that her knowledge about his thinking as a result of his completion of the learning log enabled her to learn better how to involve him in the work.

There appears to be much enthusiasm for the use of reflective diaries in the work of those who have adopted them. Many students have commented on how the developing of their portfolio and the use of reflection was the most valuable process that they had encountered during their training. It helped them to discover personal qualities of which they had previously been unaware, and to discover more about themselves and their knowledge and skills both as a person and as a professional (Woodward, 1998).

Instructions for reflective writing

Authors vary in their opinions regarding the number and type of instructions that best facilitate the keeping of a learning log. When used with pupils in schools, the approach that was most successful in producing entries that demonstrated reflection on learning was that of giving brief oral instructions (Roberts, 1989). It was emphasised that the pupils could say anything that they wished in the logs and that the teacher was interested in the pupils' feelings. Her limited instructions allowed the pupils to set their own agenda for the logs and her focus in responding was on understanding the student as a person and as a learner.

Where logs have an assessment purpose, clearer instructions are probably necessary. The following are adapted from those suggested by Roberts (1989):

The purpose of the log is twofold. Firstly, it should help you to clarify your thinking, to identify misunderstandings and to reflect upon the process of your learning as it takes place. Secondly, the log should form part of a dialogue between supervisor and supervisee through which both can learn more about the processes of therapy and supervision. The diary should record your reflections on what you have read, any links to your personal experiences, what takes place and what you have thought and felt as a therapist and in supervision, and any ideas that emerge from workshops or teaching that you attend. The diary might include:

- comments on ideas that seem useful
- comments on ideas that you would like to try out for yourself
- any confusion or puzzlement
- ideas that emerge spontaneously
- what most helpfully prompted ideas
- comments on what you have found irrelevant, impractical or de-motivating
- details of what you found difficult to understand or do
- fears, hopes and anxieties
- successes and what pleased you

Your log should demonstrate your thinking and learning over time. You may find it helpful to look forward in order to identify potential learning needs and backwards in order to review your development.

The logs used by Roberts in initial teacher education were a course requirement but were not formally assessed. In my view, where the log is assessed, supervisees are likely to develop more confidence in writing about their doubts and confusions once they have experienced the style in which the supervisor responds to their writing. A style of response which encourages further reflection and questioning, rather than making judgements about the content of the log, is desirable.

Formats

In order to be useful for the purposes of developing critical thinking and reflective practice a variety of formats for reflective writing has been proposed. One option is to adopt three headings of 'Description', 'Reflection' and 'Action'. This is proposed by Woodward (1998), who suggests that journal authors note something, reflect on it and then propose action in order to give added purpose to the reflection. It was seen as essential that the requirement to propose action did not drive the entries to the log. The use of headings can be organised in columns (Berthoff, 1978), with a left-hand column for a description of experiences, notes or quotations, and the right-hand column for reflections on these.

Other suggestions have included the use of a portable notebook in which to record ideas, questions and uncertainties as they arise.

Summary

In conclusion, an approach to learning that includes the development of critical thinking skills and reflective practice has been shown to be facilitated through supervisees engaging in reflective writing. The success of such a venture relies on the enthusiasm of supervisors and may benefit from their participation with the supervisee in an interactive writing process. Journal entries that are freely, self-critically or spontaneously written might be of particular help to the author but must be predicated upon a safe and trusting relationship with the supervisor, unless it is agreed that they are to be kept private.

Chapter 13

Challenge and evaluation

The role of evaluator is typically found difficult by supervisors (Hahn and Molnar, 1991; Holloway and Roehlke, 1987). The assertive skills of evaluating and challenging others constructively can be difficult to learn, not only in the context of the helping professions but in life more generally. Attempts to challenge others can turn into confrontation or be received as negative and unsolicited criticism, the effects of which can be to damage relationships rather than to facilitate learning and development. This has been recognised by the Probation Service in the UK in relation to the appraisal process:

> There is evidence that employees do not respond well to any substantial degree of criticism, and that it does not lead to improvement in the criticised areas of performance. It is important that this is recognised but equally important that it does not lead to the production of bland appraisal reports that fail to deal with the real developmental issues. It is more helpful and stimulating to make a concrete, time limited statement of what you expect an employee to achieve in the future, than to make critical statements of what he or she has failed to achieve in the past.
>
> (Association of Chief Officers of Probation, 1989: 2)

The nature of therapy as opposed to supervision is such that making evaluations may be contra-indicated, since the literature suggests that potential impediments to mental health can result. High levels of criticism in families (known as expressed emotion) (Jacobsen, 1998: Butzlaff and Hooley, 1998) have been shown to be associated with mental health difficulties of children in their adult lives. The core conditions for psychotherapy (Rogers, 1980: 486) include unconditional positive regard, an attitude that might be perceived as incompatible with giving feedback and making evaluations. People whose primary training has been as therapists may therefore find switching to the role of evaluator particularly difficult. Unfamiliarity may result in clumsy attempts to provide feedback. The role is therefore worthy of careful consideration, with attention given to the aims of evaluation and the conditions that best support the task.

Definition of terms

Feedback

Feedback is defined here as a response or reaction providing useful information or guidelines for further action and development. This suggests a very constructive role for feedback in skill development. However, there can be problems with feedback given by a third party such as a supervisor:

- *The recipient needs to be open to engaging with the feedback or else it will have little useful effect on learning.* This is the case irrespective of the feedback being positive or negative. If the supervisor comments, for example, that the supervisee introduced her or himself and the way of working clearly, but the supervisee does not agree, the supervisee will give precedence to her or his own self-assessment unless open to the possibility of a change of mind on this subject. The wider effect may be for the supervisee to devalue other feedback given by the supervisor – 'What does he or she know?' – evaluating the supervisor as unfit to judge.
- *The feedback should connect with the issues of the learner.* Something of particular importance to the supervisor may not yet be within the scope of the supervisee at this stage of learning. A supervisee preoccupied with surviving a session is unlikely to be able to respond to fine detail even if this is acknowledged as a future learning goal.
- *Feedback will have no positive effect unless offered in the context of a sustaining supervisory relationship.* It may be necessary to allow time for the relationship to develop prior to attempting to critique the work in order for the recipient to understand the intent of the provider. The context of the supervisory relationship is crucial. It may not be essential for the supervisee to like the supervisor, but other features such as respect and trust are necessary in order for the feedback to be accepted.
- *Feedback in respect of issues about which the recipient feels vulnerable may produce a defensive response rather than learning and development.* If perceived as hurtful to a sensitive spot supervisees may feel it necessary to disguise their vulnerabilities in general and to effect a façade of competence or withdraw from the relationship.
- *If the giver of feedback believes it to be the 'truth' rather than an opinion, it may be given in such a way as to be irrefutable.* Whilst this may be effective in some instances – 'Saying that to the client was wrong in this model of work' – feedback is more generally found acceptable when offered as an opinion – 'At that point in the session I would probably have said . . .'
- *Feedback statements beginning with 'You . . .' are more likely to be perceived as focused on personal qualities rather than on practices.*
- *Feedback implies uni-directionality rather than mutuality.* It suggests a transmission mode of teaching which is unlikely to engage the adult

learner. Feedback could be mutual and it would be important for the recipient to be able to give feedback about the feedback in order to make the view open to debate.

- *In order to be effective, the feedback must be perceived as genuine.* Where it is seen as masking the supervisor's actual opinion or given in a convoluted and clumsy fashion, the effect will be to generate uncertainty and insecurity.
- *Feedback needs to be specific.* Where a bland general comment is made – 'The session was fine' – supervisees find it difficult to identify pointers for learning.

With these issues in mind I have come to the view that feedback from a third party is of limited value except under certain conditions. In particular, it is probably helpful if the feedback is invited rather than unsolicited. This allows recipients to have a degree of control, enables them to protect their vulnerabilities, and enhances the possibility that the feedback will connect with their learning needs. It also gives some protection to supervisors, preventing them from inadvertently undermining rather than enhancing the confidence of the supervisee.

Whilst exercising caution in regard to the effectiveness of third-party feedback, I am of the view that feedback from the materials operated upon (in this case the clients) is likely to have a more profound impact on the learner. If the client responds positively to the work this is likely to produce feelings of efficacy and pleasure for the therapist. If the response of the client is perceived as ambivalent or negative, this is likely to spur supervisees into seeking changes to their approach. The task of the supervisor with regard to feedback might thus be seen as helping the supervisee to interpret the feedback from the client and to explore the options for learning from this data. Feedback from the client may not be explicit but rather comprises the responses and reactions of the client in the work.

Challenge

The meaning of challenge here is taken as an invitation or undertaking to test one's capabilities to the full. Supervisors might thus challenge supervisees to use their identified strengths and capabilities, suggesting how these may be further developed. Supervisees might also be challenged to identify new skills that they wish to learn, building on current capabilities. Particularly early in their training, supervisees tend to have difficulty in identifying their own strengths as they are unclear about the features of the skills that they are trying to learn. The supervisor can help by noticing these and inviting the supervisee to use them more widely and in different contexts. For example, the supervisor might have noticed the supervisee feeling so overwhelmed with sadness as a client described the loss of her father that he or she was unable to speak. The supervisor might challenge the supervisee through identifying the strength of the capacity to experience deep empathy and, with the supervisee's agreement, use the supervision to consider how to manage this strength, which could include allowing a period of quietness during the therapy session. The purpose of challenge is to generate new perspectives at a cognitive level and to create options for action. The challenge is to the current way of seeing or doing things.

The benefit of challenging strengths rather than weaknesses is the context of a positive frame which better supports change and development. The risk of challenging weaknesses is that of prompting defensiveness, possibly leading to confrontation and argument and a hindrance to learning.

Evaluation and assessment

Evaluation and assessment involve making a judgement of a person's work. Evaluation aimed at fostering development is known as formative evaluation and that made as a judgement of professional fitness is known as summative assessment. The issues arising in relation to formative evaluation are similar to those associated with feedback, in that a single direction is implied – from evaluator to evaluated – with its attendant difficulties.

When considering summative assessment it should be borne in mind that there is no consistent agreement about the qualities that make someone fit to be a professional helper or on the skills that make up the work. Attempts to assess competence have often defined their measures around adherence to a particular model of psychotherapy. However, the transactions between therapist and client take on particular meanings and derive their therapeutic effectiveness from the interpersonal context of the therapy (Butler and Strupp, 1986). Studies of competence have often found difficulties resulting from poor inter-rater reliability (Shaw and Dobson, 1989), poor association between measures and client outcome (Svartberg and Stiles, 1992) and difficulties in reaching agreement about what features are central to the task (Fordham, May, Boyle, Bentall and Slade, 1990). With these factors in mind, it is as well to obtain clarity about the overriding concerns that might lead to consideration of unsuitability as a helper and to share these with the supervisee early in the process of establishing the supervisory alliance.

However, the supervisor does have an evaluative role and must be satisfied that the supervisee is fit as a professional even where the arrangement for supervision is between peers. The role is particularly salient in the case of pre-registration training.

Aims of challenge

In this section 'challenge' is the preferred term for the action that supervisors might take to foster a supervisee's development. In the event of serious concerns regarding the supervisor's capability to reach a satisfactory level of competence, or in the event of impaired performance or unethical conduct, more stringent measures may be required and these are discussed in the final section of this chapter.

Ownership

The supervisor is only one element of the supervisory environment that offers opportunities for challenge. In addition to the feedback from the client, a most important element is supervisees' own assessment of their strengths and points for development. The supervisor has a role in helping supervisees to challenge themselves and this role is less likely to produce defensiveness or confrontation. In this role, the supervisor might help the supervisee to identify core skills that comprise the helping task and against which supervisees might evaluate their current functioning for evidence not of attainment, but of progress to date, prioritising some issues for learning on which they might invite the supervisor to comment. A sample list of core skills is reproduced in Appendix 4.

Principles underlying challenge

Egan (1994) helpfully outlines the principles underlying effective challenge of clients by professional helpers. In respect of supervision the following are offered as principles which can guide decisions about how and when to challenge supervisees:

- *Keep in mind the goals of challenge.* The purpose of challenge was identified earlier as formative and addressed to the supervisees' learning and development. Supervisors who keep this in mind will be trying to understand the stage of the supervisee's learning and connect their challenges to this. It is also helpful for supervisors to check that their challenges fit with the supervisee's needs and this can be achieved explicitly by the supervisor asking the supervisee whether challenges proposed or already made have been useful to learning and development.
- *Encourage self-challenge.* This can be done explicitly by asking supervisees on which topics they would wish to challenge themselves, or by choosing a specific topic and inviting supervisees to consider whether this is a good time for them to challenge themselves to develop further on this issue. The supervisor can also notice when the supervisee has seemed to be attempting to take a new stance or approach and enquire into this.
- *Work to establish a relationship in which challenge is constructive.* A fundamental requirement for a functional supervisory alliance is mutual respect. If this is absent, and where there is a choice, it is better not to begin the relationship in the first place. Where there is no choice, open

discussion of the preconceptions about the other in the beginning may be difficult but may enable a reassessment which allows for the development of mutual respect. The supervisor also needs to keep in mind the inequity of the positions of supervisor and supervisee, particularly in the context of training relationships. It may be helpful to hold a discussion early on about each person's typical defensive responses and the most constructive responses to them. The supervisor should state clearly what issues they would perceive as seriously problematic. This prevents the supervisee from having to fantasise about this, possibly including a range of issues that would not trouble the supervisor. Supervisors can usefully model positive responses to being challenged themselves. They can refer to their own difficulties with the work, their own progress and development, and thereby normalise mistakes or lack of knowledge. Such references should always be driven by the learning needs of the supervisee and not stray into meeting the affirmation needs of the supervisor.

- *Show openness to being challenged oneself.* This might be apparent through observations that the supervisee might make of the challenges made to the supervisor by clients, colleagues or the supervisee. On the other hand there may be limited opportunities, but this could be accomplished by supervisors challenging themselves about the supervision that they are offering or inviting the opinions of the supervisee.
- *Be authentic and open to learning oneself.* A useful check might be to review whether one is adhering to the values and beliefs that one holds in relation to the supervisee. This might be explored in one's own supervision and involve a process of identifying one's own values about supervision and reviewing to what extent these are being followed.
- *Balance tentativeness with assertiveness.* Messages delivered in an overly assertive manner may not leave room for disagreement, can be experienced as accusations and produce confrontation and defensiveness. On the other hand, too many qualifications can sound apologetic, devalue the point being made and can leave someone uncertain as to what the supervisor thinks. For example:

> 'You asked me to notice how the client responded to your interrupting him because you are experimenting with challenging your idea that interruptions may be disrespectful to the client. I think that maybe you were more ready to interrupt than previously and perhaps this helped the session along so that you maybe were able to stay with your plan for the session more than before.'

> 'You asked me to notice how the client responded to your interrupting him because you are experimenting with challenging your idea that interruptions may be disrespectful to the client. You certainly interrupted more than previously and I think you could easily go

further without showing disrespect. Do you want to experiment more in the next session or try it with me now?'

- *Build on success.* This links with the idea of challenging strengths that are underused or could be more widely applied. It is important not to expect great leaps in learning and to encourage even small changes, helping supervisees to notice these changes and make plans to build on them.
- *Be specific.* Vague and overly broad observations tend to be experienced as challenges to the whole being of the person rather than to specific aspects of knowledge or performance that might be developed. In addition to evoking strong feelings in the supervisee, it is much more difficult to change something that is experienced as central to one's self. For example, challenging a supervisee's whole approach to clients by saying, 'When you are with clients I observe that you are overly friendly and that limits what you can do as a therapist' is likely to be perceived as a criticism and may produce a defensive response. An alternative is to say, 'Talking to clients in the waiting room like a friend might not orient them to your professional role as a therapist. I would like us to think about how to start when clients have to be brought from the waiting area, and how you might use your strengths of warmth and friendliness in other ways in the work.'

The process of challenging

The following steps are suggested as a format for challenging a supervisee. This is not to suggest that challenge is necessarily a major undertaking, rather it can be a small part of the work of the supervisor, undertaken naturally as part of the regular supervisory process. The skills of challenging do require supervisors to acknowledge their own authority which is afforded by the role, even in peer arrangements. The format is designed to help people new to taking a position of authority to think about and practise the skills.

- *Identify the purpose of the challenge.* In planning to challenge a supervisee it is helpful to be clear that the desired outcome is some particular learning. The purpose can be described to the supervisee as a preface to introducing the subject matter, and the desired outcome should be specific and clear. The benefit to the supervisee can be included – 'I think that you could be even more effective in your work with Jane if you were to develop your skills in helping her to work harder and participate more in the sessions, perhaps by staying more quiet yourself.'
- *Decide whether you have the authority to make this challenge.* The degree of authority vested in the supervisor depends on the specific arrangement made. If in doubt, for example in a peer arrangement, ask the supervisee for their opinion on this – 'Do you want to give me the authority to

challenge your approach to this client or do you want me to help you with the approach that you're now taking?' The responsibility for some kinds of learning may lie elsewhere in the work system – for example, with a line manager or member of a training institution. In order to challenge confidently it is important to believe that one is operating within the agreed brief of the relationship.

- *Get your facts clear.* If you are unsure about what you believe it would be helpful for the supervisee to change in their work – for example, because something has been reported to you by another person, make sure that you are clear about the facts and that you subscribe to the idea that change is needed. If not, work out how to gain greater clarity before treating it as a matter on which to challenge the supervisee.

- *Practise making clear and direct statements.* If this is a new skill for you, rehearsal will help you to feel comfortable. You might also ask for feedback from the supervisee. This could be part of your learning agenda as a supervisor and could be introduced to the supervisee as such – 'I am trying to develop my skills in challenging and I would like to make a suggestion to you about your learning. I would welcome your opinion about how my suggestion affects you.'

- *Consider starting sentences with 'I'.* This indicates that you are offering an opinion which could in turn be challenged by the supervisee. 'I have noticed that I seem to be sharing more of my opinions in supervision than I usually do. I think you may have the idea that my opinions are more important than yours. I would like to talk about what I can do that would help you to develop more confidence in your own ideas.' This is clear and purposeful and less likely to be perceived as a criticism than saying, 'You need to share more of your own ideas in supervision.'

- *Use immediacy if things seem to be getting out of hand.* Immediacy in the context of supervision is using perceptions of what is currently taking place between the participants in the supervisory dialogue as information for the purposes of learning and development. The concept was introduced by Carkhuff and his colleagues (Carkhuff, 1969; Carkhuff and Anthony, 1979). If the supervisee responds defensively or aggressively to a challenge, do not be afraid to comment on what seems to be happening between you in the present. If it is appropriate, be prepared to take responsibility for the direction the conversation has taken. 'My intention in raising this is to help you to develop your confidence in your own ideas about the work but that doesn't seem to be happening. What can I do that would better achieve that?' Don't second-guess the mood of the supervisee with a 'you' statement, such as, 'You seem to be getting very angry.'

- *Offer to come back to the matter after further thought.* Sometimes you may anticipate that the issue you are planning to raise will be difficult for the supervisee to address no matter how sensitively it is raised. For example, continuing to work despite significantly poor health. 'In your position I would want to be considering whether to take a period of sick leave. One of the problems in our profession is that people are often reluctant to do that because they feel that they are letting their clients down or believe that their colleagues will be critical. Don't let me know what you think now but I would like you to think about it between now and our next supervision and put it on the agenda for then.' This can also be suggested if the conversation has proved difficult, deferring any decisions until the supervisee has been able to go beyond her or his initial response.

- *If you meet with blank refusal to consider the issue, ask the supervisee what he or she would do in your shoes.* This would more typically occur in the context of the managerial function of supervision. You may have had to raise an issue such as the supervisee coming to work with the smell of alcohol on her or his breath. The supervisee will not necessarily be thinking of your dilemma but you can introduce this by asking her or him to consider what action he or she would take in your place. You are showing authority with respect to the issue of drink and the workplace, and showing openness to learning about the process of dealing with it.
- *Be prepared to show humility.* Whilst the skills of challenging involve taking authority, this does not have to be across the board, only in relation to the specific issue raised. It is important that supervisors model a non-defensive approach with regard to their own skills in challenging.

Challenging is about the learning of the supervisee. Ultimately if the supervisee does not seem amenable to learning then supervisors will need to consider whether to exert their formal evaluative role as gate-keeper to the profession. This is explored in the final section of this chapter.

Challenge of a different kind

Sometimes supervisors find that they are in a relationship with the supervisee that differs from that desired. It is not the learning and development of the supervisee that is at stake, but rather a change in the nature of the relationship. Supervisors may feel that the relationship is too distant, that they cannot trust the word of the supervisee, or that the supervisee is acting strategically or inauthentically in supervision. However, the work carried out may meet the requirements of the profession and the issue is not therefore one of normative standards. Here, the difficulty is or may be specific to the supervisory relationship. The aim is to create a more effective and satisfying supervisory alliance.

The challenge here is to both parties, with no predetermined intent to facilitate change in the supervisee. The aim is to facilitate change in the supervisory relationship which may involve change in the supervisor.

Since the difficulty is being identified by the supervisor, it is the supervisor who is experiencing the problem and inviting the assistance of the supervisee in its solution. This may require a different approach since this is in the nature of a request which may be met or refused. There may be a consequence for the supervisee of refusing the request. Where the arrangement is voluntary the supervisor may conclude that he or she no longer wishes to participate, and where it is mandatory the supervisee who refuses to engage may find that her or his learning needs are given a reduced priority.

The challenge in this context might need to be introduced in a different way, and the value to the supervisee of agreeing to engage in solving the supervisor's problem may be part of the introduction. For example, 'I'm finding some difficulties in how my relationship with you is working and I would like to ask if you are prepared to talk to me about it because I think that we could both have a lot more enjoyment than we are having at the moment if I felt differently. Would it be OK with you if I tell you a little more about it?' Another method of introducing the topic may be first to comment on what is working well in the relationship in order to provide a context in which the supervisee is encouraged to work to preserve it. This might mean noting the professionalism of the person, her or his commitment to learning, and so on.

Attribution of the difficulty to the pattern rather than the person is probably helpful. It may also help to be specific in identifying particular examples of the difficulty, the events that have contributed to establishment of the pattern and the effects on self. For example, where the supervisor does not find the supervisee's contributions to have an authentic quality the supervisor could refer to examples. 'When you were talking to Mrs Brown I just had the feeling that you didn't mean what you said and I felt the same when you were asking to have a shorter supervision session last week. I may be misreading your tone of voice or eye-contact – I'm not sure what it is – can you help at all? Am I doing something that makes you uncomfortable or that you would rather I did differently?'

Another strategy is to work together on the pattern by enlisting the support of the supervisee in committing what is known to paper in the form of data or a diagram. In this way the parties are on the same side in studying the problem that is outside them as individuals. From time to time the best efforts of the supervisor appear to have no impact and a state of impasse is reached. In voluntary arrangements, the supervision contract can be terminated. In pre-registration arrangements the supervisor may conclude that her or his repertoire of approaches to the difficulties has been exhausted and the help of a third party may be invoked. Another conclusion may be that the supervisee is unfit to join the profession. It is important for this to be acknowledged and the supervisor will need to communicate with the training agency in order to effect the gate-keeping function.

Unsatisfactory performance

Definitions of unsatisfactory performance

From a thorough review of the literature pertaining to the training of clinical psychologists in the USA, Forrest, Elman, Gizara and Vacha-Haase (1999) conclude that there is a lack of clear, shared and consistent language to represent different types of problematic behaviour. They recommend distinguishing between impairment, incompetence and unethical practice. Impairment refers to diminished functioning after reaching an adequate level of professional competence. This is likely to arise from situations of extreme personal stress, or alcohol or substance misuse. Incompetence refers to an absence of qualities or skills necessary to attain adequate levels of professional performance (Kutz, 1986). Unethical practice refers, for example, to entering into a sexual relationship with a client where there is no temporarily diminished functioning.

Forrest *et al.* note that current definitions of impairment mix descriptions of problematic behaviour (e.g. defensiveness in supervision) with descriptions of explanations (e.g. depression, personality disorder) and that this creates confusion for both supervisors and supervisees. They make a number of recommendations through which training courses may develop helpful policies and procedures in order to fulfil their gate-keeping role.

Palmer Barnes (1998) offers another model for classifying unacceptable practice into the categories of 'mistakes', 'poor practice', 'negligence' and 'malpractice'. Mistakes feature in the work of all practitioners, although the degree of severity will differ. They are defined by Palmer Barnes as, 'an unintended slip in good practice'. At the other end of the continuum, malpractice usually involves a practitioner following a course of action designed to meet her or his own needs. For a wider discussion of these categories the reader is referred to Daniels (2000).

Supervisors, faced with managing unsatisfactory performance, need to find a path that takes into account the needs of clients and of the supervisee that is as pain-free as possible for all. Balancing educational responsibilities with gate-keeping obligations continues to be a struggle for supervisors (Hahn and Molnar, 1991; Holloway and Roehlke, 1987).

Dealing with unsatisfactory performance of a supervisee in training

In the contracting process, the supervisor's requirements of the supervisee should have been made clear. For example, the supervisor may have agreed that supervision will take place at a regular time and venue and that this should also be the case for the work carried out by the supervisee with the client. If the supervisee shows unreliable time-keeping then this will need to be addressed in supervision. The supervisor needs some skills in challenging in order to accomplish this, and these skills may differ from those required in the role of therapist. In pre-registration training, students have a right of due process, violation of which allows them recourse to legal redress. This is explored more fully in Chapter 7. Since a future career can weigh in the balance, supervisors need to take a well-considered and ethical approach to the management of unsatisfactory performance.

There is sometimes a temptation for the supervisor to hope that supervisees' evaluations of their own performances equate with those of the supervisor. There may be a temptation to ask a question rather than to make a statement. The question, 'How satisfied were you with the way the session ended?' can be asked either from a position of genuine curiosity or can be asked when the supervisor has already decided that the supervisee needs to develop skills in closing down sessions. In the latter case, the supervisor is faced with a continuing dilemma regarding how to pursue this unless the supervisee responds to the question with the same opinion as the supervisor regarding endings. Whatever the supervisee's response, be it neutral, with openness, or defensively, supervisors can make diagnostic use of this in order to judge their next action.

It may be helpful for supervisors to practice making preference and purpose statements and evaluative statements in which they make their opinions and requirements clear. Some examples follow:

> 'In the contact we agreed that I would need to hear you working and next week I would like you to bring a recording of a session of your choice. This week I would like us to spend the first 15 minutes or so working out how to use the tape in ways that you are comfortable with.'

> 'When you asked Janet to keep a diary record of her automatic thoughts, I felt that she would find the task too difficult without more structure. I tend to make a record during the session of an example, and then ask the client to do this for a second example so that any uncertainties can be dealt with at the outset. What do you think about trying that?'

> 'When we discussed how to keep case-files in this service I explained that they needed to be completed each time you saw a client. I was very surprised to find that the files are a month behind and completing them must be a priority for this week. Can you tell me how they came to be so far behind?'

> 'When you come to supervision I would prefer it if you have thought about a focus for the session in advance as at this stage I think it is no longer necessary to take a look at each of your cases every week.'

> 'We have talked a lot about how anxious the work makes you feel and how when you feel anxious one way of coping is to avoid seeing clients.

Now we are half way through the placement and I'm worried that when we reach the end you will not have achieved the aims and activities that we agreed at the beginning because you will not have had enough contact with the clients. If this happened you would not pass the placement so I think that we need to work out how to deal with the anxiety in a different way. There has to be a change but we can work out together what would be needed to help you to make the change.'

The last example leads on to failure and the gate-keeping role of the supervisor in the context of pre-registration training.

When to fail a supervisee

It is important that the supervisor and supervisee are both aware at the outset of the criteria upon which the assessment of the supervisee's work will be made. These may be set by the training institution, but with room for modification according to the individual judgement of the supervisor. The kinds of behaviours that might lead to failure are usually within the domain of unprofessional behaviour, unethical behaviour, and unwillingness or inability to learn. Occasionally the supervisor may judge the candidate to be unsuitable for the profession because of an unwillingness to examine blind spots that are considered central to conducting the work soundly. The following are some examples of what might prompt a consideration of failure:

- The supervisee makes appointments with clients but is unreliable in turning up for them, or is repeatedly late and unresponsive to suggestions for change.
- The supervisee shows hostility in interactions with staff, losing her or his temper and attributing the difficulty to others. A pattern of such behaviour emerges particularly in relation to authority figures. Attempts to discuss the difficulties lead to further expressions of hostility, with the supervisee walking out of meetings arranged to explore the difficulties.
- The supervisee violates the rules of the organisation in which the work is conducted to the extent of stepping over the boundary of events that constitute gross professional misconduct (for example, turning up to work when under the influence of drugs or alcohol, or engaging in a sexual relationship with a client).
- The supervisee achieves only a superficial level of engagement with clients, talking about them rather as objects than people. Clients typically fail appointments after the first one or two sessions. When these issues are raised the supervisee takes sick leave.
- The supervisee's work is adversely influenced by earlier life experiences which constitute major blocks to her or his work with certain issues and

clients. It is inappropriate to continue in training until these have been addressed in personal development work.

- The supervisee engages in inappropriately immature or defensive behaviour such as attempting to lie her or his way out of a difficulty rather than engaging actively with the issue and taking responsibility for the difficulties.
- The supervisee presents with very unbalanced professional capabilities. For example, there is a mismatch of skills in an academic high flyer who has very limited interpersonal skills for work in a people-centred profession.

When a supervisee's performance is unsatisfactory supervisors often try to find alternatives to failing the practice placement. Some of these alternatives do not help with the problem. Wilson (1981) describes the following:

- Ignore the problematic performance and award a 'satisfactory' grade.
- Lower performance expectations.
- Wait and see if the supervisee's performance improves in the next practice placement.
- Make the supervisee's experience so miserable that he or she withdraws from the training programme.

Since these solutions are unsatisfactory in relation to future clients and probably also for the supervisee, it would be better for supervisors to 'bite the bullet' and raise their concerns with the training institution.

How to fail a supervisee

When serious difficulties arise it is essential to keep records of the reasons for concern, the attempts that have been made to raise them with the supervisee and what would be required in order for the supervisee's performance to be assessed as adequate. Where possible it is also desirable to involve the training institution at an early stage. When such decisions are to be made it is usually wise to involve a group of people or a committee in order to ensure fairness and to establish that the difficulty is not arising from a single problematic supervisory relationship. It is essential that the supervisee has had the opportunity to make improvements – discussed in Chapter 7 under the issue of due process.

To fail a placement is a very difficult decision for one individual to make. It is important not to avoid the issue, however. A test of the level of one's concern is to imagine the supervisee being consulted by one's best friend, partner or child. If upon such consideration it is concluded that there is an unacceptable risk of the loved one being damaged by the contact, then it would surely be irresponsible not to take action.

Following from the decision to fail is either the construction of a plan for remediation or a decision to dismiss, the latter being a process which is likely to be informed by, but not taken by, the supervisor. Whilst a decision to fail a training placement is usually a source of anxiety and heart-searching for supervisors, it can be the crisis that enables a supervisee to face up to her or his difficulties in a constructive way since they can no longer be avoided.

Dealing with impairment and unethical behaviour

When the supervisor has serious concerns regarding the practice of a supervisee who is a qualified practitioner, the path for dealing with this may be even more complex and challenging than in the case of pre-registration training. A range of explanations for the impairment or unethical conduct may suggest different approaches in the longer term. Schoener and Gonsiorek (1988) reported their work in the rehabilitation of more than a thousand cases of therapists who had committed sexual transgressions with clients. They concluded that their sample varied from individuals whose conduct had arisen from naivety to those who showed psychotic symptoms. They identified the need for careful assessment of practitioners whose performance is believed to be impaired or unethical. This entails the use of clinical judgement.

Supervisors experience contradictory pulls between their nurturing and evaluative roles and are likely to have to deal with impairment in supervisees only on rare occasions. They may also fear the reaction of the supervisee to their attempts to take the matter forward. When the level of supervisors' concerns leaves them with no alternative but to act, this needs to be done with care for the individual and concern for the practitioner's clients. Supervisors in such circumstances would be wise to take advice and guidance from their professional network, out of which consultation process should emerge a suitable plan for action. This will almost certainly involve the supervisee, although her or his consent to the action may be unobtainable. Many psychologists self-report continuing to work, even when they are too distressed to function effectively (Pope, Tabachnick and Keith-Spiegel, 1987; Wood et al., 1985). Supervisors are in a pivotal position to help such practitioners to make the difficult decision to stop work, or in extreme circumstances to take the decision for them.

Summary

This chapter discusses the evaluative role of the supervisor, the role of feedback and the development of skills in constructive challenge as a preferred approach to effecting the evaluative role in facilitating supervisee development. It also discusses the issues of failure to achieve competence and of supervisee impairment. Supervisors tend to have little experience of dealing with issues of failure and impairment. This results from the fortunate occurrence that, in my experience, the majority of supervisory relationships are rewarding and satisfactory to the participants most of the time. If they were not, it would be difficult to understand why supervision continues to be regarded as an essential requirement in training in the helping professions.

Chapter 14

The supervisor's role in coursework

This chapter is addressed specifically to supervision in which supervisees are participating in a course of training, either for registration purposes or as part of their continuing professional development.

Whilst it is not the supervisor's responsibility to help supervisees who are training with their coursework requirements, many are likely to have been approached for such help and in some cases the input of the supervisor is required by the training course. The supervisor may also be responsible for providing work for supervisees that could serve as material for their coursework.

Issues in regard to coursework assignments

Finding suitable material or subjects

A common coursework assignment is that of case study. Other popular tasks are essays, placement-based research and the compilation of logs of work carried out. Supervisors benefit from clear guidance from courses as to the specific requirements for such assignments and this information will often need to be fed into the placement planning process so that suitable cases or projects can be established at the outset, training placements usually being time-limited.

A number of factors are likely to influence the suitability of the work carried out on the placement for the purposes of coursework assignments. Where supervisees need to write up their work with a client, for example, it is important that the client is accessible to them, keeps her or his appointments, and that the case is of sufficient depth and/or duration to allow for adequate assessment of the supervisee's work by the course staff. These requirements map more readily onto some placements than others. Appointments for clients being seen in a family therapy service may be more widely spaced than is suitable, rates of client non-attendance may be high, the supervisor may operate in a brief therapy model, or the work with some client groups may proceed at a slower rate than the assignment demands. Supervisors may feel more or less willing to search for suitable clients outside of their usual referral sources, particularly if this risks establishing a demand for services where none previously existed. Nevertheless, clear information about assignments and advance planning enable supervisors better to help supervisees with finding work that meets course requirements. The training course needs to be alerted early if suitable work cannot be found so that alternative arrangements can be made.

Knowledge of the service

The supervisor's knowledge of the service, the nature of its policies and practices, and the supervisor's established relationships with staff can also be of help to supervisees. Permission to carry out the work within the particular service may be needed and the supervisor is often in a good position to know key people from whom this should be obtained. There may be a need for access to the employer's policy documents or data about the local population served. The supervisors' knowledge of the system can enable them to help smooth the way for supervisees.

Confidentiality

Where assignments involve clients or services, supervisors may have concerns regarding the confidentiality of material written up or of the client files from which information may be extracted. It is as well to know the policy of the employing organisation with respect to such matters. The educational institution will probably insist on the removal of all identifiers from work submitted for assignments, but in my experience supervisees are not always adequately vigilant about this and it is quite easy involuntarily to leave in an occasional name. Supervisors need to make clear to supervisees their own concerns and the policy of their employer. They might also read any proposed submissions to ensure that they comply with this requirement.

A further issue of confidentiality is the extent to which clients might be informed that the work undertaken with their therapist is to be written up in an assignment. Whilst this is essential in the event of published work, there is less clarity with respect to submitted work which is not in the public domain. It seems likely that the need to inform the client will affect the way in which the work is written up and may constrain the nature of the writing or even the way in which the work is conducted. Monaghan (2000) suggested that whilst clinical work typically shapes the case study, the case study may also shape the clinical work since the therapist may have the write-up in mind during clinical sessions. She experienced feeling uncomfortable when the client had not been informed that the work was to be submitted as an assignment, but also wondered how informing the client might have impacted on the transference and affected the work.

Informing the client may constrain the write-up, but not necessarily to its disadvantage. There are potentially creative ways of involving the client in writing about the work. For example, Woskett (1999) agreed with a client that each would write up their own account of the sessions and these were used both to inform the work and for publication. Some clinicians write joint notes of sessions together with their clients and this method could be adapted for the purpose of case study. However, these approaches are not typically included in assignment guidelines.

One alternative approach to this issue is to inform clients that their agreement to be seen by a practitioner in training automatically carries their consent to possible write-up of the work. Providing the client with this information can be part of the general process of obtaining informed consent and it benefits from careful planning. An opt-out clause is desirable, if not essential. Appendix 5 contains an example of a notice that might be included in an initial appointment letter to clients as a preliminary way of introducing the idea.

The effects of the assignment on the tripartite arrangement

Coursework assignments represent a visible presence of the training institution in the fieldwork placement. This is likely to make a greater impact where the assignment draws on work carried out on the placement but can have an indirect effect even if the coursework is not connected with the placement. For example, the levels of energy that the supervisee brings to the practical work can adversely be affected by the demands of assignments, particularly as deadlines approach. Supervisors may experience themselves in a three-way relationship with their supervisee and the supervisee's assignments in which their own needs and the needs of the supervisee's clients appear to have lowest priority. This can be frustrating and disappointing.

Ideally the demands of coursework assignments and the nature of the practical work dovetail, but this is not necessarily the case. The potential for conflicts and irritations is likely to be lessened by exploration in supervision, possibly involving staff from the educational institution when resolution seems difficult. Supervisors do not want to feel that they are overburdening supervisees with practical work when assignments dominate because the spectre of course failure often looms large in the supervisee's consciousness. On the other hand, they will not wish trainee practitioners to qualify with an inadequate practical experience.

Supervisors may experience greater or lesser degrees of confidence in their abilities to help trainees with assignments and this is likely to be influenced by their knowledge of the coursework requirements and possibly the extent to which they themselves have produced such work in their own training. A lack of confidence may encourage the supervisor to remain distant from the assignment, for fear of providing a misleading input. Supervisors who wish to help and who are experiencing feelings of lacking confidence might take a different tack by seeking to educate themselves more fully about the requirements. It might also be seen as the responsibility of courses to provide supervisors with relevant training. Feelings of uncertainty may be associated more with some assignments than others. Small-scale research projects or larger pieces of work for a dissertation may be perceived as more 'academic' and best left in the hands of the training course. Such perceptions will depend on the research experience of the supervisor and this can be clarified to the supervisee.

Sometimes supervisors might experience a re-evocation of anxiety about or hostility towards training left over from their own past experiences. In such instances it would be important for the supervisor to recognise these and to consider their impact on the supervisor's input with the supervisee. Mutual denigration of the nature of the assignment is unlikely to benefit the supervisee's progress and development.

If the supervisor does perceive a problem with the assignment requirements it would be appropriate and helpful to raise this with a member of the course staff. The underlying principle here is for the supervisor and the course to present a coherent approach to supporting trainees' assignment work, rather than to leave trainees to sort out any incompatibilities themselves.

The potential for conflicting advice

Supervisors' roles in relation to the practical work completed on the placement are usually much clearer than their role in coursework. In the former, the supervisor has defined responsibilities; in the latter, other supervisors are also likely to be involved in the shape of course tutors who may be the 'official' supervisors of the work. Where more than one supervisor is involved in the same piece of work there is potential for conflicting input and advice. Supervisees may find it difficult to integrate input from both.

Multiple consulting is a strategy sometimes adopted by anxious supervisees who believe that they will be helped if only they can find the 'right' helper. This process may also be encouraged by supervisors who are themselves anxious about their knowledge of coursework requirements. Failure to make good progress with the coursework may be located by supervisees in what they see as an inadequate supervisor. Multiple consulting can thus serve to confuse rather than clarify.

Over- and under-conscientiousness

A dimension along which supervisees appear to differ is reflected in the standards that they set for themselves in regard to their work. I have encountered problems at both extremes. Overly high standards are exacting and can be anxiety-producing. Sometimes levels of anxiety are so high that performance is significantly impaired, and supervisees in this state are often unable to think clearly. At the other end of the spectrum are those who set unduly low standards for themselves. For them an attitude of 'What is the minimum I need to do in order to complete this course?' can generate an implicit invitation to the supervisor to do the work for them. These supervisees need different kinds of help from their supervisors.

Possible roles of the supervisor in relation to coursework

Bearing in mind the above issues, supervisors can nevertheless be very helpful to supervisees with their coursework. It is probably in the supervisor's interest to know what work supervisees are currently engaged in for their course even if the supervisee does not ask for help. This provides information about the more global demands on the supervisee and any implications for the nature of the work carried out on the placement. Supervisors may also legitimately insist on involvement, for example, should they feel that evaluation of the coursework also reflects on their own practice, or in order to ensure that the requirements of their agency have been honoured.

Normaliser

Either through their own training or through previous involvement in coursework, supervisors may have developed a good knowledge of course requirements and of appropriate standards for the work. They are also likely to have supervised other practitioners in training who have experienced the same worries and practical difficulties with their coursework. A supervisee sometimes can feel that he or she is the only person who is having difficulty, or may start to panic that the end of the placement will be reached without having found material suitable for an assignment. A supervisor's knowledge can serve to reassure, as can the construction of back-up plans in the event of client non-attendance or false starts.

In my experience trainee practitioners usually take their training very seriously. This is right and proper unless they become handicapped by such an attitude. Sometimes the seriousness can wear them down and the supervisor can help by the use of humour to bring the issues into a more suitable sense of proportion and to lighten the burden of the assignment. The supervisor can use strategies described elsewhere in this book, including, for example, asking the supervisee to role-reverse with the assignment. Questions such as 'If the assignment had a voice, what would it be saying to you about how much more time to spend? Would it prefer you to work harder for longer and go for an outstanding mark, or would it want you to get finished and go for adequate?' may be useful. Another method might be to represent other elements in the supervisee's life on paper, investigating the size and location of the assignment in relation to these factors such as her or his family, socialising, holidays, clinical skills, hobbies and so on, the aim being to put the assignment into perspective against the other facets of the supervisee's life.

Thought-organising assistant

A significant way in which supervisors can use their skills is in helping students to clarify and focus their ideas about coursework. Helping people to organise and structure their thoughts can be achieved through judicious questioning, and possibly by sketching out the responses in a diagram which links key concepts and ideas. It is not necessary for the supervisor to have detailed knowledge of the topic in order to perform this service. Supervisees may have collected a great deal of information from a client, or from wide reading around a research topic, but have reached a position in which they cannot see the wood for the trees.

Diagrams are a useful aid to case formulation since large amounts of data can be presented within a confined space, showing how they link together to provide an understanding from which intervention may proceed. This is preferable to an alternative strategy of ignoring much of the data if it does not appear to fit neatly into a single conceptual model.

Questions which address the basics of the assignment such as 'What question are you trying to answer?', 'Who are the key characters?', 'How does X link with Y?', can help in the organising process.

Theory-provider

The course on which the supervisee is registered has a role as theory-provider for the practice placement, but supervisors themselves may be an equally good source. Courses cannot address all relevant theory and supervisees may look to the supervisor to help narrow down their literature searches or to help link theory and practice. Supervisors may also have their own research specialisms and supervisees' experience may be enriched by drawing on this expertise.

Reassurer-encourager

A supervisee beset by doubts about her or his capability to complete an assignment can be reassured by a supervisor who shows genuine confidence in the supervisee's ability to be successful. Uncertainty about capability can lead supervisees to avoid starting an assignment and the supervisor can have a useful role in co-constructing a timetable and encouraging the supervisee to stick to it.

When it is unclear what form the encouragement might helpfully take, a dialogue may be of use. This might involve helping supervisees to think about how they have successfully completed previous assignments, and what has helped them to learn and progress with the task. For example, someone with a block about writing might be encouraged to begin with a tape-recorded dialogue explaining her or his work to the supervisor, a friend or colleague. The transcript of such a dialogue can be edited into a first draft of a project.

Beginning with a first draft is sometimes alien to supervisees who equate first and final drafts. Encouragement to write anything at all as a starting point can serve to unblock the writing process. The supervisor may also agree to help in the tidying process as each redraft is made.

Boundary setter

There are a number of ways in which supervisors can usefully set boundaries for supervisees in relation to their coursework. Not least is to help the supervisee to select a 'do-able' topic. There is sometimes a desire in supervisees to produce a startlingly original or very extensive piece of work. This is laudable, but is probably unrealistic in the supervisee's circumstances. The supervisor may be able to offer reassurance that the successful completion of a more modest piece of coursework may be more valuable than an ambitious unfulfilled study. Supervisees can be encouraged to see their very ambitious goals as more suited to post-qualification work. Thus supervisors can encourage supervisees to constrain their projects, to narrow down the field of literature that they intend to critique and to say 'this is enough' when they are concerned that the supervisee is spending too long, or extending too broadly or too deeply into the topic at issue. In order to take this role supervisors need to be confident that they have an accurate picture of course requirements by consultation with course staff and coursework guidelines.

The role of boundary setter can also be of help to supervisees who have become engaged in unhelpful multiple consulting. A discussion regarding the inputs of the different consultants and the effects of the inputs on the progress of the assignment might help the supervisee to give up the idea of finding the 'right' helper. Such a conversation might address issues about the future such as for how long and with how many consultants the supervisee will persist, and how many times he or she will face disappointment before changing perspective on how to progress the work.

Motivator

The role of motivator may be of help to supervisees who appear to be taking an approach to coursework of the 'What is the minimum I have to do to pass the course?' type. Such an attitude may be explained by different factors, and these could be explored in supervision. The process of training itself can contribute to the experience of reduced or fluctuating motivation (Stoltenberg, McNeill and Delworth, 1998) and it may help supervisees who are suffering in this way to understand that they are not alone in their responses.

In psychodrama, the concept of 'warming up' describes the process of establishing a state of motivation that renders tasks exciting and enjoyable. The development of this state is facilitated by participation in warm-up exercises. Such exercises may be related only indirectly to the subsequently enacted drama. If it is taking hours or weeks for supervisees to progress a coursework assignment then they are probably not warmed up to the task. Supervisors might help by exploring with them the types of activity that have been effective as warm-up exercises in their past experience.

How much to help

Earlier in this chapter it was noted that different supervisees may need different kinds of help, often in constraining their ambitions for and anxieties about the work, but sometimes in investing sufficient effort in their work.

In either case it can be tempting for the supervisor to do the work for the supervisee. Supervisees can experience feelings of being infantilised by the demands of assignments, take a passive position in relation to the work, and this can create in supervisors feelings of needing to take over. It is hard to see how this will help in the long run, since it is the supervisees' capabilities that are at issue. Supervisors are advised to consider the long-term goals of their interventions rather than short-term solutions to immediate problems.

Conclusion

J. Hughlings Jackson wrote in 1915, 'We speak, not only to tell others what we think, but to tell ourselves what we think' (p. 82). Writing this book has helped me to know better what I think about supervision and I have enjoyed writing it.

I wonder what you have made of it. I hope that it will have led you to ask questions about what you are doing in supervision and to think about what you want to do in the future.

Self-assessment schedule for supervisees

(adapted from Pomerantz, 1992; Wilson, 1981)

Introduction

The following Self-Assessment Schedule is designed to shape your thinking before engaging in an initial meeting with a placement supervisor. Previous experience has shown that supervisees and supervisors do not necessarily share common ideas about supervision. There is no supervision manual dictating formal structures or procedures other than some general guidelines and some formal course requirements. Within these constraints there is a great deal of flexibility to tailor supervision to meet the individual needs of the participants.

It is recommended that this schedule be completed as a private exercise. You may then wish to identify matters for discussion that might enable your supervisor better to understand your needs.

- Most people will already have had some experience of being supervised in a job or when undertaking research and so on. What specific activities during supervision do you recall as being particularly helpful?
- There are many different ways to offer supervision. What are the conditions that would be most helpful to you?
- What would you personally expect to gain from being supervised?
- What would you want to get from supervision but anticipate that will not be on offer? What could you do about this?
- There are a number of difficult issues that can arise in supervision. Below is a list on which to indicate issues where you expect that there may be some problems for you. Feel free to add other issues to the end of the list:

    - Having too much to do.
    - Having too little to do.
    - Having insufficient guidance as to what is required.
    - Having too little autonomy to plan and carry out your work.
    - Feeling constrained during supervision by the fact that your supervisor is also your assessor.
    - Receiving too much negative criticism during supervision.

- Receiving too little critical appraisal from your supervisor.
- Not getting enough time from your supervisor for adequate supervision.
- Being given too few opportunities to see your supervisor working.
- Being given too few opportunities to be observed working by your supervisor.
- Disagreeing with your supervisor on how to proceed with some aspects of the work.
- Disagreeing with your supervisor on how some aspects of supervision should proceed.
- Holding values concerning the role of a professional helper that seem incompatible with those of your supervisor.
- Having to cope with different styles of work and supervision from your supervisor compared to previous supervisors.
- Having to cope with different styles of work and supervision from your supervisor compared to your course tutors.
- Feeling that your supervisor is too formal with you.
- Feeling that your supervisor is too informal with you.
- Experiencing problems from having more than one supervisor during your placement.
- Add in any other issues that concern you.

- Now return to the above list and identify the two issues which seem to be the most important ones for you. What steps can be taken now to minimise the chances that these two issues will seriously interfere with your placement?
- Going into this supervisory relationship what would you consider to be your greatest strengths that you would expect your supervisor to notice? List three.
- Likewise, list three points for your development that may or may not be obvious to your supervisor. Try to be specific.
- Practitioners frequently find themselves in face-to-face contact with people labelled by society as belonging to a particular sub-group. Which sub-groups make you feel uncomfortable for any reason? Do you want to do anything about this during supervision?
- What background information do you think your supervisor needs to know about you at the outset? This might include a curriculum vitae listing your relevant previous experience. What would be the best way to convey this information?
- Is there any difference between what you want out of this placement and what you feel you need from it? Be specific.
- What background information about this placement and this supervisor do you have? How does this make you feel? Is there any more information that you need?

- What do you hope and expect your supervisor to focus on in supervision?
- What roles would you like your supervisor to take in relation to you and your work?
- What media of supervision would you like to experience (e.g. taped, 'live', reported)? How do you feel about these? What do you want to do about your feelings?
- Consider your feelings now about your work being evaluated at the end of placement by your supervisor. Do you have a reasonable idea of how that evaluation will be conducted? If the answer is 'no' what do you need to clarify with your supervisor?

Examples of rating scales of supervision

Supervisory Styles Inventory

(Friedlander and Ward, 1984; unpublished instrument.
Printed in Bernard and Goodyear, 1998)

A 33-item measure with 7-point rating scales. The same version may be completed by supervisors or supervisees. Each item lists a single-word descriptor of supervisor style (e.g. sensitive, affirming, creative, didactic). Sub-sets of scores are summed to give scores on three dimensions of 'Attractive', 'Interpersonally Sensitive' and 'Task Oriented'.

Supervisory Working Alliance Inventory

(Efstation, Patton and Kardash, 1990.
Reprinted in Bernard and Goodyear, 1998)

There are two versions for supervisors and supervisees. A 23-item supervisor form with 7-point rating scales and a 19-item supervisee form with 7-point rating scales. The supervisor form has three scales of 'Rapport', 'Client Focus' and 'Identification' scored by summing and taking the mean of sub-sets of items. The supervisee form has two scales of 'Rapport' and 'Client Focus' scored by taking the mean of a sub-set of items. Includes items such as 'I encourage my trainee to talk about the work in ways that are comfortable for him/her.' 'My supervisor stays in tune with me in supervision.'

Supervisee Perceptions of Supervision

(Olk and Friedlander, 1992. Reprinted in Bernard and Goodyear, 1998)

A 29-item measure with 5-point scales for supervisees. Lists issues with which supervisees may have found difficulty in their current or most recent supervision. There are two scales of 'Role Ambiguity' and 'Role Conflict' derived by summing scores on two sub-sets of items. Includes items such as 'My supervisor's criteria for evaluating my work were not specific.' 'My supervisor gave me no feedback and I felt lost.'

Self-Assessment Questionnaire for Supervisors

(Hawkins and Shohet, 1989)

A 35-item questionnaire with 5-point rating scales for supervisors designed to help self-identification of learning needs. Includes sub-scales of 'Knowledge', 'Supervision Management Skills', Supervision Intervention Skills', 'Traits or Qualities', 'Commitment to Own Ongoing Development', and optional scales for group supervisors and senior organisational supervisors. There is no summing of scores.

Psychotherapy Supervisory Inventory

(Shanfield, Mohl, Matthews and Hetherly, 1989)

Rating scales include the dimensions of 'Intellectual and Experiential Orientation', 'Number of Clarifying and Interpretive Comments', 'Intensity of Confrontation', 'Depth of Exploration', 'Comfort and Tension Levels', 'Degree of Focus on the Therapist and on the Patient', 'Verbal Activity Level', 'Dominance', 'Comfort and Tension Levels' and 'Empathy'. The measure is designed for completion by an observer.

The Supervisory Focus and Style Questionnaire

(Yager, Wilson, Brewer and Kinnetz, 1989)

A 60-item scale for supervisors that has nine scores in the areas of 'Personality' (Affection, Inclusion and Control), 'Supervisory Focus' (Process, Conceptualisation and Personalisation) and 'Supervisory Style' (Teaching, Counselling and Consultation).

Other scales include the Supervisor Role Analysis (Johnston and Gysbers, 1966), Supervisor Questionnaire (Worthington and Roehlke, 1979), Trainee Personal Reaction Scale (Holloway and Wampold, 1983), Psychotherapy Supervisor Development Scale (Watkins, Schneider, Haynes and Nieberding, 1995), and the Training Reaction Questionnaire (Berg and Stone, 1980).

Sample consent form

As part of our aim in offering a high-quality service, we have found it helpful to the work that people do with us to make recordings of sessions. Review of tapes usually gives us more ideas that you might find helpful in your circumstances. It is also sometimes helpful in training people who are learning the job.

Please read the following, and if you are in agreement, sign where indicated.

•   I/we consent to video/audiotapes being made of these sessions and to these tapes being used to aid the work.

Dated ....   Signed ....

     ....

•   I/we consent to extracts from these recordings, or descriptions of them, being used by (name of agency) staff for the purposes of teaching and/or research. I/we understand that the (name of agency) staff will edit out from these recordings, or from the descriptions of the recordings, as much identifying information as is possible.

Dated ....   Signed ....

     ....

On behalf of (name of agency), I undertake that, in respect of any video/audiotapes made, every effort will be made to ensure professional confidentiality and that any use of tapes, or descriptions of tapes, will be for professional purposes only and in the interests of improving professional standards through research or training programmes. Every effort will be made to protect the anonymity of all those involved in the session.

I undertake that the recordings made will be kept secure at all times. Where the use does not include teaching and research purposes, the tapes will be wiped on completion of the work unless otherwise requested by yourself.

Dated ....

Signed ....

member of the (name of agency)

Core skills in the helping professions

The following list is not offered as a professional canon but as a set of statements about skills that, in the author's view, collectively provide a sound account of practice.

Management of sessions
- Engagement and establishment of rapport with clients.
- Introduction of the service/session/method to the client.
- Explaining confidentiality and obtaining informed consent.
- Ending/closing a session/episode of care.
- Noticing and responding to expressions of emotion.
- Developing a range of understandings and responses to silence.
- Developing skills in interrupting clients.
- Dealing with boundary issues.
- Maintaining a 'change' focus/orientation.
- Managing non-talking methods of communication (drawing/gesture etc.).
- Keeping client and self safe.
- Other.

Relationship factors
- Maintaining attention to client under difficult circumstances.
- Recognising own feelings and using them to inform the work.
- Recognising own preferred/habitual defences and considering the impact for the work.
- Identifying own values and how these affect/are affected by the work.
- Identifying own personal style and personal qualities.
- Identifying issues from own personal history and current circumstances and how they may affect the work.
- Considering how much to control/show own emotions.
- Retaining openness to hostility and criticism from the client.

- Identifying and using own fears in the work.
- Managing feelings of affection for clients.
- Feeling comfortable/showing confidence in professional role.
- Choosing when and how to challenge clients.
- Other.

Data-gathering

- History taking.
- Managing/co-managing the unfolding of the client's story.
- Use of formal assessment measures – selecting/administering/recording/ interpreting.
- Making meaning of non-verbal communication.
- Use of observational methods.
- Explaining and constructing methods of self-monitoring by the client (e.g. diaries/analogue scales/charts).
- Choosing assessment strategies.
- Communication of findings of assessment to client/carer/referrer.
- Other.

Thinking and planning

- Distilling ideas from the data gathered and connecting this with theory.
- Creating a coherent formulation or explanation and understanding of the client's difficulties.
- Planning the session.
- Generating and choosing interventions that follow from the understanding of the case.
- Maintaining a balance between executing a plan and responding to the client.
- Reviewing progress of the work.
- Other.

Intervention

- Contracting for the method and duration of the work.
- Asking questions that fit with the method of the work.
- Giving advice.
- Taking an educational role.
- Constructing and making interpretations.
- Creating and explaining a task.
- Creating and managing a role-play/enactment.
- Reflecting and summarising.
- Other appropriate to the model.

Professional issues

- Taking a responsible approach (e.g. staying within codes of conduct/ communication with staff and clients.
- Awareness of issues of power.
- Prioritising – case load/self-care.
- Maintaining openness to learning.
- Showing respect for clients and colleagues.
- Addressing issues of confidentiality.
- Consulting appropriately with colleagues.
- Staying within boundaries of clinical competence.
- Reflecting on the effect of self on others.
- Being aware of and managing dependency needs of clients.
- Maintaining appropriate documentation.
- Awareness of legal issues.

Supervision

- Creating a contract for supervision.
- Identifying own expectations of supervision.
- Using process notes/tapes/role-play in supervision.
- Selecting a focus for supervision.
- Asking for specific feedback from the supervisor.
- Dealing with challenges in supervision.
- Taking responsibility for own agenda in supervision.
- Experiencing live supervision.
- Negotiating with supervisor.
- Using a supervision diary/learning log.
- Other.

The service context

- Developing knowledge of the range of services available to the client group.
- Developing knowledge of the specific features and issues associated with the client group.
- Developing knowledge of methods and approaches appropriate to the client group.
- Understanding the contribution of and relationship with other relevant disciplines.
- Understanding the politics of the setting.
- Other.

Sample notice for clients

We ask you for information about yourself so that we can give you proper care and treatment.

We keep this information and notes about your care on a file to help if we see you again.

Wherever possible we keep this information confidential to the service. Your file is kept locked away.

Information must sometimes be passed on by law. This might be where a court demands it or where a serious criminal offence is concerned.

You have a right to see your own file and if you wish to do so we will tell you how to go about this.

Within our service, information may be shared between workers to help give you the best care and treatment, and to train staff. If you are seen by a person in training they may write about the work that they have carried out with you because it is required by their course. If this happens they will do their utmost to make sure that you cannot be identified.

Information is sometimes needed by the National Health Service for other reasons, such as to plan services, to make correct payments or to investigate complaints. Wherever possible, steps will be taken to make sure that you cannot be identified.

If you are at all worried about telling anything to a member of staff, ask them about what they will write down or whether they will have to pass on the information.

When you come to your first appointment we will be pleased to talk to you further about any queries you may have about confidentiality.

References

Adair, J.E. (1983) *Effective Leadership: A Self-Development Model.* Aldershot: Gower Publishing Company.

Albee, G.W. (1998) Fifty years of clinical psychology: Selling our soul to the devil. *Applied and Preventive Psychology,* 7, 189–194.

Alderfer, C. and Lynch, B. (1987) Supervision in two dimensions. *Journal of Strategic and Systemic Therapies,* 5, 70–73.

American Association for Counseling and Development (1988) Ethical Standards (3rd revision, AACD Governing Council). *Journal of Counseling and Development,* 67, 4–8.

Amundson, N.W. (1988) The use of metaphor and drawings in case conceptualisation. *Journal of Counseling and Development,* 66, 391–393.

Anderson, H. (1997) *Conversation, Language and Possibilities. A Post-modern Approach to Therapy.* New York: Basic Books.

Anderson, H. and Goolishian, H. (1988) Human systems as linguistic systems. *Family Process,* 27, 371–395.

Anderson, T. (1987) The reflecting team: Dialogue and meta-dialogue in clinical work. *Family Process,* 26, 415–428.

Apps, J.W. (1982) *Study Skills for Adults Returning to School.* New York: McGraw-Hill.

Arnheim, R. (1969) *Visual Thinking.* London: Faber and Faber.

Ashforth, B.E. and Humphrey, R.H. (1995) Emotion in the workplace: A reappraisal. *Human Relations,* 48(2), 97–125.

Association of Chief Officers of Probation (ACOP) (1989) *Staff Appraisal in the Probation Service.* Wakefield: ACOP.

Aveline, M. (1997) The use of audiotapes in supervision of psychotherapy. In G. Shipton (ed.) *Supervision of Psychotherapy and Counselling.* Buckingham: Open University Press.

Baldwin, S. and Barker, P.J. (1991) Putting the service to rights. In P.J. Barker and S. Baldwin (eds) *Ethical Issues in Mental Health.* London: Chapman Hall.

Barnat, M.R. (1977) Spontaneous supervisory metaphor in the resolution of trainee anxiety. *Professional Psychology,* 8, 307–315.

Barnes, L.H. and Pilowsky, I. (1969) Psychiatric patients and closed-circuit television teaching: A study of their reactions. *British Journal of Medical Education,* 3, 58–61.

Bartlett, W.E. (1983) Supervision in counseling II. The framework: A multidimensional framework for the analysis of supervision of counseling. *Counseling Psychologist*, 11, 9–17.

Bateson, G. (1972) *Steps to an Ecology of Mind*. New York: Chandler.

Bauman, W.F. (1972) Games counselor trainees play: Dealing with trainee resistance. *Counselor Education and Supervision*, 11, 251–256.

Beail, N. (1998) Personal communication.

Beauchamp, T.L. and Childress, J.F. (1994) *Principles of Biomedical Ethics* (4th edition). Oxford: Oxford University Press.

Beck, A.T. (1988) *Love is Never Enough*. New York: Harper and Row.

Beck, J.S. (1995) *Cognitive Therapy: Basics and Beyond*. New York: Guilford.

Berg, K.S. and Stone, G.L. (1980) Effects of conceptual level and supervision structure on counselor skill development. *Journal of Counseling Psychology*, 27, 500–509.

Berger, M and Dammann, C. (1982) Live supervision as context, treatment and training. *Family Process*, 21, 337–344.

Bernard, J.L. and O'Laughlin, D.L. (1990) Confidentiality: Do training clinics take it seriously? *Law and Psychology Review*, 14, 59–69.

Bernard, J.M. (1979) Supervisor training: A discrimination model. *Counselor Education and Supervision*, 19, 60–68.

Bernard, J.M. (1981) In-service training for clinical supervisors. *Professional Psychology*, 126, 740–748.

Bernard, J.M. (1989) Training supervisors to examine relationship variables using IPR. *The Clinical Supervisor*, 7, 103–112.

Bernard, J.M. and Goodyear, R.K. (1992) *Fundamentals of Clinical Supervision*. Boston: Allyn and Bacon.

Bernard, J.M. and Goodyear, R.K. (1998) *Fundamentals of Clinical Supervision* (2nd edition). Boston: Allyn and Bacon.

Berthoff, A. (1978) *Forming Thinking Writing: The Composing Imagination*. Portsmouth: Boynton/Cook Publishers.

Binder, J.L. and Strupp, H.H. (1997) Supervision of psychodynamic psychotherapies. In C.E. Watkins Jr, *Handbook of Psychotherapy Supervision*. New York: John Wiley and Sons.

Bion, W.R. ([1961] 1974) *Experiences in Groups and Other Papers*. New York: Ballantine.

Boltuch, B.S. (1975) The effects of a pre-practicum skill training program: Influencing human interaction: On development of counselor effectiveness in a master's level practicum. Unpublished doctoral dissertation, New York University. Reported in N. Kagan (1984) Interpersonal process recall: Basic methods and recent research, in D. Larson, *Teaching Psychological Skills*. Monterey, Calif.: Brooks/Cole.

Bond, T. (1993) *Standards and Ethics for Counselling in Action*. London: Sage.

Bonney, W. (1994) Teaching supervision: Some practical issues for beginning supervisors. *The Psychotherapy Bulletin*, 29, 331–336.

Borders, L.D. and Ledick, G.R. (1987) *Handbook of Counseling Supervision*. Alexandria, Va.: ACES.

Bordin, E.S. (1979) The generalizability of the psychodynamic concept of the working alliance. *Psychotherapy: Theory, Research and Practice*, 16, 252–260.

Bordin, E.S. (1983) A working alliance model of supervision. *Counseling Psychologist*, 11, 35–42.

Bostock, J. (1998) From clinic to community: Generating social validity in clinical psychology. *Clinical Psychology Forum*, 121, 2–6.

Bradley, I. (ed.) (1989) *Counselor Supervision: Principles, Process and Practice*. Muncie, Ind.: Accelerated Development Inc.

Bransford, J.D and Vye, N.J. (1988) Research on cognition and its implications for instruction: An overview. Unpublished manuscript. Vanderbilt University, Nashville, Tenn.

British Association of Counselling (1988) *Code of Ethics and Practice for the Supervision of Counsellors*. Rugby: BAC.

British Psychological Society (BPS) (1995) *Professional Practice Guidelines, Division of Clinical Psychology*. Leicester: BPS, 27–28.

British Psychological Society (BPS) (1998a) *Guidelines for Clinical Psychology Services, Division of Clinical Psychology*. Leicester: BPS, 18–23.

British Psychological Society (BPS) (1998b) *Responsibility and Accountability in Clinical Psychology: Professional Practice and Multidisciplinary Teamwork*. Leicester: BPS.

Brookfield, S. (1986) *Understanding and Facilitating Adult Learning*. Buckingham: Open University Press.

Burnham, J. (1986) *Family Therapy. First Steps Towards a Systemic Approach*. London: Tavistock.

Burnham, J. (2000) Internalised other interviewing: Evaluating and enhancing empathy. *Clinical Psychology Forum* (in press).

Butler, S.F. and Strupp, H.H. (1986) Specific and nonspecific factors in psychotherapy: A problematic paradigm for psychotherapy research. *Psychotherapy*, 23, 30–40.

Button, D. and Davies, S. (1996) Experiences of encouraging student-centred learning within a wellness-oriented curriculum. *Nurse Education Today*, 16, 407–412.

Butzlaff, R.L. and Hooley, J.M. (1998) Expressed emotion and psychiatric relapse. *Archives of General Psychiatry*, 55(6), 547–552.

Byng-Hall, J. (1982) The use of the earphone in supervision. In R. Whiffen and J. Byng-Hall (eds) *Family Therapy Supervision: Recent Developments in Practice*. London: Academic Press.

Byng-Hall, J. (1995) *Rewriting Family Scripts*. New York: Guilford Press.

Caligor, L. (1984) Parallel and reciprocal processes in psychoanalytic supervision. In L. Caligor, P.M. Bromberg and J.D. Meltzer (eds) *Clinical Perspectives on the Supervision of Psychoanalysis and Psychotherapy*. New York: Plenum, 1–28.

Cann, H.M. (1998) Human genome diversity. *Comptes Rendus de l'Academie des Sciences Serie III Sciences de la Vie*, 321, 443–446.

Carey, J.C., Williams, K.S. and Wells, M. (1988) Relationships between dimensions of supervisors' influence and counselor trainees' performance. *Counselor Education and Supervision*, 28, 130–139.

Carkhuff, R.R. (1969) *Helping and Human Relations* (Vols 1 and 2). New York: Rinehart and Winston.

Carkhuff, R.R. and Anthony, W.A. (1979) *The Skills of Helping: An Introduction to Counseling*. Amherst, Mass.: Human Resource Development Press.

Carroll, M. (1996) *Counselling Supervision: Theory, Skills and Practice*. London: Cassell.

Casement, P. (1988) *On Learning from the Patient*. London: Routledge.

Casement, P. (1990) *Further Learning from the Patient*. London: Routledge.

Cecchin, G. (1987) Hypothesising, circularity, and neutrality revisited: An invitation to curiosity. *Family Process*, 26, 405–413.

Clark, A. and Millard, E. (1998) *Gender in the Secondary Curriculum*. London: Routledge.

Clarke, P. (1997) Interpersonal process recall in supervision. In G. Shipton (ed.) *Supervision of Psychotherapy and Counselling*. Buckingham: Open University Press.

Cochrane, R. and Bal, S. (1989) Mental hospital admission rates of immigrants to England – A comparison of 1971 and 1981. *Social Psychiatry and Psychiatric Epidemiology*, 24, 2–11.

Cogan, M.L. (1973) *Clinical Supervision*. Boston: Houghton Mifflin Co.

Corey, G., Corey, M.S. and Callanan, P. (1993) *Issues and Ethics in the Helping Professions* (4th edition). Pacific Grove, Calif.: Brooks/Cole.

Costa, L. (1994) Reducing anxiety in live supervision. *Counselor Education and Supervision*, 34, 30–40.

Coulshed, V. (1990) Soapbox. *Social Work Today*, 11 October: 42.

Covner, B.J. (1942) Studies in phonographic recordings of verbal material. I: The use of phonographic recordings in counseling practice and research. *Journal of Consulting Psychology*, 6, 105–113.

Czander, W.M. (1993) *The Psychodynamics of Work and Organizations: Theory and Application*. New York: Guilford Press.

Daniels, J. (2000) Whispers in the corridors and kangaroo courts: The supervisory role in mistakes and complaints. In B. Lawton and C. Feltham, *Taking Supervision Forward: Enquiries and Trends in Counselling and Psychotherapy*. London: Sage.

Dennett, D.C. (1991) *Consciousness Explained*. London: Penguin.

Dewald, P.A. (1997) The process of supervision in psychoanalysis. In C.E. Watkins Jr, *Handbook of Psychotherapy Supervision*. New York: John Wiley and Sons.

Disney, M.J. and Stephens, A.M. (1994) *Legal Issues in Clinical Supervision*. Alexandria, Va.: American Counseling Association.

Dodenhoff, J.T. (1981) Interpersonal attraction and direct–indirect supervisor influence as predictors of counselor trainee effectiveness. *Journal of Counseling Psychology*, 28, 47–62.

Dodge, J. (1982) Reducing supervisee anxiety: A cognitive-behavioural approach. *Counselor Education and Supervision*, 22, 55–60.

Doehrman, M.J.G. (1976) Parallel processes in supervision and psychotherapy. *Bulletin of the Menninger Clinic*, 40, 9–104.

Doi, T. (1974) Amae: A key concept for understanding Japanese personality structure. In T. Lebra and W. Lebra (eds) *Japanese Culture and Behaviour*. Honolulu: University of Hawaii Press.

Donaldson, M. (1978) *Children's Minds*. London: Fontana.

Edelman, G. (1992) *Bright Air, Brilliant Fire: On the Matter of Mind*. London: Penguin.

Efstation, J.F., Patton, M.J. and Kardash, C.M. (1990) Measuring the working alliance in counselor supervision. *Journal of Counseling Psychology*, 37, 322–329.

Egan, G. (1976) *Interpersonal Living: A Skills–Contract Approach to Human Relations Training in Groups*. Pacific Grove, Calif.: Brooks/Cole.

Egan, G. (1994) *The Skilled Helper* (5th edition). Monterey, Calif.: Brooks/Cole.

Ekstein, R. and Wallerstein, R.S. (1972) *The Teaching and Learning of Psychotherapy* (2nd edition). New York: International Universities Press Inc.

Elliott, R. (1986) Interpersonal Process Recall (IPR) as a psychotherapeutic process research method. In L.S. Greenberg and W.M. Pinsof (eds) *The Psychotherapeutic Process: A Research Handbook*. New York: Guilford.

Ellis, A. and Dryden, W. (1987) *The Practice of Rational–Emotive Therapy (RET)*. New York: Springer.

Ellis, M.V., Ladany, N., Krengel, M. and Schult, D. (1996) Clinical supervision research from 1981 to 1993: A methodological critique. *Journal of Counseling Psychology*, 43(1), 35–50.

Engel, A., House, R., Pearson, C. and Sluman, S. (1998) Report of a supervisors' workshop. *Training Link*, 28, 1–2. Sheffield: University of Sheffield.

Engel, M. (1971) Preface. In G. Bateson (1972) *Steps to an Ecology of Mind*. New York: Chandler Publishing Company.

Entwistle, N.J. (1981) *Styles of Teaching and Learning*. Chichester: Wiley.

Epston, D. (1993) Internalised other questioning with couples: The New Zealand version. In S. Gilligan and R. Price, *Therapeutic Conversations*. New York: W.W. Norton and Co.

Errek, H. and Randolph, D. (1982) Effects of discussion and role-playing activities in the acquisition of consultant interview skills. *Journal of Counseling Psychology*, 29, 304–308.

Fiedler, F.A. (1950) A comparison of therapeutic relationships in psychoanalytic, non-directive and Adlerian therapy. *Journal of Consulting Psychology*, 14, 436–445.

Fiedler, F.A. (1951) Factor analyses of psychoanalytic, non-directive and Adlerian therapeutic relationships, *Journal of Consulting Psychology*, 15, 32–38.

Flanagan, O. (1992) *Consciousness Reconsidered*. London: Bradford Books.

Flemons, D.G., Green, S.K. and Rambo, A. (1996) Evaluating therapists' practices in a postmodern world: A discussion and a scheme. *Family Process*, 35, 43–56.

Ford, N. (1985) Learning styles and strategies of postgraduate students. *British Journal of Educational Technology*, 2(16), 65–77.

Fordham, A.S., May, B., Boyle, M., Bentall, R.P. and Slade, P. (1990) Good and bad clinicians: Supervisors' judgements of trainees' competence. *British Journal of Clinical Psychology*, 29, 113–114.

Forrest, L., Elman, N., Gizara, S. and Vacha-Haase, T. (1999) Trainee impairment: A review of identification, remediation, dismissal and legal issues. *The Counseling Psychologist*, 27, 627–686.

Friedlander, M.L. and Snyder, J. (1983) Trainees' expectations for the supervisory process: Testing a developmental model. *Counselor Education and Supervision*, 23, 342–348.

Friedlander, M.L. and Ward, L.G. (1983) Dimensions of supervisory style. Cited in R.K. Goodyear, P.D. Abadie and F. Efros (1984) Supervisory theory into practice: Differential perceptions of supervision by Ekstein, Ellis, Polster and Rogers. *Journal of Counseling Psychology*, 31, 228–237.

Friedlander, M.L. and Ward, L.G. (1984) Development and validation of the Supervisory Styles Inventory. *Journal of Counseling Psychology*, 31, 542–558.

Friedmann, C.T., Yamamoto, J., Wolkon, G.H. and Davis, L. (1978) Videotape recording of dynamic psychotherapy: Supervisory tool or hindrance? *American Journal of Psychiatry*, 135, 1388–1391.

Frostig, M. (1972) Visual perception, integrative functions and academic learning. *Journal of Learning Disabilities*, 5, 1–15.

Fryer, P. (1984) *Staying Power: The History of Black People in Britain*. London: Pluto.

Gagné, R.M. (1967) Instruction and the conditions of learning. In L. Siegel (ed.) *Instruction: Some Contemporary Viewpoints*. San Francisco: Chandler.

Gergen, K. (1985) The social constructionist movement in modern psychology. *American Psychologist*, 40, 266–275.

Gershenson, J. and Cohen, M. (1978) Through the looking glass: The experiences of two family therapy trainees with live supervision. *Family Process*, 17, 225–230.

Gilbert, T.F. (1957) Overlearning and the retention of meaningful prose. *Journal of General Psychology*, 56, 281–289.

Gill, D. and Levidow, L. (eds) (1989) *Antiracist Science Teaching*. London: Free Association Books.

Gillborn, D. (1990) *'Race', Ethnicity and Education*. London: Unwin Hyman.

Gilligan, C. (1982) *In a Different Voice*. Cambridge, Mass.: Harvard University Press.

Gilmore, S.K., Fraleigh, P.W. and Philbrick, R. (1980) *Communication at Work*. Eugene, Oreg.: Friendly Press.

Glaser, R.D. and Thorpe, J.S. (1986) Unethical intimacy. *American Psychologist*, 41, 43–51.

Goffman, E. (1968) *Asylums*. Harmondsworth: Penguin.

Goldhammer, R., Anderson, R.H. and Krajewski, R.J. (1980) *Clinical Supervision: Special Methods for the Supervision of Teachers*. New York: Holt, Rinehart and Winston.

Goncalves, O.F. and Craine, M.H. (1991) The use of metaphors in cognitive therapy. *Journal of Cognitive Psychotherapy*, 4(2), 135–149.

Goodrich, T.J., Rampage, C., Ellman, B. and Halstead, K. (1988) *Feminist Family Therapy: A Handbook*. New York: W.W. Norton.

Goodyear, R.K., Abadie, P.D. and Efros, F. (1984) Supervisory theory into practice: Differential perceptions of supervision by Ekstein, Ellis, Polster and Rogers. *Journal of Counseling Psychology*, 31, 228–237.

Goodyear, R.K., Bradley, F.O. and Bartlett, W.E. (1983) An introduction to theories of counselor supervision. *The Counseling Psychologist*, 11, 19–20.

Greenslade, L. (1991) From visible to invisible – the health of Irish people in Britain. *Social History of Medicine*, 4, 390.

Hagan, T. and Smail, D. (1997) Power-mapping: Background and basic methodology. *Journal of Community and Applied Social Psychology*, 7, 257–267.

Haggard, E.A., Hiken, J.R. and Isaacs, K.S. (1965) Some effects of recording and filming on the psychotherapeutic process. *Psychiatry*, 28, 169–191.

Hahn, W.K. and Molnar, S. (1991) Intern evaluation in university counseling centers: Process, problems and recommendations. *Counseling Psychologist*, 19, 414–430.

Hall, E.T. (1976) *Beyond Culture*. Garden City, N.Y.: Anchor Books.

Hampden-Turner, C. (1981) *Maps of the Mind*. New York: Collier Books.

Harrar, W.R., Vandercreek, L. and Knapp, S. (1990) Ethical and legal aspects of clinical supervision. *Professional Psychology: Research and Practice*, 21, 37–41.

Hawkins, P. (1985) Humanistic psychotherapy supervision: A conceptual framework. *Self and Society: European Journal of Humanistic Psychology*, 13, 69–77.

Hawkins, P. (1997) Organisational culture: sailing between evangelism and complexity. *Human Relations*, 50, 417–440.

Hawkins, P. and Miller, E. (undated) *Psychotherapy in and with Organisations*. Bath: Bath Consultancy Group.

Hawkins, P. and Shohet, R. (1989) *Supervision in the Helping Professions*. Milton Keynes: Open University Press.

Hawkins, P. and Shohet, R. (2000) *Supervision in the Helping Professions (2nd edition)*. Milton Keynes: Open University Press.

Hellman, S. (1999) The portfolio: A method of reflective development. In E. Holloway and M. Carroll, *Training Counselling Supervisors*. London: Sage.

Heppner, P.P. and Handley, P.G. (1982) The relationship between supervisory expertness, attractiveness, or trustworthiness. *Counselor Education and Supervision*, 22, 23–31.

Hildebrand, J. (1998a) Personal communication.

Hildebrand, J. (1998b) *Bridging the Gap: A Training Module in Personal and Professional Development*. London: Karnac Books.

Hillman, J. (1983) *Interviews*. New York: Harper Row.

Hinshelwood, R.D. (1994) *A Dictionary of Kleinian Thought*. London: Free Association Books.

Hitchings, P. (1999) Supervision and sexual orientation. In M. Carroll and E. Holloway (eds) *Counselling Supervision in Context*. London: Sage.

Hoffman, L. (1991) A reflexive stance for family therapy. *Journal of Strategic and Systemic Therapies*, 10, 4–17.

Holloway, E.L. (1992) Supervision: A way of teaching and learning. In S. Brown and R. Lent (eds) *The Handbook of Counseling Psychology* (2nd edition). New York: Wiley.

Holloway, E.L. (1995) *Clinical Supervision: A Systems Approach*. Thousand Oaks, Calif.: Sage.

Holloway, E.L. and Neufeldt, S.A. (1995) Supervision: Its contribution to treatment efficacy. *Journal of Consulting and Clinical Psychology*, 63, 207–213.

Holloway, E.L. and Roehlke, H.J. (1987) Internship: The applied training of a counseling psychologist. *Counseling Psychologist*, 15, 205–260.

Holloway, E.L. and Wampold, B.E. (1983) Patterns of verbal behaviour and judgements of satisfaction in the supervision interview. *Journal of Counseling Psychology*, 30, 227–234.

Holt, J. (1969) *How Children Fail*. Harmondsworth: Penguin.

Honey, P. and Mumford, A. (1992) *The Manual of Learning Styles*. Maidenhead: Honey (10 Lindon Avenue SL6 6HB).

Horton, I. (1993) Supervision. In R. Boyne and P. Nicholson (eds) *Counselling and Psychotherapy for Health Professionals*. London: Chapman Hall.

Houston, G. (1997) *The Red Book of Counselling and Supervision*. London: Rochester Press (9 Rochester Terrace, London N1).

Howells, W.D., Karp, M., Watson, M., Sprague, K. and Moreno, Z.T. (1994) *Psychodrama Since Moreno: Innovations in Theory and Practice*. London: Routledge.

Hughes, J. and Massey, C. (2000) Personal communication.

Hughlings Jackson, J. (1915) Hughlings Jackson on aphasia and kindred affections of speech. *Brain*, 38, 1–190.

Inskipp, F. and Proctor, B. (1988) Skills for Supervising and Being Supervised (cassette). Twickenham: Cascade Publications (4 Ducks Walk, Twickenham, Middlesex).

Inskipp, F. and Proctor, B. (1993) *The Art, Craft and Tasks of Counselling Supervision. Part 1. Making the Most of Supervision*. Twickenham: Cascade Publications (4 Ducks Walk, Twickenham, Middlesex).

Inskipp, F. and Proctor, B. (1995) *The Art, Craft and Tasks of Counselling Supervision. Part 2. Becoming a Supervisor*. Twickenham: Cascade Publications (4 Ducks Walk, Twickenham, Middlesex).

Inskipp, F. and Proctor, B. (1997) Personal communication. Trent Region supervisors' workshop.

Ishiyama, F.I. (1988) A model of visual case processing using metaphors and drawings. *Counselor Education and Supervision*, 28, 153–161.

Ivey, A.E. (1974) Micro-counselling: Teacher training as facilitation of pupil growth. *British Journal of Educational Technology*, 5, 16–21.

Jacobsen, T. (1998) Delay behaviour at age six: Links to maternal expressed emotion. *Journal of Genetic Psychology*, 159(1), 117–120.

Johnston, J.A. and Gysbers, N.C. (1966) Practicum supervisory relationships: A majority report. *Counselor Education and Supervision*, 6, 3–10.

Jones, S. (1996) *Training Link*. Newsletter of the Universities of Leicester and Sheffield Clinical Psychology Training Courses, April. Sheffield: University of Sheffield.

Jung, C.J. (1963) *Memories, Dreams, Reflections*. London: Collins/Routledge and Kegan Paul.

Kagan, N. (1984) Interpersonal Process Recall: Basic methods and recent research. In D. Larson, *Teaching Psychological Skills*. Monterey, Calif.: Brooks/Cole.

Kagan, N. and Kagan, H. (1991) Teaching counselling skills. In K.R. Cox and C.E. Ewan (eds) *The Medical Teacher*. Edinburgh: Churchill Livingstone.

Kagan, N. and Krathwohl, D.R. (1967) *Studies in Human Interaction: Interpersonal Process Recall Stimulated by Videotape*. East Lansing: Michigan State University.

Kagan, N., Krathwohl, D.R. and Miller, R. (1963) Stimulated recall in therapy using videotape: A case study. *Journal of Counselling Psychology*, 10, 237–243.

Kagan-Klein, H. and Kagan, N. (1997) Interpersonal Process Recall: Influencing human interaction. In C.E. Watkins Jr (ed.) *Handbook of Psychotherapy Supervision*. New York: John Wiley and Sons, Inc.

Kalff, D. (1980) *Sandplay: A Psychotherapeutic Approach to the Psyche*. Santa Monica, Calif.: Sigo Press.

Karp, M., Holmes, P. and Tauvon, K.B. (1998) *The Handbook of Psychodrama*. New York: Routledge.

Katz, J.H. (1985) The sociopolitical nature of counseling. *The Counseling Psychologist*, 13, 615–624.

Keith-Spiegler, P. and Koocher, G.P. (1985) *Ethics in Psychology*. New York: Random House.

Kent, G. and McAuley, D. (1995) Ethical difficulties faced by trainee clinical psychologists. *Clinical Psychology Forum*, June, 26–30.

Kerka, S. (1996) *Journal Writing and Adult Learning*. ERIC digest no. 174. Columbus, OH: Eric Clearing House on Adult, Career and Vocational Education.

King, D. and Wheeler, S. (1999) The responsibilities of counsellor supervisors: A qualitative study. *British Journal of Guidance and Counselling*, 27, 215–228.

Kingston, P. and Smith, D. (1983) Preparation for live consultation and live supervision when working without a one-way screen. *Journal of Family Therapy*, 5, 219–233.

Kolb, D.A. (1984) *Experiential Learning – Experience as the Source of Learning and Development*. Englewood Cliffs, N.J.: Prentice-Hall.

Kopp, R.R. (1995) *Metaphor Therapy: Using Client-Generated Metaphors in Psychotherapy*. New York: Brunner/Mazel.

Kuhn, T.S. (1962) *The Structure of Scientific Revolutions*. Chicago: University of Chicago Press.

Kurpius, D., Gibson, G., Lewis, J. and Corbet, M. (1991) Ethical issues in supervising counseling practitioners. *Counselor Education and Supervision*, 31, 48–57.

Kutz, S.L. (1986) Defining 'impaired psychologist'. *American Psychologist*, 41, 220.

Ladany, N., Hill, C.E., Corbett, M.M. and Nutt, E.A. (1996) Nature, extent and importance of what psychotherapy trainees do not disclose to their supervisors. *Journal of Counseling Psychology*, 43, 10–24.

Lambert, M.J. (1980) Research and the supervisory process. In A.K. Hess (ed.) *Psychotherapy Supervision: Theory, Research and Practice*. New York: Wiley, 423–450.

Lang, W.P., Little, M. and Cronen, V. (1990) The systemic professional: Domains of action and the question of neutrality. *Human Systems*, 1, 1.

Laplanche, J. and Pontalis, J.B. (1973) *The Language of Psychoanalysis*. London: Hogarth Press.

Larson, P.C. (1982) Counseling special populations. *Professional Psychology*, 13, 843–858.

Lawson, D.M. (1989) Using family sculpting in groups to enrich current intimate relationships. *Journal of College Student Development*, 30, 171–172.

Lawton, B. (2000) 'A very exposing affair': Explorations in counsellors' supervisory relationships. In B. Lawton and C. Feltham, *Taking Supervision Forward: Enquiries and Trends in Counselling and Psychotherapy*. London: Sage.

Lee, E.P. (1997) The learning response log: An assessment tool. *English Journal*, 86, 41–44.

Lesage-Higgins, S.A. (1999) Family sculpting in premarital counseling. *Family Therapy*, 26, 31–38.

Lev-Ran, A. (1974) Gender role differentiation in hermaphrodites. *Archives of Sexual Behaviour*, 3, 391–424.

Levine, F.M. and Tilker, H.A. (1974) A behaviour modification approach to the supervision of psychotherapy. *Psychotherapy: Theory, Research and Practice*, 2, 182–188.

Lewontin, R. (1982) Are the races different? In D. Gill and L. Levidow (eds) (1987) *Anti-racist Science Teaching*. London: Free Association Books.

Liddle, B.J. (1986) Resistance in supervision: A response to perceived threat. *Counselor Education and Supervision*, 26, 117–127.

Liddle, H.A., Breunlin, D.C. and Schwartz, R.C. (eds) (1988) *Handbook of Family Therapy and Training Supervision*. New York: Guilford.

Liese, B.S. and Beck, J. (1997) Cognitive therapy supervision. In C.E. Watkins Jr, *Handbook of Psychotherapy Supervision*. New York: John Wiley and Sons Inc.

Liese, B.S., Barber, J. and Beck, A.T. (1995) The Cognitive Therapy Adherence and Competence Scale. Unpublished instrument. University of Kansas Medical Centre, Kansas City. Reproduced in B.S. Liese and J. Beck (1997) Cognitive therapy supervision. In C.E. Watkins Jr, *Handbook of Psychotherapy Supervision*. New York: John Wiley and Sons Inc.

Littrell, J.M., Lee-Borden, N. and Lorenz, J.A. (1979) A developmental framework for counseling supervision. *Counselor Education and Supervision*, 19, 119–136.

Loganbill, C., Hardy, E. and Delworth, U. (1982) Supervision: A conceptual model. *Counseling Psychologist*, 10, 3–42.

Lowenfeld, M. (1979) *The World Technique*. London: Allen and Unwin.

Lowenstein, S.F., Reder, P. and Clark, A. (1982) The consumer's response: Trainees' discussion of the experience of live supervision. In R. Whiffen and J. Byng-Hall (eds) *Family Therapy Supervision: Recent Developments in Practice*. London: Academic Press.

Mac an Ghaill, M. (1988) *Young, Gifted and Black*. Milton Keynes: Open University Press.

McCann, D., Gorrell Barnes, G. and Down, G. (2000) Sex and sexuality: The supervisory challenge. In G. Gorrell Barnes, G. Down and D. McCann (eds) *Systemic Supervision: A Portable Guide for Supervision Training*. London: Jessica Kingsley Publishers.

McCarthy, P., Kulakowski, D. and Kenfield, J.A. (1994) Clinical supervision practices of licensed psychologists. *Professional Psychology: Research and Practice*, 25, 177–181.

McElfresh, T.A. and McElfresh, S.J. (1998) How being a psychotherapist can imperil personal relationships. In L. Vandercreek and S. Knapp (eds) *Innovations in Clinical Practice: A Source Book*. Sarasota, Fla.: Professional Resource Press.

McNeill, B.W. and Worthen, V. (1989) The parallel process in psychotherapy supervision. *Professional Psychology: Research and Practice*, 20, 329–333.

Macran, S. and Shapiro, D. (1998) The role of personal therapy for therapists: A review. *British Journal of Medical Psychology*, 71, 13–25.

Mahoney, M.J. (1986) The tyranny of technique. *Counseling and Values*, 30, 169–174.

Mauzey, E. and Erdman, P. (1997) Trainee perceptions of live supervision phone-ins: A phenomenological inquiry. *The Clinical Supervisor*, 15, 115–128.

Meredith, R. and Bradley, L. (1989) Differential supervision: Roles, functions and activities. In L. Bradley (ed.) *Counselor Supervision*. Muncie, Ind.: Accelerated Development, 301–373.

Meyer, R.G., Landis, E.R., and Hays, J.R. (1988) *Law for the Psychotherapist*. New York: W.W. Norton.

Meyer-Bahlburg, H.F. (1982) Hormones and psychosexual differentiation: Implications for the management of intersexuality, homosexuality, and transsexuality. *Journal of Clinical Endocrinology and Metabolism*, 11, 681–701.

Mezirow, J. (1985) A critical theory of self-directed learning. In S. Brookfield (ed.) *Self-Directed Learning: From Theory to Practice*. San Francisco: Jossey-Bass.

Mezirow, J. (1988) Principles of good practice in continuing education. Unpublished paper.

Miars, R.D., Tracey, T.J., Ray, P.B., Cornfeld, J.L., O'Farrell, M. and Gelso, C.J. (1983) Variation in supervision process across trainee experience levels. *Journal of Counseling Psychology*, 30, 403–412.

Middleman, R.R. and Rhodes, G.B. (1985) *Competent Supervision: Making Imaginative Judgments*. Englewood Cliffs, N.J.: Prentice-Hall.

Miller, N. and Crago, M. (1989) The supervision of two isolated practitioners: It's supervision, Jim, but not as you know it. *Australian and New Zealand Journal of Family Therapy*, 10, 21–25.

Minardi, H.A. and Ritter, S. (1999) Recording skills practice on videotape can enhance learning – a comparative study between nurse lecturers and nursing students. *Journal of Advanced Nursing*, 29, 1318–1325.

MIND Publications (n.d.) *Getting the Best from your Counsellor or Psychotherapist*. London (ISBN: 1–87469–048–0).

Moldawsky, S. (1980) Psychoanalytic psychotherapy supervision. In A.K. Hess (ed.) *Psychotherapy Supervision: Theory, Research and Practice*. New York: Wiley, 126–135.

Mollon, P. (1989) Anxiety, supervision and a space for thinking: Some narcissistic perils for clinical psychologists in learning psychotherapy. *British Journal of Medical Psychology*, 62, 113–122.

Monaghan, L. (2000) Personal communication.

Montalvo, B. (1973) Aspects of live supervision. *Family Process*, 2, 343–359.

Morrison, T. (1990) The emotional effects of child protection work on the worker. *Practice*, 4(4). Cited in T. Morrison (1993) *Staff Supervision in Social Care*. Harlow: Longman.

Morrison, T. (1993) *Staff Supervision in Social Care*. Harlow: Longman.

Nelson, G.L. (1978) Psychotherapy supervision from the trainee's point of view: A survey of preferences. *Professional Psychology*, 9, 539–550.

Neufeldt, S.A. (1999) Training in reflective processes in supervision. In E. Holloway and M. Carroll, *Training Counselling Supervisors*. London: Sage.

Neufeldt, S.A., Karno, M.P. and Nelson, M.L. (1996) A qualitative analysis of experts' conceptualization of supervisee reflectivity. *Journal of Counseling Psychology*, 43, 3–9.

Newman, A.S. (1981) Ethical issues in the supervision of psychotherapy. *Professional Psychology: Research and Practice*, 12, 690–695.

Niemi, P.M. (1997) Medical students' professional identity: Self-reflection during the preclinical years. *Medical Education*, 31, 408–415.

Niland, T.M., Duling, J., Allen, V. and Panther, E. (1971) Student counselors' perceptions of videotaping. *Counselor Education and Supervision*, 11, 97–101.

Noddings, N. (1984) *Caring: A Feminine Approach to Ethics and Moral Education*. Berkeley: University of California Press.

Noucho, A.O. (1983) The use of visual imagery in training professional helpers. In J. E. Shorr, G. Sobel-Whittington, P. Robin and J. Conella (eds) *Imagery*. Vol 3: *Theoretical and Clinical Applications*. New York: Plenum, 72–85.

Nourry, C., Samba, D. and Bieder, J. (1978) The mosaic test of Margaret Lowenfeld applied to schizophrenics. *Annales Medical Psychologiques*, 136, 1217–1224.

Nuttall, D., Goldstein, H., Prosser, R. and Rasbash, H. (1989) Differential school effectiveness. *International Journal of Educational Research*, 13, 769–776.

Olk, M. and Friedlander, M.L. (1992) Trainees' experiences of role conflict and role ambiguity in supervisory relationships. *Journal of Counseling Psychology*, 39, 389–397.

Padesky, C.A. (1994) Schema change processes in cognitive therapy. *Clinical Psychology and Psychotherapy*, 1, 267–278.

Page, S. and Wosket, V. (1994) *Supervising the Counsellor: A Cyclical Model*. London: Routledge.

Palazzoli, M., Boscolo, L., Cecchin, G. and Prata, G. (1980) Hypothesising, circularity, neutrality: Three guidelines for the conductor of the session. *Family Process*, 19, 3–18.

Palmer Barnes, F. (1998) *Complaints and Grievances in Psychotherapy: A Handbook of Ethical Practice*. London: Routledge.

Pask, G. (1973) Educational Methods Using Information about Individual Styles and Strategies of Learning. Final Report of SSRC Project HR 1424/1 (2 vols). (Unpublished research project.)

Pask, G. (1976) Styles and strategies of learning. *British Journal of Educational Psychology*, 46, 128–148.

Patterson, C.H. (1997) Client-centred supervision. In C.E. Watkins Jr, *Handbook of Psychotherapy Supervision*. New York: John Wiley and Sons Inc.

Pearce, W.B. and Cronen, V.E. (1980) *Communication, Action and Meaning: The Creation of Sound Realities*. New York: Praeger.

Pederson, P. (1987) Ten frequent assumptions of cultural bias in counseling. *Journal of Multicultural Counseling and Development*, 9, 16–24.

Pegg, P.F. and Manocchio, A.J. (1982) In on the Act. In R. Whiffen and J. Byng-Hall, *Family Therapy Supervision: Recent Developments in Practice*. London: Academic Press.

Perr, H.M. (1986) The use of audio-tapes in psychotherapy. *Journal of the American Academy of Psychoanalysis*, 13, 391–398.

Piaget, J. (1972) *The Principles of Genetic Epistemology* (translated by W. Mays). London: Routledge.

Polanyi, M. (1958) *Personal Knowledge*. London: Routledge and Kegan Paul.

Pomerantz, M. (1992) Personal communication.

Pomerantz, M., Leydon, G., Lunt, I., Osborne, E., Powell, M. and Ronaldson, J. (1987) *Report of the Joint DECP/Course Tutors' Working Party on Fieldwork Supervision*. Leicester: British Psychological Society.

Poortinga, Y.H. (1995) Cultural bias in assessment – historical and thematic issues. *European Journal of Psychological Assessment*, 11, 140–146.

Pope, K.S. and Vasquez, M.J.T. (1991) *Ethics in Psychotherapy and Counseling: A Practical Guide for Psychologists*. San Francisco: Jossey-Bass.

Pope, K.S., Tabachnick, B.G. and Keith-Spiegel, P. (1987) Ethics of practice: The beliefs and behaviours of psychologists as therapists. *American Psychologist*, 42, 993–1006.

Proctor, B.M. (2000) *Group Supervision: A Guide to Creative Practice*. London: Sage.

Putney, M.W., Worthington, E.L. and McCullough, M.E. (1992) Effects of supervisor and supervisee theoretical orientations on supervisors' perceptions. *Journal of Counseling Psychology*, 39, 258–265.

Raichelson, S.H., Herron, W.G., Primavera, L.H. and Ramirez, S.M. (1997) Incidence and effects of parallel process in psychotherapy supervision. *Clinical Supervisor*, 15, 37–48.

Randall, R. and Southgate, J. (1980) *Co-operative and Community Group Dynamics*. London: Barefoot Books.

Reavis, C.A. (1976) Clinical supervision: A timely approach. *Educational Leadership*, 33, 360–363.

Reiss, M.J. (1993) *Science Education for a Pluralist Society*. Buckingham: Open University Press.

Riding, R. (1992) Cognitive styles: An overview and integration. *Educational Psychology*, 11(3–4), 193–215.

Riding, R. (1994) *Personal Style Awareness and Personal Development*. Birmingham: Learning and Training Technology.

Robbins, A. and Erismann, M. (1992) Developing therapeutic artistry: A joint counter-transference supervisory seminar/stone sculpting workshop. *The Arts in Psychotherapy*, 19, 367–377.

Roberts, C.A. (1985) Viewpoint: The multi-disciplinary team in psychiatry. *Psychiatric Journal of the University of Ottawa*, 10, 147–152.

Roberts, M. (1989) Writing as reflection. In F. Slater (ed.) *Language and Learning in the Teaching of Geography*. London: Routledge.

Rogers, C.R. (1942) The use of electronically recorded interviews in improving psychotherapeutic techniques. *American Journal of Orthopsychiatry*, 12, 429–434.

Rogers, C.R. (1974) *On Becoming a Person*. London: Constable.

Rogers, C.R. (1980) Client-centred therapy. In C.H. Patterson, *Theories of Counseling and Psychotherapy*. New York: Harper and Row.

Rosenblatt, A. and Mayer, J.E. (1975) Objectionable supervisory styles: Students' views. *Social Work*, May, 184–189.

Ross, W.D. (1930) *The Right and the Good*. Oxford: Clarendon Press.

Rowan, J. (1989) *The Reality Game: A Guide to Humanistic Counselling and Therapy*. London: Routledge.

Rowell, J.A. (1989) Piagetian epistemology: Equilibration and teaching of science. *Synthese*, 80, 141–162.

Rudduck, J. and Sigsworth, A. (1985) Partnership supervision (or Goldhammer revisited). In D. Hopkins and P. Wiser, *Rethinking Teacher Education*. London: Croom Helm.

Rule, W.R. (1983) Family therapy and the pie metaphor. *Journal of Marital and Family Therapy*, 9, 101–103.

Russell, R.K., Crimmings, A.M. and Lent, R.W. (1984) Counselor training and supervision: Theory and research. In S.D. Brown and R.W. Lent (eds) *Handbook of Counseling Psychology*. New York: Wiley, 625–681.

Ryan, F. (1991) Taking care with responsibility. *Clinical Psychology Forum*, Sept. 36–37.

Salzberger-Wittenberg, I. (1983) Part 1: Beginnings. In I. Salzberger-Wittenberg, G. Henry and E. Osborne, *The Emotional Experience of Teaching and Learning*. London: Routledge and Kegan Paul.

Scaife, J.A. and Scaife, J.M. (1996) A general supervision framework: Applications in teacher education. in J. Trafford (ed.) *Learning to Teach: Aspects of Initial Teacher Education*. Sheffield: USDE Papers in Education.

Scaife, J.M. (1993a) Setting the scene for supervision: The application of a systems framework to an initial placement consultation. *Human Systems*, 4, 161–173.

Scaife, J.M. (1993b) Application of a general supervision framework: Creating a context of cooperation. *Educational and Child Psychology*, 10(2), 61–72.

Scaife, J.M. (1993c) Hierarchy and Heterarchy in Systemic Therapy: Reflexivity in Therapy and Consultation. Unpublished research dissertation. University of Birmingham.

Scaife, J.M. (1995) *Training to Help: A Survival Guide*. Sheffield: Riding Press.

Scaife, J.M. and Pomerantz, M. (1999) A survey of the record-keeping practices of clinical psychologists. *Clinical Psychology and Psychotherapy*, 6, 210–226.

Schoener, G.R. and Gonsiorek, J. (1988) Assessment and development of rehabilitation plans for counselors who have sexually exploited their clients. *Journal of Counseling and Development*, 67, 227–232.

Schön, D.A. (1987) *Educating the Reflective Practitioner*. San Francisco: Jossey-Bass.

Schutz, W.C. (1967) *Joy: Expanding Human Awareness*. New York: Grove/Atlantic Incorporated.

Schutz, W.C. (1989) *Joy – Twenty Years Later*. Berkeley, Calif.: Ten Speed Press.

Schwartz, R.C., Liddle, H.A. and Breunlin, D.C. (1988) Muddles in live supervision. In H.A. Liddle, D.C. Breunlin and D.C. Schwartz (eds) *Handbook of Family Therapy Training and Supervision*. New York: Guilford Press.

Scott, C. and Spellman, D. (1992) Clinical psychology and family therapy training. *Clinical Psychology Forum*, 48, 31–34.

Searles, H.F. (1955) The informational value of the supervisor's experience. In *Collected Papers on Schizophrenia and Related Subjects*. London: Hogarth Press.

Shainberg, D. (1983) Teaching therapists to be with their clients. In J. Westwood. (ed.) *Awakening the Heart*. Boston, Mass.: Shambhala.

Shanfield, W.B., Mohl, P.C., Matthews, K. and Hetherly, V. (1989) A reliability assessment of the Psychotherapy Supervisory Inventory. *American Journal of Psychiatry*, 146, 1447–1450.

Sharpe, M. (1995) *The Third Eye: Supervision of Analytic Groups*. New York: Routledge.

Shaw, B.F. and Dobson, K.S. (1989) Competency judgements in the training and evaluation of psychotherapists. *Journal of Consulting and Clinical Psychology*, 56, 666–672.

Shem, S. (1985) *The House of God*. London: Black Swan.

Shem, S. (1999) *Mount Misery*. London: Black Swan.

Sills, C. (ed.) (1997) *Contracts in Counselling*. London: Sage.

Skovholt, T.M. and Ronnestad, M.H. (1992) *The Evolving Professional Self: Stages and Themes in Therapist and Counsellor Development*. Chichester: Wiley.

Smith, D. and Kingston, P. (1980) Live supervision without a one-way screen. *Journal of Family Therapy*, 2, 379–387.

Smith, E.J. (1981) Cultural and historical perspectives in counseling blacks. In D.W. Sue (ed.) *Counseling the Culturally Different*. New York: John Wiley and Sons, 141–185.

Smith, T.E., Yoshioka, M. and Winton, M. (1993) A qualitative understanding of reflecting teams. I. Client perspectives. *Journal of Systemic Therapies*, 12, 28–43.

Snadden, D., Thomas, M.L., Griffin, E.M. and Hudson, H. (1996) Portfolio-based learning and general practice vocational training. *Medical Education*, 30, 148–152.

Spy, T. and Oyston, C. (1999) Supervision and working with disability. In M. Carroll and E. Holloway (eds) *Counselling Supervision in Context*. London: Sage.

Stoltenberg, C.D. and Delworth, U. (1987) *Supervising Counselors and Therapists*. San Francisco: Jossey-Bass.

Stoltenberg, C.D., McNeill, B. and Delworth, U. (1998) *IDM Supervision: An*

Integrated Developmental Model for Supervising Counselors and Therapists. San Francisco: Jossey-Bass.

Stones, E. (1984) *Supervision in Teacher Education: A Counselling and Pedagogical Approach*. London: Methuen and Co.

Strosahl, K. and Jacobson, N. (1986) Training and supervision of behaviour therapists. *The Clinical Supervisor*, 4, 183–206.

Sullivan, C.G. (1980) *Clinical Supervision: A State of the Art Review*. Alexandria, Va.: Association for Supervision and Curriculum Development.

Svartberg, M. and Stiles, T.C. (1992) Predicting patient change from therapist competence and patient–therapist complementarity in short-term anxiety-provoking psychotherapy: A pilot study. *Journal of Consulting and Clinical Psychology*, 60, 304–307.

Tarasoff v. *Regents of the University of California* (1974) 118 Cal. Rptr. 129, 529 P. 2d 533.

Taylor, F.W. ([1911] 1998) *Principles of Scientific Management*. Norcross: Engineering and Management Press.

Tennen, H. (1988) Supervision of integrated psychotherapy: A critique. *Journal of Integrative and Eclectic Psychotherapy*, 7, 167–175.

Thomas, A., Chess, S. and Birch, H.G. (1968) *Temperament and Behaviour Disorders in Children*. New York: University Press.

Thorbeck, J. (1992) The development of the psychodynamic psychotherapist in supervision. *Academic Psychiatry*, 16, 72–82.

Tomm, K. (1984) One perspective on the Milan systemic approach. Part I: Overview of development, theory and practice. *Journal of Marital and Family Therapy*, 10, 113–125.

Tomm, K. (1987) Interventive interviewing: Part II. Reflexive questioning as a means to enable self-healing. *Family Process*, 26, 167–183.

Troster, A.I., Paolo, A.M., Glatt, S.L., Hubble, J.P. and Koller, W.C. (1995) Interactive video conferencing in the provision of neuro-psychological services in rural areas. *Journal of Community Psychology*, 23, 85–88.

Tuckman, B.W. (1965) Developmental sequence in small groups. *Psychological Bulletin*, 63, 384–399.

Tuckman, B.W. and Jensen, M.A.C. (1977) Stages of small group development revisited. *Group and Organizational Studies*, 2, 419–427.

University of Sheffield Clinical Psychology Training Course Supervisor's Handbook (1999) Sheffield: University of Sheffield.

Urmson, J.O. and Rée, J. (1989) *The Concise Encyclopaedia of Western Philosophy and Philosophers*. London: Routledge.

Ussher, J.M. and Nicolson, P. (1992) *Gender Issues in Clinical Psychology*. New York: Routledge.

VanderMay, J. and Peake, T. (1980) Psychodrama as psychotherapy supervision technique. *Journal of Group Psychotherapy, Psychodrama and Sociometry*, 33, 25–32.

Von Glasersfeld, E. (1991) Knowing without metaphysics: Aspects of the radical constructivist position. In F. Steier, *Research and Reflexivity*. London: Sage.

Wade, P. (1999) Human nature and race. Paper presented at the British Association Annual Festival of Science, 13–17 September, Sheffield Anthropology and Archaeology Section.

Wadsborough Solicitors (1999) Personal communication.

Walsh, S. and Scaife, J.M. (1998) Mechanisms for addressing personal and professional development in clinical training. *Clinical Psychology Forum*, 115, 21–24.

Warburton, N. (1995) *Philosophy: The Basics* (2nd edition). London: Routledge.

Wark, L. (1995) Live supervision in family therapy: Qualitative interviews of supervision events as perceived by supervisors and supervisees. *The American Journal of Family Therapy*, 23, 25–37.

Watkins, C.E. Jr (1995) Pathological attachment styles in psychotherapy supervision. *Psychotherapy*, 32, 333–340.

Watkins, C.E. Jr (ed.) (1997) *The Handbook of Psychotherapy Supervision*. New York: Wiley and Sons.

Watkins, C.E., Schneider, L.J., Haynes, J. and Nieberding, R. (1995) Measuring psychotherapy supervisor development: An initial effort at scale development and validation. *Clinical Supervisor*, 13, 77–90.

Webb, N.B. (1983) Developing competent clinical practitioners: A model with guidelines for supervisors. *The Clinical Supervisor*, 1(4), 41–55.

Weil, S. (1993) Access: Towards education or miseducation? Adults imagine the future. In M. Thorpe, R. Edward and A. Hanson. *Culture and Processes of Adult Learning*. Milton Keynes: Open University Press.

Weil, S. (1995) Learning by doing – A guide to teaching and learning methods. Personal communication.

Wetchler, J.L., Piercy, F.P. and Sprenkle, D.H. (1989) Supervisors' and supervisees' perceptions of the effectiveness of family therapy supervisory techniques. *American Journal of Family Therapy*, 21, 242–247.

Whitehead, A.N. (1926) *Science and the Modern World*. London: Cambridge University Press.

Wilbur, M.P., Roberts-Wilbur, J., Hart, G.M., Morris, J.R. and Betz, R.L. (1994) Structured group supervision (SGS): A pilot study. *Counselor Education and Supervision*, 33, 262–279.

Williams, A. (1995) *Visual and Active Supervision*. New York: Norton.

Williams, A.B. (1997) On parallel process in social work supervision. *Clinical Social Work Journal*, 25, 425–435.

Williams, B. (1982) *Moral Luck: Philosophical Essays, 1973–80*. Cambridge: Cambridge University Press.

Wilson, S.J. (1981) *Field Instruction*. New York: The Free Press.

Winnicott, D.W. (1965) *Maturational Processes and the Facilitating Environment*. Madison, Wis.: International Universities Press Incorporated.

Winter, M. and Holloway, E.L. (1991) Relation of trainee experience, conceptual level, and supervisor approach to selection of audiotaped counseling passages. *Clinical Supervisor*, 9, 87–103.

Wong, Y.-L. S. (1997) Live supervision in family therapy; Trainee perspectives. *The Clinical Supervisor*, 15, 145–157.

Wood, B.J., Klein, S., Cross, H.J., Lammers, C.J. and Elliot, J.K. (1985) Impaired practitioners: Psychologists' opinions about prevalence, and proposals for intervention. *Professional Psychology: Research and Practice*, 16, 843–850.

Woods, P.J. and Ellis, A. (1997) Supervision in Rational Emotive Behaviour Therapy. In C.E. Watkins Jr, *Handbook of Psychotherapy Supervision*. New York: John Wiley and Sons Inc.

Woodward, H. (1998) Reflective journals and portfolios: Learning through assessment. *Assessment and Evaluation in Higher Education*, 23, 415–423.

Worthen, V. and McNeill, B.W. (1996) A phenomenological investigation of 'good' supervision events. *Journal of Counseling Psychology*, 43, 25–34.

Worthington, E.L. Jr (1987) Changes in supervision as counselors and supervisors gain experience: A review. *Professional Psychology: Research and Practice*, 18, 189–208.

Worthington, E.L. and Roehlke, H.J. (1979) Effective supervision as perceived by beginning counselors-in-training. *Journal of Counseling Psychology*, 26, 64–73.

Wosket, V. (1998) Personal communication.

Woskett, V. (1999) Personal communication.

Wynne, L.C., McDaniel, S.H. and Weber, T.T. (1986) *Systems Consultation: A New Perspective for Family Therapy*. New York: Guilford Press.

Yablonsky, L. (1992) *Psychodrama: Resolving Emotional Problems Through Role-Playing*. New York: Brunner/Mazel.

Yager, G.G., Wilson, F.R., Brewer, D. and Kinnetz, P. (1989) The development and validation of an instrument to measure counseling supervisor focus and style. Paper presented at the American Educational Research Association, San Francisco. Cited in J.M. Bernard and R.K. Goodyear (1998) *Fundamentals of Clinical Supervision* (2nd edition). Needham Heights, Mass.: Allyn and Bacon

Yalom, I.D. (1989) *Love's Executioner and Other Tales of Psychotherapy*. New York: Basic Books.

Young, J., Perlesz, A., Paterson, R., O'Hanlon, B., Newbold, A., Chaplin, R. and Bridge, S. (1989) The reflecting team process in training. *Australia and New Zealand Journal of Family Therapy*, 10, 69–74.

Yourman, D.B. and Farber, B.A. (1997) Nondisclosure and distortion in psychotherapy supervision. *Psychotherapy*, 33, 567–575.

Author index

Abadie, P.D. 189
Adair, J.E. 113
Albee, G.W. 138
Alderfer, C. 52
Allen, V. 148
Amundson, N.W. 175, 177
Anderson, H. 82, 166, 201
Anderson, R.H. 79
Anderson, T. 168, 171
Anthony, W.A. 222
Apps, J.W. 206
Arnheim, R. 174
Ashforth, B.E. 80
Aveline, M. 147, 148, 153

Bal, S. 135
Baldwin, S. 122
Barber, J. 201
Barker, P.J 122
Barnat, M.R 188
Barnes, L.H. 151
Bartlett, W.E. 97, 189
Bateson, G. 18
Bauman, W.F. 153
Beail, N. 50
Beauchamp, T.L. 122, 126
Beck, A.T. 198
Beck, J.S. 198, 200, 201
Bentall, R.P. 218
Berg, K.S. 244
Berger, M 167
Bernard, J.L. 131
Bernard, J.M. 3, 4, 32, 36, 54, 74,
  75, 77, 79, 81, 96, 156, 194, 198,
  243
Berthoff, A. 213
Betz, R.L. 172

Bieder, J. 179
Binder, J.L. 16, 24, 190, 191
Bion, W.R. 70, 117, 118
Birch, H.G. 40
Boltuch, B.S. 158
Bond, T. 122
Bonney, W. 197
Borders, L.D. 69
Bordin, E.S. 57
Boscolo, L. 202
Bostock, J. 135
Boyle, M. 218
Bradley, F.O. 189
Bradley, I. 185
Bradley, L. 185
Bransford, J.D. 15
Breunlin, D.C. 161, 168
Brewer, D. 243
Bridge, S. 171
Brookfield, S. 25
Burnham, J. 83, 186, 187, 202, 203,
  204
Butler, S.F. 218
Button, D. 207
Butzlaff, R.L. 215
Byng-Hall, J. 49, 169, 204

Caligor, L. 190
Callanan, P. 122
Cann, H.M. 139
Carey, J.C., 63
Carkhuff, R.R. 222
Carroll, M. 2, 52, 69
Casement, P. 41, 42, 186, 191, 212
Cecchin, G. 202
Chaplin, R. 171
Chess, S. 40

Childress, J.F. 122, 126
Clark, A. 138, 169
Clarke, P. 156
Cochrane, R. 135
Cogan, M.L. 96
Cohen, M. 167
Corbet, M. 143
Corbett, M.M. 35, 64, 73
Corey, G. 122, 144
Corey, M.S. 122, 144
Cornfeld, J.L. 190
Costa, L. 161
Coulshed, V. 29
Covner, B.J. 159
Crago, M. 158
Craine, M.H. 175
Crimmings, A.M. ix
Cronen, V. 203
Cronen, V.E. 32
Cross, H.J. 229
Czander, W.M. 73

Dammann, C. 167
Daniels, J. 225
Davies, S. 207
Davis, L. 148
Delworth, U. 3, 64, 70, 93, 94, 95, 122,
153
Dennett, D.C. 19
Dewald, P.A. 191
Disney, M.J. 131, 133
Dobson, K.S. 218
Dodenhoff, J.T. 64
Dodge, J. 153
Doehrman, M.J.G. 11, 35, 60, 70, 76, 88,
190
Doi, T. 137
Donaldson, M. 23
Down, G. 134
Dryden, W. 198
Duling, J. 148

Edelman, G. 19, 20, 26
Efros, F. 189
Efstation, J.F. 243
Egan, G. 63, 88, 101, 219
Ekstein, R. 11, 189
Elliot, J.K. 229
Elliott, R. 156
Ellis, A. 189, 190, 197, 198
Ellis, M.V. ix
Ellman, B. 141

Elman, N. 225
Engel, A. 5
Engel, M. 206
Entwistle, N.J. 22
Epston, D. 83, 186
Erdman, P. 170
Erismann, M. 188
Errek, H. 185

Farber, B.A. 64, 145
Fiedler, F.A. 189
Flanagan, O. 19
Flemons, D.G. 203
Ford, N. 21, 22
Fordham, A.S. 218
Forrest, L. 225
Fraleigh, P.W. 110, 111
Friedlander, M.L. 64, 97, 190, 243
Friedmann, C.T. 148
Frostig, M. 18
Fryer, P. 27

Gagné, R.M. 21
Gelso, C.J. 190
Gergen, K. 201
Gershenson, J. 167
Gibson, G. 143
Gilbert, T.F. 18
Gill, D. 135
Gillborn, D. 135
Gilligan, C. 201
Gilmore, S.K. 110, 111
Gizara, S. 225
Glaser, R.D. 128
Glatt, S.L. 158
Goffman, E 38, 80
Goldhammer, R. 79
Goldstein, H. 136
Goncalves, O.F. 175
Gonsiorek, J. 229
Goodrich, T.J. 141
Goodyear, R.K. 3, 4, 32, 36, 96, 189, 194,
198, 243
Goolishian, H. 201
Gorrell Barnes, G. 134
Green, S.K. 203
Greenslade, L. 135
Griffin, E.M. 207, 208
Gysbers, N.C. 244

Hagan, T. 138
Haggard, E.A. 151

Hahn, W.K. 215, 225
Hall, E.T. 137
Halstead, K. 141
Hampden-Turner, C. 174
Handley, P.G. 64
Hardy, E. 3, 94
Harrar, W.R. 143
Hart, G.M. 171
Hawkins, P. 33, 52, 55, 71, 80, 84, 86, 87, 88, 89, 244
Haynes, J. 243
Hays, J.R. 132
Hellman, S. 207
Heppner, P.P. 64
Herron, W.G. 88
Hetherly, V. 243
Hiken, J.R. 151
Hildebrand, J. 22, 41
Hill, C.E. 35, 64, 73
Hillman, J. 52
Hinshelwood, R.D. 42
Hitchings, P. 134
Hoffman, L. 32, 166, 168, 202
Holloway, E.L. ix, 2, 96, 97, 215, 225, 244
Holt, J. 42
Honey, P. 22
Hooley, J.M. 215
Horton, I. 89
House, R. 5
Houston, G. 112
Howells, W.D. 188
Hubble, J.P. 158
Hudson, H. 207, 208
Hughlings Jackson, J. 239
Humphrey, R.H. 80

Inskipp, F. 2, 4, 7, 23, 67, 68, 69, 71, 73, 84, 99, 119, 120, 174, 176
Isaacs, K.S. 151
Ishiyama, F.I. 177, 178
Ivey, A.E. 83, 97

Jacobsen, T. 215
Jacobson, N. 185
Jensen, M.A.C. 70
Johnston, J.A. 244
Jones, S. 161
Jung, C.J. 207

Kagan, H. 77, 83
Kagan, N. 77, 83, 156, 158

Kagan-Klein, H. 156
Kalff, D. 179
Kardash, C.M. 243
Karno, M.P. 152
Karp, M. 185, 188
Katz, J.H. 138
Keith-Spiegel, P. 122, 229
Kenfield, J.A. 145
Kent, G. 123
Kerka, S. 210
King, D. 8, 9, 51
Kingston, P. 166
Kinnetz, P. 244
Klein, S. 229
Knapp, S. 143
Kolb, D.A. 27, 208
Koller, W.C. 158
Koocher, G.P. 122
Kopp, R.R. 175
Krajewski, R.J. 79
Krathwohl, D.R. 83, 156, 158
Krengel, M. ix
Kuhn, T.S. 11
Kulakowski, D. 145
Kurpius, D. 143
Kutz, S.L. 225

Ladany, N. ix, 35, 64, 73
Lambert, M.J. 3
Lammers, C.J. 229
Landis, E.R. 132
Lang, W.P. 203
Laplanche, J. 42
Larson, P.C. 135
Lawson, D.M. 182
Lawton, B. 13, 53
Ledick, G.R. 69
Lee, E.P. 211
Lee-Borden, N. 96
Lent R.W. ix
Lesage-Higgins, S.A. 182
Levidow, L. 135
Levine, F.M. 74, 81, 83, 84, 160
Lev-Ran, A. 141
Lewis, J. 143
Lewontin, R. 139
Leydon, G. 113
Liddle, B.J. 57, 153
Liddle, H.A. 161, 168
Liese, B.S. 200, 201
Little, M. 203
Littrell, J.M. 96

Loganbill, C. 3, 94
Lorenz, J.A. 96
Lowenfeld, M. 179
Lowenstein, S.F., 169
Lunt, I. 113
Lynch, B. 52

Mac an Ghaill, M. 140
Macran, S. 50
Mahoney, M.J. 149
Manocchio, A.J. 169
Matthews, K. 244
Mauzey, E. 170
May, B. 218
Mayer, J.E. 91
McAuley, D. 123
McCann, D. 134
McCarthy, P. 145
McCullough, M.E. 189
McDaniel, S.H. 35
McElfresh, S.J. 74
McElfresh, T.A. 74
McNeill, B. 64, 70, 88, 93, 95, 122, 153, 237
Meredith, R. 185
Meyer, R.G. 132
Meyer-Bahlburg, H.F. 141
Mezirow, J. 25, 26
Miars, R.D. 190
Middleman, R.R. 36
Millard, E. 138
Miller, N. 158
Miller, R. 83, 156
Minardi, H.A. 148
Mohl, P.C. 244
Moldawsky, S. 190
Mollon, P. 37, 38, 41, 73, 167
Molnar, S. 215, 225
Monaghan, L. 232
Montalvo, B. 204
Moreno, Z.T. 188
Morris, J.R. 171
Morrison, T. 3, 31, 143
Mumford, A. 22

Nelson, G. L. 152
Nelson, M.L. 5
Neufeldt, S.A. 152
Newbold, A. 171
Newman, A.S. 134
Nicolson, P. 142
Nieberding, R. 244

Niemi, P.M. 207
Niland, T.M. 148
Noddings, N. 124
Noucho, A.O. 188
Nourry, C. 179
Nutt, E.A. 35, 64, 73
Nuttall, D. 136

O'Farrell, M. 190
O'Hanlon, B. 171
O'Laughlin, D.L. 131
Olk, M. 243
Oyston, C. 134
Osborne, E. 113

Padesky, C.A. 197
Page, S. 13, 52, 69, 71, 89, 91, 92, 125
Palazzoli, M. 202
Palmer Barnes, F. 225
Panther, E. 148
Paolo, A.M. 158
Pask, G. 21, 22
Paterson, R. 171
Patterson, C.H. 196, 197
Patton, M.J. 243
Peake, T. 174
Pearce, W.B. 32
Pearson, C. 5
Pederson, P. 136, 137, 138
Pegg, P.F. 169
Perlesz, A. 171
Perr, H.M. 191
Philbrick, R. 110, 111
Piaget, J. 23, 24, 26, 29
Piercy, F.P. 145
Pilowsky, I. 151
Polanyi, M. 3
Pomerantz, M. 76, 81, 83, 113, 130, 240
Pontalis, J.B. 42
Poortinga, Y.H. 136
Pope, K.S. 122, 229
Powell, M. 113
Prata, G. 202
Primavera, L.H. 88
Proctor, B. 2, 4, 7, 23, 67, 68, 69, 71, 73, 84, 99, 119, 120, 174, 176
Prosser, R. 136
Putney, M.W. 189

Raichelson, S.H. 88
Rambo, A. 203
Ramirez, S.M. 88

Rampage, C. 141
Randall, R. 118
Randolph, D. 185
Rasbash, H. 136
Ray, P.B. 190
Reavis, C. A. 96
Reder, P. 169
Rée, J. 124
Reiss, M.J. 139
Rhodes, G.B. 36
Riding, R. 22
Ritter, S. 148
Robbins, A. 188
Roberts, C.A. 34
Roberts, M. 207, 208, 209, 212, 213
Roberts-Wilbur, J. 171
Roehlke, H.J. 215, 225, 244
Rogers, C.R. 20, 21, 26, 159, 189, 190, 194, 196, 197, 215
Ronaldson, J. 113
Ronnestad, M.H. 96
Rosenblatt, A. 91
Ross, W.D. 125
Rowan, J. 91
Rowell, J.A. 24
Rudduck, J. 77, 79
Rule, W. R. 174
Russell, R.K. ix
Ryan, F. 132

Salzberger-Wittenberg, I. 35
Samba, D. 179
Scaife, J.A. 15, 71, 74, 79, 81
Scaife, J.M. 4, 15, 22, 30, 32, 41, 43, 52, 62, 71, 74, 79, 81, 99, 130, 149, 192
Schneider, L.J. 244
Schoener, G.R. 229
Schön, D.A. 15, 16, 24
Schult, D. ix
Schutz, W.C. 114, 116, 118
Schwartz, R.C. 161, 168
Scott, C. 81, 145
Searles, H.F. 88
Shainberg, D. 85
Shanfield, W.B. 244
Shapiro, D. 50
Sharpe, M. 113
Shaw, B.F. 218
Shem, S. 138
Shohet, R. 33, 55, 71, 80, 86, 87, 88, 89, 244

Sigsworth, A. 77, 79
Sills, C. 108
Skovholt, T.M. 96
Slade, P. 218
Sluman, S. 5
Smail, D. 138
Smith, D. 166
Smith, E.J. 136
Smith, T.E. 171
Snadden, D. 207, 208
Snyder, J. 64
Southgate, J. 118
Spellman, D. 81, 145
Sprague, K. 188
Sprenkle, D.H. 145
Spy, T. 134
Stephens, A.M. 131, 132, 133
Stiles, T.C. 218
Stoltenberg, C.D. 64, 70, 93, 95, 122, 153, 237
Stone, G.L. 244
Stones, E. 77
Strosahl, K 185
Strupp, H.H. 16, 24, 190, 191, 218
Sullivan, C.G. 79, 97
Svartberg, M. 218

Tabachnick, B.G. 229
Tauvon K.B. 185
Taylor, F.W. 31
Tennen, H. 191
Thomas, A. 40
Thomas, M.L. 207, 208
Thorbeck, J. 190
Thorpe, J.S. 128
Tilker, H.A. 74, 81, 83, 84, 160
Tomm, K. 70, 202
Tracey, T.J. 190
Troster, A.I. 158
Tuckman, B.W. 70, 106, 115, 116, 117, 118

Urmson, J.O. 124
Ussher, J. M. 142

Vacha-Haase, T. 225
Vandercreek, L. 143
VanderMay, J. 174
Vasquez, M.J.T. 122
Von Glasersfeld, E. 201
Vye, N.J. 15

Wade, P. 139
Wadsborough 132
Wallerstein, R.S. 11
Walsh, S. 30, 41
Wampold, B.E. 244
Warburton, N. 124
Ward, L.G. 97, 190, 243
Wark, L. 167, 168
Watkins, C.E. Jr. 57, 97, 244
Watson, M. 188
Webb, N.B. 90
Weber, T.T. 35
Weil, S. 26, 28, 29
Wells, M. 63
Wetchler, J.L. 145
Wheeler, S. 8, 9, 51
Whitehead, A.N. 16
Wilbur, M.P. 171
Williams, A. 174, 179, 180, 181, 184, 185
Williams, A.B. 88
Williams, B. 124
Williams, K.S. 63
Wilson, F.R. 244

Wilson, S.J. 228, 240
Winnicott, D.W. 121
Winter, M. 96
Winton, M. 171
Wolkon, G.H. 148
Wong, Y-L. S. 167
Wood, B.J. 229
Woods, P.J. 197, 198
Woodward, H. 207, 211, 212, 213
Worthen, V. 64, 88
Worthington, E.L. 189, 244
Worthington, E.L. Jr. 95
Wosket, V. 13, 52, 69, 71, 89, 91, 92, 125, 177, 233
Wynne, L.C. 135

Yablonsky, L. 188
Yager, G.G. 244
Yalom, I.D. 41
Yamamoto, J. 148
Yoshioka, M. 171
Young, J. 171
Yourman, D.B. 64, 145

Subject index

ABC 198
Absolute duties 124
Abstract conceptualisation 27
Abstraction, dependency across cultures 137
Abuse of clients 72
Academic context 80
Accelerated learning 158
Accommodation
  in groups 115
  & learning 23
  professional accommodation syndrome 31
Accountability
  in contracting 89
  & dual relationships 144
  in groups 105
  use of tapes and 149
Accurate empathy 194
Action 213
  culture 184
  methods 183–188
  plans 92
  replay 82
Actions, events & responses 79
Active leadership 109, 110
Active listening
  in person-centred model 194
  in supervision and therapy 12
Adult learner 24
  & feedback 216
Advantages of taping 148–150
Affect needs, in groups 115
Age 62
  & ethics 134
Ageism 136

Agenda setting 5, 52
  in cognitive therapy supervision 200
  in group supervision 107
  in the General Supervision Framework 78
Agreements
  & boundary issues 95
  & learning logs 211
  in live supervising teams 203
  in managing groups 101, 102–107, 116
  with training institutions 10
Aggression from group members 112
Aide-mémoire
  & learning logs 208
  in use of tapes 149
Aims of supervision
  & features of supervision 5
  & the supervisory alliance 57
  & the supervisory relationship 1
Alcohol misuse 225
Alienation 32
Allegiance to different parties 10
Allele frequencies 139
Alliance
  client/therapist 57, 69
  & conceptual frameworks 98
  & constructive challenge 218, 223
  & contracting 57, 63
  & cyclical model of supervision 92
  & definition of supervision 2
  dos and don'ts of supervision 67
  & evaluative role 218
  & groups 102
  & learning 191
  & learning logs 210
  & live team supervision 171
  & nature of role-relationship 57

& non-disclosure 35
& parallel process 118
& sculpting 183
supervisor working alliance inventory
    243
& trust 35
Allocation
    meeting 66
    of supervisor 13, 138
    of time 101, 106
American Association for Counseling
    and Development 143
Analysis of performance 96
Analytic–holist learning style 22
Anorexia 17
Anti-depressant medication 181
Anxiety
    & academic climate 32
    & action methods 179, 188
    & clinical supervision 96
    & coursework assignments 234
    & developmental models of
        supervision 93, 96
    & engagement with clients 128
    & evaluation 57, 62, 227, 229
    & groups 115
    & learning 24
    & live supervision 82, 161, 170
    & narcissistic perils 38
    normalising 57
    & responsibility for clients 8
    state 37
    & taping 148, 153
    & uncertainty 84
Apartheid 134
Appeals
    & due process 133
    to supervisor 59
Appraisal
    critical 240
    & definition of supervision 2
    & evaluation 215
    & group reviews 101
    & line management 144
    of motivation in clients 6
    & procedural knowledge 16
Apprenticeship 16
Archaeology 139
Artificial intelligence 19
Asian 136
Assertion 111
Assertiveness

for group leaders 111
& principles of challenge 220
Assessment procedures 10
Assignments
    & contracting 53
    & issues regarding coursework 231
    & learning logs 210
Assimilation & personal and
        professional development 43
Attachment theory 57
Audience in groups 118
Audiotape 145–159
    as medium of supervision 81–83
    of supervision session 43
Authenticity
    & needs in groups 115
    & openness of supervisor 64
Authoritative
    group 108
    group and parallel process 118
    messages & use of earphone 204
    style 91
    supervision 102
Authority 3
    & challenge 221
    & counter-transference 61
    & earphone 169
    education 136
    & ethical standards 143
    feeling comfortable with 113
    figures 35
    & gate-keeping role 203
    in groups 118
    & organisations 143
    & supervisory teams 203
Automatic thoughts 198
Autonomy
    & developmental models 93
    & earphone 169
    & ethical principles 125, 128–129
    & self-assessment questionnaire 240
Auxiliaries 188

Basic assumptions 117
Bed occupancy 31
Behaviour rehearsal 18, 83
Behavioural supervisors 189
Behaviourism 17–18
    & instrumental learning 25
Being supposed to know 42
Beliefs
    about supervisee 220

& cognitive therapy 197–201
& culture 140
in groups 113
& learning 15–27
& personal and professional
    development 30–33, 39–41
& philosophical underpinnings 16
& RET 198–200
Beneficence 125–130
Bereavement 183
effects on work 38, 80
Biologist 139
Birth order 49
Black
& context 27
definition 140
& negative labelling 135
& political implications 138
& racism 136
Blind alleys 162
Blind spots 56, 129
Blurring of roles 13
Bond 57
Borderline clients 42
Boredom 163
Boundaries
with colleagues 33
& consent to taping 147
& containment 176
& contracting 89
& course-work assignments 237
& ethical dilemmas 61
& feelings 38
as focus of supervision 38
in groups 110
personal issues in supervision 41, 55,
    64
& safety 67
& self assessment 249
in sexual abuse 45–46
& supervisory relationship 7, 52, 73
time boundaries 25, 192
Boundary setter 237
Breach of confidence 132
Bridge
as aid to learning 24
between theory and practice 96
& cyclical model of supervision 89–92
Brief therapy model 231
British Association of Counsellors
code of ethics and practice 53
complaints procedure 9

British Psychological Society
& confidentiality 130
guidance on training 81
& multi-disciplinary teams 34
survey of educational psychologists 76
Bug-in-the-ear
& live supervision 81–82
& team supervision 169–170
Bureaucratic culture 33

Campaign groups 135
Cancellations 89
Cancer 181
Case conceptualisation
& supervisory style 190
& use of objects 181
& visual metaphors 175–180
Case
conference 44
drawing 177
management 144
material 10
presentation 179
record 147
study 232
Casework 60
& focus of supervision 80
Causal-linear 202
Cause and effect 137
Challenge 215–224
& agency requirements 72
& choice of supervisor 13
& cognitive behaviour therapy 197
& colleagues 87
constructive 132, 215–224
& counter-transference 61
& cyclical model of supervision 92
& developmental models of
    supervision 93
& dos and don'ts for supervisors 67
& evaluation 215
& facilitation of groups 101–121
& learning cultures 33
& live supervision 169–172
role in learning 26
& safety 67
& self assessment 247
& supervisory relationship 52
in therapy 77
& use of tapes 145–148
of values and beliefs 43–46
Changing beliefs 200

Charlatanism 149
Charles Burns Clinic 152
Charts 131
Child protection 126
Choosing a supervisor 13, 54
Circular questioning 202
Circularity 202
Clarity
   & constructive challenge 222
   & leadership of groups 109
   of purpose of learning log 210
   in purpose and preference statements
      110
   of responsibility 56
   of role in live supervision 165
   of task in group supervision 113
   & unsuitability for training 218
Client
   centred 189
   focus 243
   identifiers 147
   outcomes 50
Client–therapist relationship 155
Clinical supervision 79, 96–97
   & confidentiality 131
   definition 96
   & focus of supervision 79
   & taping 148
Cloak of privacy 148
Closing sessions 165
Coaching 24
Code of Conduct 52, 130–131, 249
Code of Ethics and Practice 52, 105,
      122
Cognitive-behavioural therapy
      supervision 189, 197–201
   & experiential learning 27
   & supervisory focus 79
   & taping 150
Cognitive case processing form 177
Cognitive Styles Analysis 22
Cognitive therapy 150
   adherence & competence scales 201
Collaboration 168
   to change 57
Collaborative exploration 92, 173
Collegial role 76, 93–96
   in groups 104
Collusion 129
Collusive avoidance 148
Colonialism 139
Community centres 141

Competence
   assessment of 218–230
   doubts about 149
   effects of training on 149
   & ethical issues 132–134
   & feedback 58
   & learning readiness 23
   & live supervision 164
   maximising 2, 3
   & reflective practice 16
   & role of personal therapy 36
   self assessment 249
   & taping 154
   & transference issues 37–42
   veneer of 33, 64, 217
Competitiveness
   & academic context 32
   in groups 102
Compliments 204
Concealment from supervisor 73
Conceptualisation
   & General Supervision Framework
      74–80
Concrete experience 27–28
Conditional dependency 95
Conductors of groups 119
Conference in clinical supervision 97
Confident enough communication 110
Confidentiality
   & consent forms 245, 152
   & contracting for supervision 61, 89
   & course-work assignments 232
   & ethics 123 126, 131
   explaining to clients 17
   & group supervision 107
   limits of 150
   & note keeping 130
   & refugee status 141
   & self assessment 247
   & taping 82, 147–150
Conflict
   of beliefs and values 140
   between needs of clients and
      supervisees 8–10
   between supervisors and supervisees
      123
   cognitive conflicts in learning 23
   & developmental models of
      supervision 94–96
   & groups 102–116
   & live supervision 203
   & parallel process 190

& principles of ethics 127–130, 143
& psycho-dynamic theories 190
role conflicts 13
   & sculpting 183
   & stakeholders in supervision 31–32,
      233–234
   & taping 159
   in teams 32–34
Conflicting advice 234
Confrontation 215
Conscientiousness 234
Conscious
   competence 23
   incompetence 23
   restraint 168
Consciousness
   & course failure 233
   critical consciousness 26
   & groups 117
   & learning 16, 19
   & racism 135
   self-consciousness and taping 146
Consent
   to supervise 129
   to taping 82
Consequences of actions 124
Consequentialist theories 125
Constructive challenge
   & ethics 132
Constructivism 201
Consultant role 189
Consultation
   definition 3–4
   & groups 113
   & impaired performance 229
   in live supervision 165–170
Containment 92
   & developmental models of
      supervision 93
Content mastery 26
Context 26
Continuing professional development 2,
   231
Contracting 9, 52–69
   & action culture 184
   & characteristics of supervision 5
   & cyclical model of supervision 89–92
   & dual relationships 13
   & focus of supervision 80
   & general supervision framework 84
   & group supervision 105–114
   & learning logs 209

& principle of fidelity 125–128
& purposes of supervision 71–72
& reduction of anxiety 161
& responsibilities to stakeholders 72
& self assessment 247
& supervisory style 91
& taping 154–159
& therapeutic model 43, 194
& trust 35
& unsatisfactory performance 225
Co-operative supervision 103
Core
   conditions 194–197, 215
   qualities 102
Corrective scripts 49
Counsellor role 77
Counter-identification 191
Counter-transference 42–43, 80
   & developmental models of
      supervision 94
   & focus of supervision 80
   & parallel process 70
   & personal qualities 40
   & position of authority 61
   & psycho-dynamic models of
      supervision 190–194
   types of 87
Course requirement 209
Course-work
   guidelines 237
   & learning logs 211
   & supervision contract 53
   supervisor's role in 231–238
Co-work 161–163
Creative methods 173–188
Creativity
   & double matrix model of supervision
      86
   & transference 43
Criteria
   for evaluation 196
   & learning logs 211
   & self assessment 243
   & unsatisfactory performance 227
Critical
   attack 156
   consciousness 26
   incidents 97
   reflection 26–29
   thinking skills 214
Cultural
   dissonance 135

encapsulation 137
unawareness 137
Culture
  & contracting process 62
  & ethics 126, 134–139
  group culture 102, 121
  of helping professions 20, 26, 34
  learning cultures 33
  organisational cultures 33
  of origin and effects on work 39
  & selection 20
Curiosity
  & concealment 64
  & enquirer role 76
  & group supervision 110
  & internalised-other interviewing 187
  & systemic approaches 202
  & unsatisfactory performance 226
Current knowledge 21–23
Curriculum
  delivery of 32
  relationship to thinking and learning
    206
  personal 12
  & self assessment 241
  of training institution 15
  vitae 241
Customers 32
Cycle of arousal 45
Cyclical model of supervision 89–92

Dance 120
Data collection 97, 224
Darwin 19
Deadlines 233
De-briefing 83, 174
De-centre 23
De-roling 174
Declarative knowledge 15
Defensiveness
  & contracting 61–62
  & failure 228
  & feedback 216
  in groups 116
  in learning contexts 24
  & live supervision 164
  & responsibilities of supervisees 7
  & taping 152–158
  & unsatisfactory performance 225
Dependence 93, 117
Dependency of trainee 93–94
Dependency–autonomy conflicts 94

Depression 44, 181, 225
Deprivation 140
De-consulting 161–163
De-roling 186
Descartes 18
De-skilling 104
Description 213
Descriptive writing 209
Deviance 135
Developing needs 114
Development of self 30–51
Developmental
  models of supervision 70,
    93–96
  stage of group leader 121
Diagnosis 197
Diagrams 224, 236
Dialogic learning 25
Diary 206–214
Didactic 191, 197
Didactic-consultative style 91
Difference
  & ethics 134
  individual 23, 62
  & life expectancy 135
  of opinion 60, 112
  & the plastic brain 20
Differences of opinion 34, 60
  in groups 112, 171
Dilemma
  & creative approaches 173
  & dual responsibility 8–9, 162
  & ethnicity 140
  as focus of supervision 85, 91
  & learning logs 210
  & personal responses 49
  & supervisor role-behaviour 76
Directive 198
Directives and taping 153–159
Disability 134, 141
Disciplinary procedures 10
Disclosure to supervisor 123
Discovery 198
Discovery learning 28
Discrimination 134–136, 141
Discussion 200
Dis-equilibration 24
Disposal of tapes 147
Disruptions 88
Dissertation 234
Distance learning 158
Distancing 175

Distress
  of clients 50
  & focus of supervision 81
  & live supervision 164
  & negative evaluation 57
  & stopping work 229
Disturbance 197
Diversity in groups 102–107
Do-able projects 237
Domain
  of action 203
  of aesthetics 203
  of explanation 203
  of production 203
Dominant group 134
Dos and don'ts
  & context of safety 67
Double Matrix Model 84
Doubling 188
Drafts 237
Drama 120, 188
Drawing 175–179
  the client as a fish 176
Dress style 140
Dual relationships 4, 12–13, 55
  & ethics 128, 142–144
Dual responsibility for client 8
Dualism 18
Due process 133, 226
Duty to warn 132
Dynamics
  & focus of supervision 80
  in live supervision 166
  & psycho-dynamic supervision 190
  of therapeutic relationship 69
Dysfunctional group behaviour 110,
      117

Earphone 169, 204
Eastern philosophies 137
Ecological analysis 135
Economic cogs 31
Edge of awareness 173
Education institution 233
Educational
  psychology 60
  role 198
Elective arrangements 63
Emergencies 55
Emotional
  climate 30–51, 160
  expression 145

Emotions
  in group leaders 112
  & restorative function of supervision 73
  suppression of 40
  at work 12, 30–51
Empathy
  effects of taping on 146
  enhanced 149
  in group leaders 102
  in groups 106–115
  & life events 47
  & person-centred supervision 194
  in supervisees 218
  in supervisors 64
Empiricism 16, 25
Employer
  aims of 10
  constraints of 72
  supervisor's responsibility to 8–10
Empty chairs 184
Enculturation 20
  & multi-disciplinary teams 34
Engagement
  with clients 227
  in groups 111
Enquirer role of supervisor 75, 156–158
Equity 134
Enquiry
  & creative methods 180
  & experiential learning 27
  & role of supervisor 12, 56
  & sculpting 183
Episode of care 147
Equilibration 23
Equity 126
  & due process 133
Errors 162
Establishment of supervisory team
      171
Ethical
  considerations 197
  dilemmas 122–144
    & aims of employer 10
    & contracting process 61
    in groups 107
    & normalising 61
  principles 122–130
  responsibilities to clients 72, 76
  standards 143
Ethics of care 124
Ethnicity 134–141
  & contracting process 62

& detentions in school 135
& justice 126
Ethnographic study 135
Ethos 31
Evaluation 215–230
    & anxiety 57–58
    & clinical supervision 97
    & contracting process 53–61
    & ethics 132
    & expectations 163
    fear of negative 8
    forms 96
    & function of supervisor 35
    & restorative role of supervisor 73
    & review stage of cyclical model 92
    of self 58
    & taping 150
Evaluative
    role 229
    statements 226
writing 209
Evolution, & brain structure 19
Exclusion 141
Existential 189
Experiential exercises 119–120
Experiential learning cycle 27–29, 208
Experiential learning theory 27–29
Expert 153
Explanation 156
Exposure 167
Expressed emotion 215
Expression of feelings 209
External supervisor 191
Externalisation 176
Extracts from tapes 154
Eye contact 165, 224

Façade of competence 64, 216
Facilitation
    & creative methods 178
    & experiential learning 29
    of groups 113
Failed appointments 85
Failure 227–229
    & contracting process 54–61
    & course-work 233
    & due process 133
    & ethics 123, 128
    & process of learning 23
Fair opportunity rule 126
Family
    of origin 26

relationships 48
scripts 49
system in groups 120
therapy 64
    & live supervision 82, 160–172
Fear of instruction 156
Feedback 2, 20, 215–217
    & clinical supervision 96
    in groups 107–114
    & learning logs 208
    & level 1 supervisors 95
    & live supervision 171
    reciprocal 57
    from supervisor 18, 36
    & supervisor role behaviour
        76
    staying in control of 8
    & tapes 155
Feelings
    as focus of supervision 11
    as information 86
    oriented 91
Felt sense 120, 160
Feminism 201
Fidelity 125–130
Field settings 96
Fight/flight 117
First impressions 39
Flexibility of supervisor 84
Focus of supervision
    & developmental models of
        supervision 94
    & expectation of supervisees 7
    & general supervision framework
        74–81
    identification of 46
    & live supervision 163
    narrowing in review of tapes 155
    & organisational context 32
    preferred 79
Focusing, in cyclical model of
    supervision 89–91
Following the client 196
Formal assessment 10
Formative
    assessment 11, 211
    function 5, 29, 72
    role 101
Formats
    for group supervision 120
    of learning logs 213
Forming process 106–116

Formulation
  & creative methods 176
  & diagrams 236
  & General Supervision Framework 80
  hasty 84
Fragmentation 137
Framework for case drawing 177–179
Frameworks
  for group supervision 110–121
  for supervision 70–98
Free association 49, 191
Free-flow group supervision 119
Frequency of supervision 52
Freud 52

Gate-keeping 5
  & challenge 223
  & responsibility to clients 132
  & supervisory role-relationship 76
Gaze avoidance 165
Gender
  & contracting process 62
  & ethics 134–142
  identity 141
  & justice 126
  relevance to work 46
  roles 49, 141
  stereotyping 142
Gene frequencies 139
Generalisation 191
Genetic diversity studies 139
General
  practitioners 207
  Supervision Framework 74–84
Genogram 43, 48
Genuineness 196
Gestalt 189
Gestures 87
Goal-oriented 92
Goals
  of supervision 57, 96
  of therapy 92
Goals of challenge 219
Good enough group work 99, 121
Grievance procedures 10
Gross professional misconduct 133
Ground rules 55
  in groups 107–111
Grounding questions 186
Group
  awareness 101
  development frameworks 110–112

  dynamics 113
  inter-disciplinary 121
  managers 101
  manners 100–114
  movement 115–117
  needs 113
  process 102, 110–113
  supervision 99–121
  theories 70
  work 41
    roles 100
    tasks 100
Guidance 160
Guided
  discovery 200
  imagery 185

Habitual patterns 37
Hard contract 108
Hearing impairment 141
Helplessness 94
Hierarchy 171, 203
High context cultures 137
History
  client's 192
  & ethnic groups 140
  neglect of 138
  taking 248
Holist 21
Holistic 137
Homework tasks 150, 200
Host agency 53
Humanistic 189
Humility 223
Humour 40, 95, 235
Hungarian position 190
Hypotheses 156, 168

Identification 242
Identity needs 116
Illegal immigrant 130
Ill-health 72
  and taping 146
Images
  & creative methods 174
  as focus of supervision 86–87
  in group leaders 112
Imbalance 111
Imitation 99
Immaturity 228
Immediacy 222
  & supervisor's experience 88

Impairment 219–230
Imperialism 139
Improvisation 16, 24
    in groups 109
Inability to learn 227
Inclusion exercises 115
Inclusion needs 114
Incompetence
    feelings of 41
    identification of 225
Incubation period 208
Independence 137
Indian 136
Individual
    differences 23, 62
    emphasis on 136
    needs 102–114
    responsibility 106
Individuation 136
Induction 55
    of session 162
Inductor of groups 101
Inequity 130
Infantilisation 238
Influence needs 114
Informal, contact with supervisor 55
Inform–assess 75–76
Information
    absorber 206
    giving 12, 56
    regurgitator 206
Informed consent 125
    in groups 107
    to taping 150
Innatism 16
Inner London Education Authority
    136
Inquirer role 156–158
Inquiry 200
Insecurity of supervisee 93–94
    & creative methods 175
Insight-oriented 91
Institution of higher education 6
Institutionalised racism 136
Instructions 169
Instrumental learning 25
Insurance companies 138
Integration 207
Intellectualisation 153
Intelligence tests 136
Intensity 204
Intentionality 102–109

Intergenerational patterns 49
Interactive learning logs 209–210
Internal
    dialogues 119
    experience of therapist 86
    landscape 97
    market 130
    supervisor 191, 212
Internalised images 191
Internalised-other 83, 186–187
Internet 158
Interpersonal
    dynamics 69
    processes 24, 158
    relationships 63, 70
    process recall 77, 82, 156–158
    skills 228
Interpersonally sensitive 243
Interpretation
    of parallel process 191
    & sculpting 183
    & tapes 155–156
Interpreters 141
Inter-rater reliability 218
Interrupting 166
Interruptions 60
Inter-subjective processes 208
Intervention 168
Interviewing for a role 187
Intimacy
    & different cultures 137
    & live supervision 166
    needs for at work 33
    sexual 143
Introduction of taping to client
    150
Introjection 191
Intrusiveness 74
    & earphone 169
    & live supervision 82
    & taping 191
Invited feedback 217
Irish 135
Irrational thoughts 198

Japanese culture 137
Job description 129
Joint
    notes 233
    work 165
Journals 206–214
Jumping through hoops 158

Jung 206
Justice 125–130
Justifying 116

Kantian ethics 124
Key concepts 236
Kibbutz 137
Knowledge-in-action 15
Knowledge
　of the head 16
　of the heart 16
　thinking and planning 79

Laissez-faire
　group 104
　style 91
Language 140
Laws of nature 25
Lead therapist 165
Leadership of groups 3,
　　101–103
Learning 15–29
　agenda 222
　alliance 191
　cultures 33
　cycle
　history 90
　logs 206–214
　styles 15, 90
Legal
　framework 140
　precedents 122, 130
　in private practice 8
　requirements 130
　redress 226
　statutes 123
Level playing field 136
Liability
　of employing agency 10
Life
　events 11, 38, 47
　expectancy 135
　history 39
　preserver 177
Lifelines 48
Linear
　processes in groups 116
　thinking 137
Line-management
　& dual relationships 12, 143
　& responsibilities 222
　supervision 143

Listening role of supervisor 56, 74
　& developmental models 94
　& general supervision framework 77
Listen-reflect 75
Literature searches 236
Litigation
　increase in 130
　protecting self from 8, 125
Live supervision 160–172
　& clinical supervision 97
　after failed placement 128
　in family therapy 65
　& General Supervision Framework 82
　& systemic therapy supervision 201
Locke 16
Longitudinal census data 135
Low context cultures 137
Lowenfield World Technique 179

Macmillan nurse 181
Maintenance needs 114
Malpractice 225
Managed care networks 130
Managerial
　responsibilities 3
　function of supervisor 72, 223
　role in groups 101–106
　supervision 12, 61
Manual
　of Learning Styles 22
　of supervision 240
Maps 113, 120
Marketplace 32
Mass disorder 138
Master class 104
Medical students 207
Medium of supervision, & General
　　Supervision Framework 74
Mental health 215
Mental Health Act 133
Mental hospital 133
Meta-cognitive 97, 211
Meta-perspective 201
Metaphor
　& creative methods 174–175
　& developmental models 94
　& double matrix model 84–87
　& group leadership 112
　& learning styles 22
Metaphysical knowledge 16
Micro-analysis 150
Micro-counselling 82

Mid-session consultation 164–168
Migrant groups 135
Mime 120
Mind 18–21
Mini-contracting 68–69, 89
Minority 135
  groups 136
Mistakes 73, 99
  & taping 153
  & unsatisfactory performance 225
Misunderstandings 212
Mode of supervision 81
Modelling
  & action methods 184
  & behaviourism 17
  in groups 102–111
  & live supervision 160
  role 190
  as teaching strategy 3
Moral philosophy 124
Mortality rates 135
Motivation
  to change 6
  & developmental models of
      supervision 93
  & ethics 123
  fluctuating levels of 237
Motivator 237
Mourning 117
Multi-disciplinary teams 34
Multiple
  consulting 234
  hypotheses 201
  lenses 34
  perspectives 148, 168–171
Music in groups 120
Mutual
  recall 158
  respect 165
Mutuality 97
Myth of sameness 136
Myths and taping 150

Naivety 229
Narcissistic insults 73, 167
Narrative approaches 201
National Health Service 130, 249
Natural
  helpers 137
  science 16
  selection 19
Nativism 16

Nature–nurture 17, 47
Negative
  automatic thoughts 198
  criticism 239
  evaluation 148
    & contracting process 57
    & dual role-relationships 13
    & learning logs 210
  labelling 135
  power differential 136
Negligence 132, 225
Negotiation of disagreements 7
Neo-Aristotelianism 124
Nerve-racking 164
Neuroscience 19
Neuronal pathways 19–20
Neutrality 202
Nondisclosure 35
Non-judgemental attitude 64
Non-maleficence 125–130
Non-participatory observation 81
Non-threatening 158
Non-verbal
  communication 146
    & live supervision 163
  cues 155
Normal developmental stage 94
Normalising 220, 235
Normality 135–136
Normative
  function 5, 72
  meanings 25
  role 101
Norming 116
Norms in groups 106, 115
Note-keeping 130
Notes 131
Nurse 62, 181
Nurturing role 229

Objects 179
Objectifying 85
Objectives 90
Observable characteristics 139
Observation 160–172
  & behaviourism 17
  & clinical supervision 97
  & cognitive-behavioural supervision
      200
  frequency of 81
  & General Supervision Framework 82
  indirect 82, 145

& live supervision 163–167
& qualification 129
supervisee's views of 8
Observer
perspective 86
role 164–167
One-way screen 82, 167–168
Open ended questions 157
Openings 74
Openness
& clinical supervision 96
& contracting process 53, 58
to experience 28
to learning 7, 35
& live supervision 165
& taping 149–155
Oppression 115
Oppressive systems 138
Oral instructions
Organic presentations 197
Organisational context 32
& emotional experiences of employees
73
Outnumbering the client 166
Over-confidence 95
Over-learning 23
Over-protection 170
Ownership
of points for development 219
of tapes 147

Pairing 117
Pakistani 136
Palaeontology 139
Parallel process
& double matrix model 84–88
& frameworks for supervision 70
& group supervision 104, 118
& psycho-dynamic supervision 190
Participant
management 203
observation 89
Participative
management 165
supervision 102, 118
Partnership
with clients 168
models 79
supervision 77
& role behaviour 76
Passive role 163
Pathological systems 138

Patterns
analysis of 97
attribution to 224
of crisis 193
of interaction 167
of referral 142
& systemic therapy supervision 201
in tape review 154
in therapeutic process 85, 163
Peer consultation
& definitions 3
Peer group supervision 103–120
Peer supervision
& challenge 221
& contracting 61
& definitions 3
People-work 80
Performance
assessment 210
anxiety 93, 148
& tapes 155
focus on 154
Performing 116
Permission
in contracting process 59
for recording 147
Person-centred therapy supervision
190–197
Personal
and professional development
30–51
& boundary issues 11
& developmental models of
supervision 93–95
& learning logs 208
adjustment 196
analysis 190
bias
characteristics 39–40, 62–63
conflicts 190
development needs 5, 228
ethical code 122
growth 125
identity 60
information 67
issues 11, 30–51, 201
learning styles 20–22
needs 77
pathology culture 33
qualities 212
responsibility 132
therapy 36, 41–51, 190

& General Supervision Framework
   80
& person-centred supervision 196
Personality 40
   disorder 225
   dynamics 197
Person-centred therapy supervision
   194–197
Phenotype 139
Philosophical underpinnings 19
Phone-ins 170
Physical
   action 184
   pick-up 112
   scaling 184
   sensations 112
Piaget 23–24
Pictures 120
Placement planning 231
Plastic brain 18–19
Plato 17
Play 179
Playfulness 173
Pluralist society 140
Points for development
   of supervisees 7, 241
   & taping 154
Police 132
Policies regarding confidentiality 131
Policy documents 232
Political climate 32
Poor practice 225
Population
   geneticist 139
   statistics 232
Portfolios 206–214
Positive
   action 136
   constructions 203
feedback 18
frames 170, 218
Positivism 16
Post-modernism 201
Post-qualification 237
Post-registration supervision,
   supervisor responsibility for
   case-work 8
Poverty 141
Power
   balance/imbalance 141
   of feelings 192
   needs 114

struggles 115
& western society 135
Practical arrangements 101
Practice 185
Practitioner supervision, & definitions 3
Praise 94
Preference statements 110, 226
Preferences of supervisors 63
Prejudice 135
Preparation
   for groups 109
   & mini-contracting 68
Pre-registration supervision 3
   responsibility of supervisor in 8–11
Pre-session consultation 168
Presentation 91
Presenting in groups 107
Primitive emotions 192
Principles of ethics 122
Prioritising 112, 200
Privacy 210
Private practice, legal responsibilities in 8
Private records 209
Privileged communications 131
Probation officer 45, 161
Probation Service 215
Problem
   detection 24
   posing 26
Problem-solving 22, 24–26
   clients' skills in 40
Procedural manuals 29
Process
   as focus of supervision 95
   notes 163
Processes of change, in therapy and
   counselling 6
Procedural knowledge 15, 24
Professional Accommodation Syndrome
   31
Professional
   body 72
   community and ethics 125
   contract 117
   discipline 171
   genogram 22
   identity 37, 60
   misconduct 133, 227
   roles and ethics 122
Projection 51, 150, 193
Protagonists 185
Psychoanalysis 41

Psychoanalytic school 11, 189
Psychodrama 120, 174–188
Psychodynamic model 60
    & group supervision 118
    & taping 150
Psychodynamic therapy supervision
        189–194
    & focus of supervision 79
Psychological methods 36
Psychotherapy Supervisor Development
        Scale 244
Psychotic symptoms 229
Pseudo-science 27
Public services 147
Punctuation 202
Punitiveness 144
Pupil-teacher 89
Purchaser of supervision 10
Purpose statements 110, 226
Purposes of supervision 2–3, 52
    a model of 71–74

Questionnaires
    as awareness exercises 120
    pre-supervision 55
    for supervisees 58
Questions 155, 209

'Race' 134–139
Race Relations Act 140
Racism 135, 141
    & clients 136
    & pseudo-science 27
Rapport 243
Rating scales 58
Rational Emotive Therapy 189,
        198–201
Rationalisation 153
Rawness 173
Reactive crisis culture 33
Reading 200
Reassurer-encourager 236
Recaller 156–158
Receptivity 110–111
Reciprocal feedback 57
Reciprocity 75
Reconstruction 197
    of knowledge 207
Recording of sessions 82
Re-enactment 42
Referral criteria 66
Reflecting team 82, 170

Reflection
    in action 16, 24
    on action 211
    on experience 33
    & experiential learning 27
    & feedback 172
    & General Supervision Framework 77
    in groups 111
    & learning logs 206–214
Reflective
    alliance 92
    diary 206–214
    practice 101
    practitioner 1, 99
    observation 27
    process & taping 152
    space 32, 104–119
    writing 206–214
Reflexive questions 202
Reflexivity 202
Re-framing 202
Refugee status 141
Register, child protection 44
Registration 231
Rehearsal 184
Reinforcement 18, 94
Relationship
    with colleagues 33, 133
    model 189
    with supervisors 35, 52–69
        & disclosure 123
        & role play 84
Relaxation training 185
Religion 140
Remediation, of problems shown by
        supervisee 8, 229
Remuneration 55
Reparation 133
Replicative scripts 49
Reporting, as medium of supervision
        81
Reputations 13
Research
    & frameworks for supervision 74
    & taping 150
Residence arrangements 66
Resistance
    in groups 121
    in learning 23
Resolution of personal issues 48
Respect 102–115, 196
Response statements 172

Responsibilities
    to clients 132
    of stakeholders in supervision 7–11
Restorative function of supervision 5, 12,
        32
    & framework for supervision 72
    & groups 99
    & personal and professional
        development 50
Restorative needs of supervisee 56
Restorative role of supervisor 101
Retrospective reporting 81
Review
    & cyclical model of supervision 89
    of groups 101
    of supervision contract 57
    of tapes 148
Right fights 112
Risk
    clients at 8
    in groups 104
    taking 35
    of topics studied 47
Rituals 202
Role
    ambiguity 242
    behaviour 74–79
    conflict 13, 243
    expectations of supervisee 7
    model 95, 122
    play
        & action methods 183–186
        & cognitive-behavioural supervision
            200
        & earphone use 169
        & General Supervision Framework
            81–84
        & live supervision 165
        & modelling 18
        of problem in supervision 59
    reversal 83, 164–166
    rehearsal 89
    relationships 48, 52
        & co-working 162
        & purposes of supervision 71
        & systemic therapy supervision
            203
    switching 92
    of supervisor 74
    training 183
Ruptures 36
Russian dolls 105–106

Safeguard
    & live supervision 160–166
    supervision as a 123
    of taping 149
Safety
    constructing a climate of 1, 25, 33
        & contracting process 67
        & developmental models 93
        & live supervision 166–167
        & taping 155
        & experiential learning 29
        & focus of supervision 89
        & groups 104–120
        & peer groups 105
    of work with clients 60
Scene setting 85
Schemas 27, 197
Scientific management 31
Scientist-practitioner 1,
Sculpting 181–183
    in groups 120
Secret knowledge 14
Security of tapes 147
    of client materials 131
Selection
Self-actualisation 125
Self-assessment
    exercises 55
    Questionnaire for Supervisees 240–242
    Questionnaire for Supervisors 244
Self-awareness 158
Self-care 51
Self-consciousness 146
Self-development 30–51
Self-exploration 157
Self-disclosure 12, 143
Self-discovered learning 20
Self-doubt 179
Self-esteem 25
Self-evaluation 196
Self-expression 18
Self-harm 127
Self-neglect 50
Self-reflective learning 25–26
Self-report 229
Self and other awareness 93
Sensory feedback 112
Sentence stems 116
Serialist 21
Session content 84
    as scene setting 85
Sex of assignment 141

Sexism 136
Sexual
    abuse 44, 161
    advances 128, 142
    attraction 142
    intimacy 128
    orientation
        of clients 142
        and justice 126
    relationships with clients 227
    therapy 17
Shadow doll 108
Shame 51
Shared
    desire 118
    leadership 166
Short Inventory of Approaches to Study
        22
Sign language 141
Silences 155
Six-eyed supervisor 84
Skilled performance 15
Skills
    development & clinical supervision 79
    focus 189
    of the supervisee 7
    learning 36
Sleep problems 6
Small-scale research 234
Social
    constructionism 201
    conventions 17
    influence 99
    influence theory 63
    reference 165
    services 44, 161
Socialisation into profession 11
Socio-cultural context of referred
        problems 6
Socio-drama 120
Sociograms 181–182
Socio-political nature of helping
        professions 138, 141
Socrates 17
Socratic questioning 157, 184
Soft contract 108
Sound quality 148
South Africa 134
Space, & cyclical model of supervision
        89
Specificity of challenges 221
Spurious compliance 91

Stage
    of development 81
    in process 197
    model of supervision 93
Stakeholders
    & contracting process 54
    & frameworks for supervision 98
    in supervisory process 5
Stammering 27
Standards of practice 101
Status 171
Stigmatisation 135
Stone sculpting workshop 188
Stopping work 51
Storming 116
Straightforwardness 102
Strategies 189
Strengths
    challenging 218
    of supervisees 7, 96, 198
Stress levels 68, 225
Structure
    & level 1 supervisors 95
    of supervisory session 89
Structured group supervision model 119,
        171
Structuring the supervisory relationship
        197
Stuckness
    & gender of therapist 39
    in groups 117
    & live supervision 164–166
Study groups 135
Study Preference Questionnaire 22
Substance misuse 225
Suicide 17
Summarising 111
Summative assessment 11, 211
Supervisee-centredness 196
Supervisee Perceptions of Supervision
        243
Supervision Management Skills 244
Supervisor Questionnaire 243
Supervisor Role Analysis 244
Supervisory Focus and Style
        Questionnaire 244
Supervisory relationship & aims of
        supervision 1
Supervisory style 91
Supervisory Styles Inventory 243
Supervisory Working Alliance Inventory
        243

Support
  && groups 100–101
  && live supervision 168
  role of supervisor in 11, 73
  systems of client 137
Surrogate therapist 91
Survival 93–96, 216
Symbolic use of objects 179–180
Symptom reduction 197
Systemic therapy
  model 40
  supervision 190, 201–204
Systems theory
  && group supervision 70

Tacit rules 149
Tangential issues 153
Taping
  && cognitive-behavioural supervision
    201
  consent form 245
  && course-work assignments 237
  introducing to clients 150
  && person-centred supervision 196
  && psycho-dynamic supervision 191
Tarasoff 132
Task
  needs 114
  oriented 243
Tasks of supervision 57, 102
Teachers 190
Teaching/direction 168
Team supervision 65
  && live supervision 168
Technical skills 148
Technique
  && the bridge stage of cyclical model 92
  && cognitive-behavioural supervision
    201
  && contracting process 69
  && focus of supervision 86, 95
  && person-centred supervision 196
  && personal qualities 36
  && psycho-dynamic supervision 191
  && practice 18
  && role play 185
Technology 145, 168
Telephones 169
Temperament 40
Tentativeness 220
Test results 131
Themes in tape review 154

Theoretical model
  && contracting process 56
  && focus of supervision 81
  && supervisory process 189–205
Theory && cultural basis of 140
Theory-practice links 15, 92
Theory-provider 236
Therapeutic
  alliance 70, 118
    && live supervision 171
  process 95, 163
  role 191
  supervision 91
Therapist role 189
Thinking 206
Third party 146, 224
Thought-organising assistant 236
Threatening, supervisees' own experience
    of 7
Time
  boundaries 25
  consuming review of tapes 154
  frame 156
  keeping 60, 225
  management in groups 106
  table 236
Timing of supervision 52
Tokenism 137
Tone of voice 145, 224
Tool-kit 112
Trainee Personal Reaction Scale 244
Training institution
  && contracting process 56
  && coursework assignments 53
  && failure 227
  && priorities 32
  supervisor responsibility to 8–10
Training placements 56
Training Reaction Questionnaire 244
Training supervision
  && contracting 61
  && definitions 3
  && learning of supervisee 71
Transactions as focus of supervision 86
Transcripts 148
Transferable notes 130
Transference
  && consent to case studies 232
  && double matrix model 84–86
  as focus of supervision 42, 80
  && psycho-dynamic supervision 191
  && review of tapes 155

Transitions
   in life of supervisee 38, 47
   & parallel process 70
   & sculpting 183
Transitory records 147
Transmission
   of information 28
   mode of teaching 216
Treatment manuals 24
Trustworthiness
   & contracting process 69
   & earphone use 169
   & ethics 124
   in groups 102–118
   of professionals 151
   & systemic therapy supervision 203
   & trainee performance 63
Tutoring role of group leader 119
Typology of groups 102

User-led services 135
Uncertainty
   early in training 84
   in learning 24
Unconditional positive regard 215
Unconscious
   competence 23
   enactments with clients 191
   incompetence 23
   material 188
   processes 79, 117
Underachievement 138
Understanding
   as an aspect of mind 19
   & role-relationships 67
Unethical practice 225–228
Unprofessional behaviour 227
Unsolicited criticism 215
Unsupportive style 91
Unwillingness to learn 227
Use of objects 179–181
Utilitarianism 124

Validation of group members' needs 115
Value
   judgements 134
   system, of Edelman 19

Values
   clients' 140
   & contracting process 53
   & dialogic learning 25
   & family of origin 43
   & learning 20
   & personal biases 40–47
   & role of helper 140
   of supervisee 87
   in work systems 26
Verbal reporting 81
Verbaliser–imager learning style 22
Vicarious responsibility 132
Videoconferencing 158
Video-link 167–168
Videotape 145–159
   & comparison of supervision 189
   of client 182
   as medium of supervision 81–83, 96
   in teaching 24
Vienna position 190
Violations of professional ethics 143
Virtue theory 124
Visual
   imagery 188
   methods 174–181
Visualisers 175
Vulnerability
   of employees 30
   & feedback 216
   & live supervision 166
   of participants in supervisory
      relationship 1
   of supervisees 64
   & taping 152–156

Waiting lists 31
Warming-up 185, 238
Watch-your-back culture 33
Weaknesses 96, 198
Western bias 136
Working agreements 101, 117
Working alliance
   & definition of supervision 2
   in groups 109
Working arrangements in groups 107
Written consent 147